C000125818

Fuzzy Sets and Economics

To my mother, Suad Azizieh Mansur

Fuzzy Sets and Economics

Applications of Fuzzy Mathematics to Non – Cooperative Oligopoly

Yusuf M. Mansur

University of Oklahoma
Norman, Oklahoma

Edward Elgar

© Yusuf M. Mansur 1995

All rights reserved. No part of this publication may be reproduced, stored in a retrieval system, or transmitted in any form or by any means, electronic, mechanical, photocopying, recording, or otherwise without the prior permission of the publisher.

Published by
Edward Elgar Publishing Limited
Gower House
Croft Road
Aldershot
Hants GU11 3HR
England

Edward Elgar Publishing Company
Old Post Road
Brookfield
Vermont 05036
USA

British Library Cataloguing in Publication Data
Mansur, Yusuf M.
  Fuzzy sets and Economics: Applications of Fuzzy
  Mathematics to Non−cooperative Oligopoly.
  I.Title
  330.0151132

Library of Congress Cataloguing in Publication Data
Mansur, Yusuf M. 1957−
  Fuzzy sets and economics: applications of fuzzy mathematics to
  non−cooperative oligopoly/Yusuf M. Mansur.
    p.   cm.
  Includes bibliographical references and index.
  ISBN 1 85898 206 5
    1. Oligopolies − Mathematical models. 2. Fuzzy Sets. I. Title.
  HD2757.3.M36 1995
  338.8'2−dc20   94−34104
                                                              CIP
Printed in Great Britain at the University Press, Cambridge

Contents

Figures and Tables

FIGURES

TABLES

Preface

This book presents certain elementary but fundamental concepts and properties of fuzzy set theory, a relatively new mathematical subdiscipline. It then proceeds to demonstrate the applicability of this mathematical system to non−cooperative oligopoly markets. The widespread use of fuzzy mathematics in almost every science attests to its intuitive appeal and the many insights it offers. Most fundamentally, fuzzy set theory provides a tool for studying non−stochastic uncertainty, which mathematics is especially relevant to any evaluation of the behavioral uncertainty intrinsic to oligopoly markets. It is unfortunately the case to this point in time that notwithstanding its obvious applicability to the business world, fuzzy mathematics has remained largely outside of the mainstream of economic analysis.

The objectives of this book are threefold: Initially, it provides the reader with a penetrating, yet concise introduction to fuzzy mathematics; then it demonstrates its full applicability to non−cooperative oligopoly markets; and finally, it indicates how the economic evaluation of oligopolistic competition changes when fuzzy set mathematics is used.

Among other important results, the neo−classical view that oligopolistic competition is inefficient is shown to apply only to the short run; moreover, such policy matters as antitrust are revealed to be altered by the fuzzy math framework; and we further find that even basic economic fundamentals, such as the supply/demand paradigm are affected by the view of rational behavior in a fuzzy world. These are but a few of the myriad impacts that fuzzy set theory has already had (and will have) on economic theory.

Chapter 1 provides a brief, yet detailed, introduction to the theory of fuzzy sets and its arithmetic. The non−utilization of fuzzy techniques in theoretical economic analysis necessitates the inclusion of basic fuzzy set operations in order to acquaint the reader with the concepts utilized in this work. While the presentation is not exhaustive, the basic tools, concepts and references provided in this chapter will equip the enthusiast with a modest level of expertise in this relatively new mathematical subdiscipline.

In Chapter 2, fuzzy sets are employed to quantitatively define and describe the oligopoly market as viewed by the entrepreneur; it also demonstrates the uncertainty level arising in oligopoly markets from the conjectural mode of competition. In significant contrast to existing models, an entropy measure is used to calculate the oligopolistic uncertainty. We further deviate from existing models by utilizing a model of fuzzy signalling to demonstrate short−run competition in oligopoly markets, whereby the short run is demonstrated to be chaotic and non−determinate.

Chapter 3 establishes the personal/human dimensions of the entrepreneur and provides a method for imputing the opportunity cost of the entrepreneur which includes individual entrepreneurial characteristics. Fuzzy approximate measures are utilized to demonstrate the opportunity cost associated with the conjectural uncertainty in oligopoly markets. The calculation of this conjectural uncertainty involves uncertain estimates with respect to investments, payoffs, and discount rates. Additionally, the entrepreneur's personal preferences as to venture choice are included in the opportunity cost estimation process. In distinction from other economic models, that which is presented in Chapter 3 utilizes possibilistic distributions which are deterministic; i.e., not random (probabilistic).

Chapter 4 illustrates the imputation of the opportunity cost of the entrepreneur to the cost, revenue relationships of the differentiated product oligopolist. The homogeneous product oligopoly market is then demonstrated to be a special case of the analysis. Chapter 4 further demonstrates that oligopolistic competition leads in the long run to results similar to those obtained under pure competition. This equilibrium is derived in two stages: The first stage is fuzzy occurring in the intermediate run, where the intermediate run is defined as the intersection of the two fuzzy sets 'long run' and 'short run'. In the second stage, the equilibrium is crisp and occurs solely in the long run. Homogeneous and differentiated product results are established.

Moreover, Chamberlin's monopolistic competition and equilibrium are shown to be a special case in oligopoly markets.

In Chapter 5, the dynamic path of the long−run equilibrium is mapped at different levels of market uncertainty. At low levels of market uncertainty, the long−run equilibrium is shown to be stable. As the level of market uncertainty increases, the dynamic path of the long−run equilibrium becomes less and less stable until it is completely chaotic. The attributes of fuzzy math are further manifested as a natural counterpart to the 'real−life' role of the entrepreneur in the oligopoly market setting.

Chapter 6 delineates additional applications of fuzzy sets to economics. The demand and supply model is generalized via fuzzy sets to allow for the non−homogeneity of inputs and market outputs. In addition to the neo−classically recognized supply/demand forces, consumers and entrepreneurs are shown to be active determinants of the resulting market equilibrium. Also, we re−interpret market power indices via fuzzy sets to demonstrate the subjectivity inherent in such determination. Words and fuzzy summaries are used to describe market shares, firms, and market structures.

In writing this book, as with virtually every writer, throughout time, I have been the recipient of significant intellectual advantages. I am indebted first and foremost to my mentor and teacher Professor M.L. Greenhut. He stimulated my interest in microeconomics in my first graduate course in economic theory, then years later he supervised my dissertation, and subsequently encouraged me to write this book. Over the same period of time, he has helped me with his vast knowledge, doing this on innumerable occasions. To him my academic debt is clearly the greatest.

My wife, Brenda Joyce Crockett, has been my favorite critic and editor. She has for many months put her own career as a public policy researcher on hold to see this work move towards its completion. In no way at all could this book have been finished without her everlasting help, participation, and love.

I would also like to thank Professors David Huettner, chairman of the Department of Economics at the University of Oklahoma and Tim Gronberg, chairman of the economics department at Texas A&M University, each for providing me with research and administrative support. I want further to thank the secretarial staff at both universities, especially Tami Kinsey, Patricia Hardman, and Tamara Ariens, for assisting me in this endeavor.

1. Introduction to Fuzzy Set Theory

The purpose of this chapter is to acquaint the reader with the basic operations of fuzzy sets and their arithmetic. To complement the presentation of basic operations, concepts that are necessary for extrapolating results presented later in this work will be explained individually. Therefore, we reassert that the goal of this chapter is to provide a brief introduction to fuzzy set arithmetics.[1]

Initial formulation of fuzzy set theory was by Zadeh (1965). He presented it as a mathematical subdiscipline, a tool for decision making under what he referred to as ambiguous conditions. Zadeh (1989) later defined fuzzy logic as 'the logic underlying models of reasoning which are approximate rather than exact'.

The several evaluations and many applications of fuzzy set theory extended into a variety of fields, including more than 5,000 academic articles since its inception.[2] In addition to its intuitive appeal, fuzzy set theory is computationally simple. Moreover, its theoretical accessibility, beyond pure math, contributes further to its increasing importance.

Virtually all sciences have either benefitted from fuzzy set theory in the area of problem solving techniques or in theoretic formulation. Management science, sociology, political science, and psychology have long utilized fuzzy set theory as an analytical tool. However, economics has yet to realize the full potential of that theory.[3]

The reluctance of economists to apply fuzzy techniques as an analytical tool can be attributed to two factors: (1) The traditional and long established use of probability theory in the areas of risk, uncertainty and subjective evaluations.[4] And, equally significant, (2) the treatment of the cost of decision making under conditions of uncertainty in traditional economic theory. Under conditions of uncertainty, decision making costs become a variant part of production in a manner distinct from risk yet equally important as risk, if not more so. However, traditional economic theory has long ignored the cost of decision making under uncertainty in its concept of production costs.[5] Including uncertainty in the costs of production requires a tool to quantify the approximations that apply under uncertainty, a function which probability theory cannot fulfill accurately.[6]

Excluding the imputation of the cost of decision making under uncertainty in the neoclassical production function, as opposed to conditions of certainty, has distanced microeconomics from the reality of the firm. Abstract models that assume away numerous variables in order to create crisp and precise results are of no use to the manager and/or the entrepreneur in a real setting, as will be demonstrated in later chapters. By the terminology 'real world', we denote the world as viewed from the entrepreneurs' perspective.

Reality is fuzzy; that is, it is vague. The decision maker does not possess the abilities to acquire all data relevant to decision making, nor is this individual capable of retaining the information needed to make crisp decisions.[7] The decision maker is required to make choices concerning the future of her organization based on personal (subjective) criterion. The entrepreneur's belief that a specific choice set exists, and within this set certain choices are preferred over others, signifies the start of the decision making mechanism. The set of relevant outcomes and payoffs is generated and effected by the entrepreneur's subjective rationalization, inclusive of likes and dislikes.

In a real world environment, the decision maker may not have the luxury of observing an experiment repeatedly to assert the randomness of an event. Consequently, while probabilistic criterion is applicable to certain decision making problems, it does not encompass the realm of decision making in its entirety.

Observe the following example set forth by Zadeh during a presentation at the University of Oklahoma in 1991. A person inquires, 'What is the probability of your car being stolen?' The question is simple, implying an uncomplicated answer. Yet, the simplicity of the question belies the complexity of the response. To mathematical probabilists, the answer to this simple question poses a full scale challenge to their intellectual abilities. Your car is distinct in physical appearance; that is, it is distinguishable by the make, color, and specific added options, such as stereo, radar detectors, radial tires, etc. While consideration of physical characteristics alone may produce numerous variables for the analysis, the car's physical attributes are not the sole determinant of its desirability to an auto thief. Other factors affect the probability of theft, increasing the complexity of the question. Your driving and parking habits are unique. You may or may not own a garage. Your garage may be fitted with security devices, the type of device varying among security device owners. Your neighborhood is not identical to any other neighborhood in the world. The location of your home is unique. You may live in an affluent section of a city (center, periphery or median), close to a university or in proximity to a shopping center. Furthermore, the size and mix of your household is unique in terms of age, work, and consumption habits.

Is the answer to the question still obviously simple and immediate? As one can see, the answer is a difficult, time consuming one to calculate, and costly to produce. In fact, the answer may not merit investigation. Each variable requires a probability distribution which may or may not exist. All distributions require the process of collating and adjusting; that is, factoring to various degrees of significance each variable into the probability of the car being stolen, in order to obtain a simple answer. The variables are countless; the procedure represents a hardship, in the least, for those performing the necessary calculations.

Zadeh (1965) and Goguen (1967) state that the intention of fuzzy set theory is not to replace probability measures of stochastic randomness, but to provide

...a natural way of dealing with problems in which the source of imprecision is the absence of sharply defined criteria of class memberships rather than the presence of random variables.

Fuzzy set theory is described by Kaufman et al (1988) as

...a body of concepts and techniques that gave a norm of mathematical precision to human cognitive processes which in many ways are imprecise and ambiguous by the standards of classical mathematics.

Zimmermann (1985) states

Fuzzy set theory provides a strict mathematical framework (there is nothing fuzzy about fuzzy set theory!) in which vague conceptual phenomena can be precisely and rigorously studied.

Thus the utilization of fuzzy logic arises.

BASIC FUZZY SET THEORY

Fundamental to the basic ordinary set theory apparatus is the crispness of the set members; that is, an item is either a member or is not a member of a set. Once an item is a member of a set, it fully assumes all characteristics of the set and vice versa.

To indicate that an individual object x is an element or a member of a set A, we simply write $x \in A$ or $x \notin A$, where the symbols $\in$ and $\notin$ indicate respectively a member and not a member. A set can be described either by defining all of its members or by specifying well defined rules or properties which the set members satisfy.

The set A, whose members are x_1, x_2, ..., x_n, is usually written as

$$A = \{x_1, x_2, ..., x_n\}$$

Note that the above listing of set elements can only be used if the elements of the set are finite. If the elements are infinite, that is $x \in [a,b]$ where a,b are the minimum and supremum of an interval I on the real line, then $A=[a,b]$ represents the set A of infinite elements.

The set A can also contain subsets or groupings instead of simply individual elements. Thus the set A, whose members are x_1, x_2, $\{a_1, a_2\}$, can be written as

$$A = \{x_1, x_2, \{a_1, a_2\}\}$$

The characteristic or membership function of an ordinary set simply assigns values of 0 or 1 to each individual element in the universal set (the set which contains A). The membership function thus discriminates respectively between non−members and members of the crisp set. Middle values or partial memberships are not included in the crisp set.

For example, suppose the entrepreneur (decision maker) states that the firm's potential customers are composed of the set of tall people.

The word tall in ordinary set theory is a descriptor that is required to assume a certain value. People who are of the designated height are alone included in the set. Assume that tall is six feet or taller. Thus the characteristic function assigns a value of 1 to people who are six feet or taller and a value of 0 to people who are not. The entrepreneur makes the investment decision accordingly. In the less restricted real world however, some entrepreneurs (and the general public) may consider tall to include heights of 5'11" or 5'10", etc. Yet people who are 5'10" or 5'11", are not members of the crisp — ordinary set. However, if we ask a person who is 5'4" to describe a tall person, a dilemma results. Why? Because the word tall is a subjective criterion; and unfortunately we cannot include this subjectiveness in the crisp set. Consequently, it is simply lost.

Suppose the entrepreneur of the preceding paragraph clarifies the meaning of tall. The subsequent definition is given as 'by tall, I mean a height of approximately six feet.' Accordingly, we return to our ordinary set and attempt to incorporate all of the people who are approximately six foot or taller in the set. Because the characteristic function is restricted to 0,1 values (that is, people are either short or tall), the word approximately becomes meaningless and is therefore ignored. In other words, a middle value does not exist; that is to say, there is no membership between 0,1. If we attempt to solve the entrepreneur's dilemma by continuing to use crisp sets as a restricted tool, we ultimately fail again. Suppose our definition of tall is altered to include heights 5'10" or taller. Again the person who is 5'9¾" tall is excluded. Clearly the word 'approximate' cannot be fully interpreted by the crisp set.

Imagine an entrepreneur who will base the final decisions on ordinary set criteria. Is this realistic? Does not the entrepreneur lose many potential customers due to the inability of existing theory to describe true market phenomena? Furthermore, the business decision, when based on ordinary mathematics, becomes a naive abstraction that may or may not reflect that which in reality is true. How can a decision maker incorporate this vagueness into the decision set? Answer to this question lies in the characteristic function.

The characteristic function can be generalized in that the values assigned to the elements in the universal set fall within a specified range. Membership in the set falls within a range from 0 to 1, in place of 0 or 1. The values assigned to the elements in the universal set indicate the membership grade of each element in the set. Larger values indicate higher membership grades, degrees, or consistency between an element of the set and the full characteristics that the set describes. This function is called the membership function. The set defined by this membership functions is a fuzzy set. We define a fuzzy set as a set whose membership is not characterized by an either/or relationship but by a degree of membership.

The membership function is defined as a real number in the interval [0,1], where 0 membership means that the element is not in the set. A membership of 1 means that the element is definitely in the set. A membership that lies in between 0 and 1 indicates that the element is a partial member in the set. Thus elements, whose characteristics are uncertain (do not conform to the deterministic 0,1 rule of ordinary set theory), are not excluded. To represent the membership measure, we use the notation $\mu_A(x)$. A membership $\mu(5'10") = .9$ signifies that a person who is 5'10" tall is a partial member in the set A of tall people.

Clearly a removal of the scale of membership; that is, all $\mu_A(x) \in (0,1)$, reduces the fuzzy set to an ordinary (crisp) set. Therefore, ordinary set theory becomes a special case of fuzzy set theory, the latter being a claim reiterated by proponents and doubters of fuzzy set theory alike.

FUZZY SETS AND THEIR OPERATIONS

Let X denote a universal set, and μ_A the membership function by which the fuzzy set A is defined. Stated in canonical form

$$\mu_A: X \rightarrow [0,1].$$

Assume a sample size composed of four people (for simplicity) possessing heights of 5'5", 5'9", 5'11", 6'5". Let this sample be our universe of discourse, X, with the set A representing the set 'tall people'. The entrepreneur states that 5'5" is definitely short and 6.0'+ is definitely tall. 6'5" is assigned a membership of 1 and 5'5" is assigned a membership of 0. A person who is 5'5" is therefore not included in A. A person who is 5'9" is assigned (subjectively, as are

all the other elements) by the decision maker the membership grade
.8. A person who is 5'11" is assigned a membership grade of .95.

To depict the fuzzy set, a notation compatible with the fuzzy set
literature is employed. The fuzzy set A is written as follows

$$A = (1.0/6'5" , .95/5'11" , .8/5'9")$$

where the numerator indicates the membership grade and the
denominator indicates the set element (height). Note that the sum of
the membership grades is greater than 1; that is, $1 + .95 + .8 = 2.75$
> 1. Clearly, the sum of the membership grades (defined as the scalar
cardinality of the fuzzy set) is not necessarily one. Herein lies the
major difference between membership grades and probability. In
probability theory the sum of all probabilities in a probability
distribution is 1, while in fuzzy set theory such a restriction is
inapplicable as demonstrated above. The membership function does
not describe a probability (random) distribution. It describes a
possibility (non−random, subjective) distribution. That an occurrence
is possible does not mean it is probable. However, if an element is
impossible then it is also improbable.[8]

Figure 1.1 The fuzzy set A of tall people

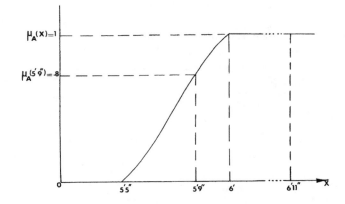

We can illustrate the fuzzy set A above in a diagram as in Figure 1.1. The vertical axis represents $\mu_A(x)$, the membership grades; the horizontal axis represents the elements in the set A, where $x \in X$, X being the universe of discourse (universal set). Note that in Figure 1.1 a membership grade of 1 is assigned for people who are 6' or taller.

Vague semantical operators, such as 'very' and 'less', can be added to the set 'tall' without any significant alteration of the set itself.[9] 'Very tall' sets, and 'less tall' sets can be established. For example: let B represent the set of tall people, s.t.

$$B = (0/5'8", \ .4/5'9", \ .7/5'11", \ 1.0/6', \ 1.0/6'5" \ ..., \ 1.0/6'9")$$

Note that set B has assigned partial membership only to people taller than 5'8" but less than 6 foot tall. Other sets, C (very tall) and D (less tall), can be represented by the membership functions

$$C = \mu_{very \ B} = \mu_B \ (x + k), \ x \geq k$$
$$D = \mu_{less \ B} = \mu_B \ (x - k), \ x \geq k$$

The sets C and D are, accordingly, derived from fuzzy set B and specified along a real line by the positive number k. Phrased otherwise, the set B is shifted along the x axis by a k amount (feet or inches in this example) chosen subjectively by the decision maker as represented in Figure 1.2.

Figure 1.2 The fuzzy sets 'tall', 'very tall', 'less tall'

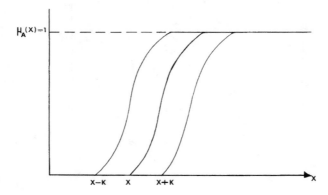

Note, that a fuzzy set may not be normal; that is, the highest membership grade in the set may be less than 1. If a fuzzy set is not normal, it can be normalized by dividing each membership grade by the maximum grade in the set, as below

$$A \text{ normalized } (x) = \frac{\mu_A(x)}{max \ \mu_A(x)}$$

The notion of normalization is non−trivial since the fuzzy set may not contain an element with full membership. The normalization technique standardizes the belief functions and thus facilitates easy comparisons between various fuzzy sets.

Return now to the original set of tall people for the purpose of recognizing a significant tool typically utilized in fuzzy set theory. The set of tall people A is defined below

$$A = (1.0/6'5" , .95/5'11" , .8/5'9")$$

Suppose the entrepreneur determines that heights with a membership grade below .95 do not merit consideration in the final set of customers. In other words, any element that has a membership grade less than .95 is eliminated from the set. Thus the entrepreneur creates a fuzzy set whose membership grades are equal to or greater than .95. Call the new set $A_{.95}$ where

$$A_{.95} = 1.0/6'5" , .95/5'11"$$

In fuzzy set terminology, the .95 value is called an α−cut. An α−cut of a fuzzy set $(A_{.95})$ serves as a threshold whereby only elements whose memberships are greater than or equal to α, the threshold value, are exhibited in the fuzzy set; that is, $A_\alpha = \{x \in X, \mu_A(x) \geq \alpha\}$. When elements with membership grades equal to α are included in the α−cut, the resulting set is called a weak α−cut. A strong α−cut is defined as

$$A_\alpha = \{x \in X \ \mu_A(x) > \alpha\}$$

The α−cut is a significant concept in fuzzy set theory, a concept which will be utilized in Chapters 2 and 3. The α−cuts are assigned arbitrarily by the decision maker. Such assignments are typically selected from the set of membership grades, but selection from membership grades not being mandatory. In other words, the decision maker may decide that all elements with membership grades less than or equal to .7 are insignificant. Clearly, the α-cut, .7, is not in the set A.

Set Operations

Let the universal set be X. Let A and B be two fuzzy sets in X. We define below the main set theoretic operations on A and B.

Intersection of A and B (the logical 'and')

$$\mu_{A \cap B}(x) = \mu_A(x) \wedge \mu_B(x)$$

where $\wedge$ denotes the minimum of the membership functions. Alternatively stated

$$\mu_{A \cap B}(x) = \min\ (\mu_A(x),\ \mu_B(x))$$

Union of A and B (the logical 'or')

$$\mu_{A \cup B}(x) = \mu_A(x) \vee \mu_B(x)$$

or alternatively

$$\mu_{A \cup B}(x) = \max\ (\mu_A(x),\ \mu_B(x))$$

Where $\vee$ denotes the maximum of the memberships.

Complementation of A

$$\mu_{A'} = 1 - \mu_A(x)$$

Properties I, II, III appear at first glance to be similar to theoretic operations on ordinary sets. However, recall that we are strictly utilizing membership functions. The complementation of a fuzzy set as demonstrated below, is not similar at all to that in an ordinary set.

We illustrate the above operations with a numerical example. Let $X = \{1, 2, 3, 4, 5, 6\}$, where X is our universe of discourse.

$$A = .8/3\ ,\ 1/5\ ,\ .7/6$$
$$B = .7/3\ ,\ 1/4\ ,\ .4/6$$
$$A \cup B = .8/3\ ,\ 1/4\ ,\ 1/5\ ,\ .7/6$$

Note that the union of fuzzy sets is, in and of itself, a fuzzy set. Furthermore, elements 5, 4 are unique to A and B respectively and thus become members of the union set. The inclusion of 5,4 in the union set does not contradict the definition of the union operation of a fuzzy set. This claim can be verified easily by extending the fuzzy set A to include another element 0/4 and the fuzzy set B by 0/5. The addition of elements with 0 memberships do not affect the union since 0 membership indicates 'not in the set'.

$$A \cap B = .7/3 \ , \ .4/6$$

This intersection is unambiguous keeping in mind the specification (0/4, 0/5 elements).

$$A' = 1/1 \ , \ 1/2 \ , \ .2/3 \ , \ 1/4 \ , \ .3/6$$

Thus far the basic logic operations (union, intersection, complementation) on fuzzy sets have been presented. However, for the purpose of thoroughness, but without unnecessary detail, consider the following operations.

Multiplication of fuzzy sets

The product operation can be stated in its canonical form as

$$AB := \sum_{j=1}^{n} \mu_A(x_j) \mu_B(x_j)/x_j$$

The expression sigma represents the union of elements in fuzzy set mathematics, not the arithmetic sum or addition.

If the sets A,B are infinite then AB can be represented as

$$AB = \int_x \mu_A(x) \mu_B(x)/x$$

Where $\int$ means the infinite union of the constituent elements.

We demonstrate the multiplication operation below with A,B having the numerical values set forth in the previous example.

$$AB = .56/3 \ , \ .28/6$$

Note the exclusion of elements not common to both sets. Moreover, if an element has a 0 membership in either set, then it is excluded from the product set.

Concentration of A

This operation is applied by the decision maker as a consistent procedure for adjusting the membership grades of the set downward; that is, deflating all the membership grades of the set. Defined as

$$A^2 = \sum_{j-1}^{n} \mu_A^2(xj)/xj$$

and exemplified below

$$A^2 = .64/3 \ , \ 1/5 \ , \ .49/6$$

Left square of A

This operation multiplies each element of the set by itself; that is, the elements of a set are squared without affecting or altering the membership grades. The left square of A is denoted as ^2A and defined as

$$^2A = \sum_{j-1}^{n} \mu_A(x^2j)/x^2j$$

and in our example

$$^2A = .8/9 \ , \ 1/25 \ , \ .7/36$$

Dilation of A

Defined as

$$A^{1/2} = \sum_{j-1}^{n} \mu_A^{1/2}(xj)/xj$$

This operation simply inflates the membership function of a set.[10]

$$A^{1/2} = .89/3 \ , \ 1/5 \ , \ .84/6$$

Addition of fuzzy sets

The addition of fuzzy sets is equivalent to adding the membership grades of identical set elements. Whenever the membership grade resulting from addition is >1 we simply write 1 for the membership grade. Provided set A contains an element that is not in B, an additional element is assigned to B with a membership grade of 0. If set B contains an element not contained in A, the same procedure is applied.

$$A + B = 1/3 \ , \ 1/5 \ , \ 1/4 \ , \ 1/6$$

Note that 1/5 occurs in $A+B$ as a result of adding 1/5 in A and 0/5 in B; that is, $(1+0)/5 = 1/5$. Additionally, 1/3 in $A+B$ occurs as a result of adding .8/3 in A and .7/3 in B as indicated by the full membership in $A+B$.

Subtraction of fuzzy sets
Subtraction also refers to membership grades, not the elements. A zero membership grade denotes that the element is removed from the final set. Furthermore since the membership grade is bounded from above and below; that is, [0,1], any subtraction of membership resulting in a negative membership grade establishes 0. In other words negative membership grades are not allowed.

One following example illustrates this last point

$$A - B = .1/3 \ , \ 1/5 \ , \ .3/6$$

FUZZY NUMBERS AND THEIR ARITHMETIC

Thus far we have presented a general framework of fuzzy sets and their operations. In this section, emphasis is placed on a subdiscipline of fuzzy sets, termed fuzzy numbers or fuzzy subsets. Our presentation of fuzzy numbers is predominately based on Kaufman and Gupta's work (1988). The pioneering work of Nahmias (1977, 1979), Dubois and Prade (1980, 1982) and others have presented and stressed the significance of fuzzy numbers as an analytical tool.

A fuzzy number is a fuzzy subset of **R** that is convex and normal.[11] Convexity in ordinary set theory means that if any two points in the set are chosen and connected with a straight line, the line remains in the set. Thus the closed interval is a convex subset of the real line. In fuzzy set theory, a fuzzy set is convex iff the membership grade of an interim element u (lying between any two elements x,y in a fuzzy set A) is not less than the minimum of the membership grades of x and y. See Figures 1.3a, 1.3b.

In Figure 1.3a, $\mu_A(u) > (\mu_A(x) \wedge \mu_A(y))$ for all x,y in A. Thus A is a convex fuzzy subset of **R**. In 1.3b, $\mu_A(u) < (\mu_A(x) \wedge \mu_A(y))$ for some x,y in A', thus A' is not a convex fuzzy subset of **R**, thus a convex fuzzy set is formally defined as

$$\forall \; x, \; y \in \mathbf{R}, \; A \subset \mathbf{R}:$$

$$\mu_A \; [\lambda x + (1-\lambda)y] \geq \mu_A(x) \wedge \mu_A(y) \quad \forall \lambda \in [0,1] \; A \text{ fuzzy subset } A \subset \mathbf{R}$$

is normal iff

$$\forall x \in \mathbf{R}, \; \vee_x \; \mu_A(x) = 1$$

Figure 1.3a   The convex fuzzy set. Note that $\mu_A(x) < \mu_A(u)$.   Also, the set A is normal since $\mu_A(m)=1$.

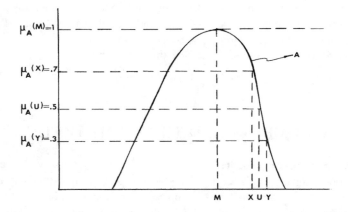

The concept of normality in fuzzy mathematics thus requires at least one element of the subset to have a membership grade equal to unity, and hence the union of the membership grades must contain at least one full member of the set.

Recall that, by definition, a fuzzy number is convex and normal. Therefore, a fuzzy number can be viewed as a generalization of the confidence interval concept. The assignment of a membership grade to an element in the set A requires an assumption by the entrepreneur that the membership grade has a certain value. This membership grade can be viewed as a presumption (or confidence) level. The convexity condition guarantees that a confidence interval can be

Figure 1.3b The non−convex fuzzy set

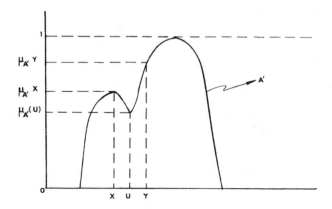

assigned to each presumption level. The normality of the fuzzy number guarantees that the maximum presumption level is equal to 1. However, as noted by Kaufmann and Gupta (1985, p. 14), a fuzzy number is not a random variable

> A random variable is defined in terms of probability, which has evolved from the theory of measurement. A random variable is an objective datum whereas a fuzzy number is a subjective datum.

Throughout this section and that which follows, fuzzy sets are presented in terms of membership functions (or grades) while fuzzy numbers are presented in terms of the concept of confidence intervals for flexibility and ease of use. Additionally, problems containing negative fuzzy numbers are solved directly through the use of the confidence intervals concept, thereby avoiding the analytical complexity arising from the use of membership functions.

Assume that a manager is forced to exercise a degree of subjectivity when imputing an uncertain argument into the cost or revenue functions. The level of subjectivity (presumption) is portrayed by use of fuzzy numbers. This concept of fuzzy numbers can be demonstrated by the following example.

Suppose a manager is asked, 'What do you expect the interest rate will be in the year 2000?' He answers, 'the interest rate will be 8 per cent'. Clearly the answer denotes an ordinary number (a singleton or crisp number). The crisp number usually has a single element (8 per cent in this example) with a membership grade of one. The crisp number, 8 per cent, is presented in canonical form below

$$\mu_{.08}(x) = 1$$

at $x = .08$ and 0 otherwise. Also see Figure 1.4.

Figure 1.4   The crisp number illustrated as a special case of the fuzzy number

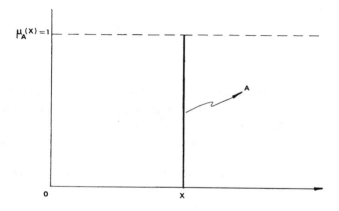

Alternatively, our manager could answer the question with a degree of uncertainty by stating, 'I am sure that the interest rate will not be below 7 per cent or above 9 per cent'. In ordinary set theory the manager is demonstrating a level of confidence where numbers between 7 per cent and 9 per cent have full memberships and all other numbers have zero membership grades. Consequently, the manager is defining a confidence interval $A = [7$ per cent, 9 per cent].

Note that although the manager has demonstrated a level of uncertainty, for lack of a better tool she fully accepts all values that fall in the confidence interval, as shown in Figure 1.5.

Assume the manager of the enterprise is introduced to fuzzy set theory. She can now state that the interest rate in the year 2000 will be 'approximately 8 per cent'. The answer is a fuzzy number. Note

Figure 1.5 The crisp range as a confidence interval

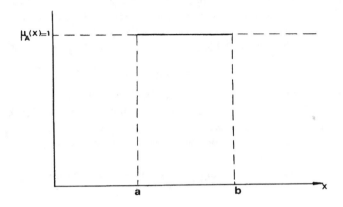

that by utilizing a fuzzy number, a more realistic response is obtained. The response contains a subjective evaluation, for in reality one cannot predict with certainty the interest rate in the future. Furthermore, observe how closely the fuzzy number mirrors and captures the subjectivity intrinsic to the human rationalization process.

Earlier in the chapter, a fuzzy number was defined as a subset of **R** which is normal and convex. We now define a fuzzy number in terms of confidence intervals as

$$\exists x \in \mathbf{R}: \vee_x \mu_A(x) = 1 \tag{1}$$

$$A_\alpha = [a_1^{(\alpha)}, a_2^{(\alpha)}] \tag{2}$$

where

$$(\alpha' < \alpha) \Rightarrow ([a_1^{(\alpha)}, a_2^{(\alpha)}] \subset [a_1^{(\alpha')}, a_2^{(\alpha')}]), \tag{3}$$
$$\forall \alpha', \alpha \in [0,1]$$

(1) implies normality; that is, there is a value (x) within the confidence interval $[a_1, a_2]$ that has a maximum membership grade of 1.

Statements (2) and (3) describe the convexity of the fuzzy number. A_α is called the α-cut where α describes the presumption level of the manager. Instead of considering the interval of confidence at one presumption level, the confidence interval is obtained at several levels (discrete membership function) or at all levels (continuous membership function) of presumption. The maximal presumption is equal to 1; that is, at a membership grade or α−cut that is equal to 1. The minimum presumption level occurs at α=0.

An $\alpha \in [0,1]$ gives the confidence interval described by statement (2)

$$A_\alpha = [a_1^{(\alpha)}, a_2^{(\alpha)}].$$

Statement (3) describes the confidence interval A_α as a monotonically decreasing function of α. In other words $A_{\alpha'} \subset A_\alpha$ for α' > α, where the confidence intervals or α−cuts $A\alpha$, $A\alpha'$ are monotonically decreasing functions of α and α' respectively.

Figure 1.6 A fuzzy number defined by confidence intervals

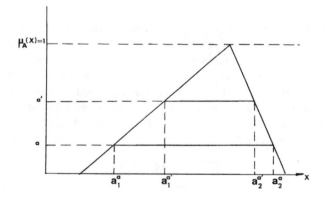

In other words, A_α (the confidence interval) never increases as α increases. Figure 1.6 illustrates a fuzzy number defined in terms of confidence intervals.

TYPES OF FUZZY NUMBERS

Many types of fuzzy numbers are used to analyze various ambiguous structures.[12] The types of fuzzy numbers we employ in this work are triangular and trapezoidal fuzzy numbers.

Triangular Fuzzy Numbers

A triangular fuzzy number (henceforth, T.F.N.) can be defined by a triplet (a_1, a_2, a_3), where a_1, a_3 are the lower and upper bounds respectively of the subject fuzzy number, with a_2 being the argument in the fuzzy subset that achieves the maximum membership grade; that is, $\mu_A(a_2) = 1$, where a_2 is also known as the mode of the fuzzy number. Incidentally, the value a_2 is *not* required to fall at the mid point of the interval. A T.F.N. is demonstrated in Figure 1.7.

Figure 1.7 A T.F.N.

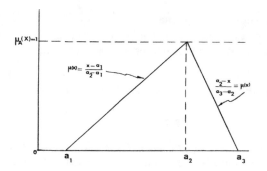

The T.F.N. represented in Figure 1.7 is defined by the triplet (a_1, a_2, a_3) and the membership function

$$\mu_A(x) = 0 \quad \text{at} \quad x < a_1 \qquad \text{I}$$

$$\frac{x - a_1}{a_2 - a_1} \quad \text{at} \quad a_1 \leq x \leq a_2 \qquad \text{II}$$

$$\frac{a_2 - x}{a_3 - a_2} \quad \text{at} \quad a_2 \leq x \leq a_3 \qquad \text{III}$$

$$0 \quad \text{at} \quad x > a_3 \qquad \text{IV}$$

Where I denotes that the elements in X with values less than a_1 (the lower bound) that are not included in the fuzzy number; that is, $\mu_A(a_1) = 0$. II, III represent the membership function in linear form, and for simplicity as monotonically increasing and decreasing in X respectively. Alternatively, the T.F.N. is defined in terms of its α−cuts (or confidence intervals) by the following formula

$$A_\alpha = \left[a_1^{(\alpha)}, a_3^{(\alpha)}\right] = \left[(a_2 - a_1)\alpha + a_1, \ -(a_3 - a_2)\alpha + a_3\right]$$

In our example the manager states that the interest rate is approximately 8 per cent. By using fuzzy numbers, upper and lower bounds for the interval can be specified; that is, let $a_1 = 7$ per cent, $a_2 = 8$ per cent, $a_3 = 9$ per cent. Then $a_2 = 8$ per cent may be based on an *a priori* data or knowledge base. The uncertainty surrounding the word 'approximately' represents the manager's own subjective opinion.[13]

For example, suppose the manager wants to obtain the confidence interval at a level of presumption equal to .7; that is, $A_{.7}$. At $\alpha = .7$, we substitute the corresponding numerical values for a_1, a_2, a_3 into the above A_α expression.

$$\begin{aligned}
A_{.7} &= \left[.07^{(.7)}, .09^{(.7)}\right] = \left[(.08 - .07).7 + .07, -(.09 - .08).7 + .09\right] \\
&= [.077 , .083] \\
&= 7.7\% , 8.3\%
\end{aligned}$$

Note that at $\alpha = 0$, $A_0 = $ [7 per cent, 9 per cent], and at $\alpha = 1$, $a_1 = $ [1 per cent + 7 per cent , $-$(1 per cent) +9 per cent] = [8 per cent, 8 per cent] = 8 per cent. Clearly, the triplet (7 per cent, 8 per cent, 9 per cent) refers to maximal and minimal presumptions. Therefore, it is only an approximation of A_α , the actual fuzzy number, since A_α contains all presumption levels.

Operations on T.F.N.

Addition
Fuzzy numbers in triplet form may be added as below

$$\begin{aligned}
A + B &= (a_1, a_2, a_3) + (b_1, b_2, b_3) \\
&= (a_1 + b_1, a_2 + b_2, a_3 + b_3)
\end{aligned}$$

Alternatively, a more accurate method of adding fuzzy numbers consists of adding the intervals of confidence at each α−level

$$A_\alpha + B_\alpha = \left[a_1^\alpha, a_2^\alpha\right] (+) \left[b_1^\alpha, \ b_2^\alpha\right]$$

$$= \left[a_1^{(\alpha)} + b_1^{(\alpha)}, \; a_2^{(\alpha)} + b_2^{(\alpha)}\right]$$

The addition operation in fuzzy sets is demonstrated in the following example

$$\text{Let } A = (-2, \; 1, \; 3)$$
$$B = (-2, \; -1, \; 0)$$

Using the triplets method

$$A + B = (-2-2, \; 1-1, \; 3+0) = (-4, \; 0, \; 3)$$

Using the confidence interval method that is at each α cut. First, we transfer the triplet expression for a T.F.N. to a confidence interval expression

$$A_\alpha = \left[a_1^{(\alpha)}; a_3^{(\alpha)}\right] = \left[(a_2-a_1)\alpha + a_1, \; -(a_3-a_2)\alpha + a_3\right]$$

Substituting for a_1, a_2, a_3, in the above expression we obtain

$$A_\alpha = \left[(1+2)\alpha + (-2) - (3-1)\alpha + 3\right]$$
$$= \left[3\alpha - 2, \; -2\alpha + 3\right]$$

Note that at $\alpha = 1$ $A_1 = (1,1) = 1$
                  $\alpha = 0$ $A_0 = (-2,3)$

Similarly for B_α we obtain

$$B_\alpha = [(-1,2)\alpha + (-2), \; -(-0-1(-1))\alpha + 0]$$
$$= [\alpha - 2, \; -\alpha]$$
$$B_0 = (-2,0)$$
$$B_1 = (-1,-1) = -1$$

$$A_\alpha + B_\alpha = [(3\alpha - 2) + (\alpha - 2), \; -2\alpha + 3 - \alpha]$$
$$= [4\alpha - 4, \; -3\alpha + 3]$$

A $\alpha = 0$ and 1 respectively

$$A_0 + B_0 = [-4, +3]$$
$$A_1 + B_1 = [0,0] = 0$$

Subtraction

$$A - B = (a_1, \; a_2, \; a_3) - (b_1, \; b_2, \; b_3)$$
$$= (a_1 - b_3, \; a_2 - b_2, \; a_3 - b_1)$$

Subtraction in T.F.N.s can also be performed by using the confidence interval expression for all levels of α. The subtraction procedure is identical to the addition procedure of T.F.N.s.

Multiplication

Triplets cannot be used in multiplication operations, or with multiplicative inverse operations (that is, division). However, confidence intervals can be easily applied to triplets provided all values are positive reals; that is, $x \in \mathbf{R}^+$.

In **R** computations of multiplication, inverse and division require the decomposition of the membership functions to investigate the minimum and maximum with positive and negative values when α increases from 0 to 1.[14]

We illustrate the multiplication operation for T.F.N.s in $\mathbf{R}^+$ by an example.

Let
$$A = (2, 4, 5)$$
$$B = (3, 5, 8)$$

$$A\alpha = [2\alpha + 2, \; -\alpha + 5]$$
$$B\alpha = [3\alpha + 3, \; -2\alpha + 8]$$

$$A\alpha(\cdot)B\alpha = [2\alpha + 2, \; -\alpha + 5] \, (\cdot) \, [3\alpha + 3], \; -2\alpha + 8]$$
$$= [(2\alpha + 2)(3\alpha + 3), \; (-\alpha + 5)(-2\alpha + 8)]$$

$$A_\alpha(\cdot)B_\alpha = [6\alpha^2 + 12\alpha + 6, \; 2\alpha^2 - 18\alpha + 40]$$

Let $\qquad C_\alpha = A_\alpha(\cdot)B_\alpha$
at $\quad \alpha = 0 \; A_\alpha(\cdot)B_\alpha = [6, 40]$, $\alpha = 1 \; A_1(\cdot)B_1 = [24, 24] = 24$

The result of multiplication is a parabola, not a straight line.[15] The parabola occurs due to the α^2 in the product of the T.F.N. as shown in Figure 1.8.

The multiplication process can be approximated by

$$A \cdot B = (6,24,40)$$

However, with α−cuts, we can substitute α for α^2 in C_α; that is, we approximate the fuzzy product by straight line segments in place of parabolas, as below.

$$C_\alpha = [6\alpha + 12\alpha + 6, \; 2\alpha - 18\alpha + 40]$$

$$C_\alpha = [18\alpha + 6, \ -16\alpha + 40]$$

Where C_α is the approximate T.F.N.[16]

Figure 1.8 Multiplication of Two T.F.N.s

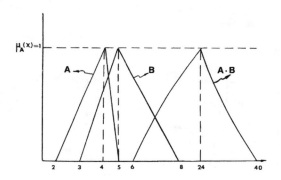

The inverse operation

To illustrate the division operation of T.F.N.s in $\mathbf{R}^+$ we must also be aware of any 0 values since an inverse of 0 is undefined as in ordinary arithmetic.

Let N be an approximation of A^{-1}, where A is a T.F.N; that is, $A^{-1} \approx N$ and $A \subset \mathbf{R}_0^+$.

Let $\qquad\qquad A = (a,b,c)$

Then $\qquad\qquad A_\alpha = [a + (b-a)\alpha, \ -(c-b)\alpha + c]$

$$A_\alpha^{-1} = \left[\frac{1}{c(c-b)\alpha}, \ \frac{1}{a + (b-a)\alpha} \right]$$

$$N = \left[\frac{1}{1}, \frac{1}{b}, \frac{1}{a} \right]$$

$$N_\alpha = \left[\frac{1}{c} + \left(\frac{1}{a} - \frac{1}{b} \right)\alpha, \ \frac{1}{a}, \ \left(\frac{1}{a} - \frac{1}{b} \right)\alpha \right]$$

To investigate the divergence of the approximation, we derive both the left and right divergency and then estimate the maximum divergence.[17]   The approximation N is shown in Figure 1.9 by the broken line. The parabolic A^{-1} is the actual inverse of the T.F.N.

Figure 1.9   Inverse of the T.F.N. A and its approximation N. A is represented by the triplet (a,b,c), N = approximation of A^{-1}, therefore N = (1/c, 1/b, 1/a). Note the divergence of the actual inverse A^{-1} from its approximation.

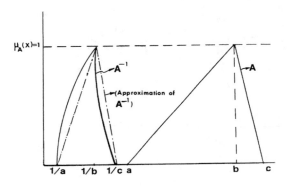

The division operation

The division operations of two T.F.N.s A, B where $A \subset \mathbf{R}^+$ and $B \subset \mathbf{R}_0{}^+$ is illustrated below.

Let $A = (a_1, a_2, a_3)$, $B = (b_1, b_2, b_3)$, where $A_\alpha = (a_1+(a_2-a_1)\alpha, a_3-(a_3-a_2)\alpha)$ and $B_\alpha = (b_1+(b_2-b_1)\alpha, b_3-(b_3-b_2)\alpha)$

$$A_\alpha : B_\alpha = [a_1+(a_2-a_1)\alpha, a_3-(a_3-a_2)\alpha] :$$
$$[b_1+(b_2-b_1)\alpha, b_3-(b_3-b_2)\alpha]$$

$$= \left[\frac{a_1+(a_2-a_1)\alpha}{b_3-(b_3-b_2)\alpha} \; , \; \frac{a_3-(a_3-a_2)\alpha}{b_1+(b_2-b_1)\alpha} \right],$$

Let D be the approximation of $A : B$; that is, at $\alpha=0, 1$

Then $D = \left[\dfrac{a_1}{b_3}, \dfrac{a_2}{b_2}, \dfrac{a_3}{b_1} \right]$

$$D_\alpha = \left[\frac{a_1}{b_3} + \left[\frac{a_2}{b_2} - \frac{a_1}{b_3} \right] \alpha, \ \frac{a_3}{b_1} - \left[\frac{a_3}{b_1} - \frac{a_2}{b_2} \right] \alpha \right]$$

The divergence of the approximation, D, is measured by the same technique utilized in the multiplication operation. [18]

Trapezoidal Fuzzy Numbers

Trapezoidal fuzzy numbers (Tr.F.N.) are the most widely used type of fuzzy numbers. A (Tr.F.N.) model includes statements such as 'the interest rate next year will be approximately 6 per cent to 9 per cent', where values respectively between 6 per cent and 9 per cent are assigned full memberships in the fuzzy subset and values above or below 9 per cent and 6 per cent are respectively assigned partial memberships.

A trapezoidal fuzzy number (Tr.F.N.) is viewed to be the general form of the triangular fuzzy number; that is, a T.F.N. is a special case of the Tr.F.N.. Recall from the previous section, that a T.F.N. is represented by the triplet (a,b,c), with the singleton b attaining the full membership; that is, 1. Tr.F.N.s are represented by quadruplets such as (a,b,c,d) with the segment (b,c) having a full membership; that is, $x \in [b,c]$ has $\mu_A(x)=1$ for $A \subset \mathbf{R}$. Trapezoidal fuzzy numbers (Tr.F.N.) convert to triangular fuzzy numbers (T.F.N.) when only one element x in the support of A attains a membership grade equal to 1.

Let A be a (Tr.F.N.) represented by a quadruplet $(a,b,c,d,)$; alternatively, it can be represented by its $\alpha-$cuts, $\alpha \in [0,1]$ which yield particular values for a, b, c, and d at each α.

$$A_\alpha = [(b-a)\alpha + a, \ -(d-c)\alpha + d]$$

The membership function of A is characterized as

$$\mu_a(x) = \frac{x-a}{b-a} \qquad a \leq x \leq b$$
$$= 1 \qquad b \leq x \leq c$$
$$= \frac{d-x}{d-c} \qquad c \leq x \leq d$$
$$= 0 \qquad \textit{otherwise; i.e., at } x < a, \ x > d$$

Operations on Tr.F.N.s are similar to the operations on T.F.N.s. By converting the quadruplet expression to an A_α, the algebraic operations

on Tr.F.N.s are identical to those on T.F.N.s. Figure 1.10 illustrates
a Tr.F.N.

Figure 1.10   A Tr.F.N.

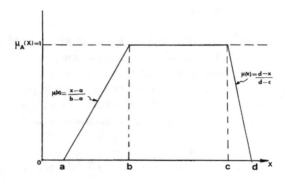

A statement such as 'the interest rate in the year 2000 will be
approximately between 6 per cent and 7 per cent' exemplifies a
Tr.F.N. In other words, the manager admits all values between 6 per
cent and 7 per cent with full membership into the fuzzy set and
assigns partial memberships to values that are close to 6 per cent from
below and close to 7 per cent from above. Uncertainty belies the
boundaries of the Tr.F.N.   The entrepreneur, based on prior
knowledge, experience and relevant yet incomplete data, surmises that
an interest rate of 2 per cent or below, is impossible and an interest
rate above 21 per cent is also impossible.   Thus the entrepreneur
specifies the boundaries to the interest rate prediction as (2 per cent,
21 per cent).   The Tr.F.N. can be represented by the triplet (2 per
cent, 6 per cent, 7 per cent, 21 per cent) or by its α-cut

$$A_\alpha = [(.06-.02)\alpha + .02, \; - (-.21-.07)\alpha + .21]$$
$$A_\alpha = [.04\alpha + .02, \; - .14\alpha + .21]$$
$$A_0 = [.02, .21] \, , \, A_1 = [.06, .07]$$

For a graphical representation of the Tr.F.N., see Figure 1.11.

Figure 1.11 A Tr.F.N. (an interest rate, approximately between 6 per cent and 7 per cent)

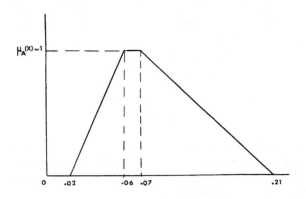

FUZZY VERSUS CRISP LINEAR PROGRAMMING: AN APPLICATION

The following simple example demonstrates the general applicability and advantages of fuzzy mathematics in economic science.[19] Additionally, the reader will see why crisp number mathematics can be misleading and why related uses of the calculus are less valid in economics than in physics.

Consider the following linear program

$$\max X_1 + 2X_2 = Z$$

subject to

$$3X_1 + 5X_2 \leq 14$$
$$X_1 + 7X_2 \leq 10$$
$$X_1, \ X_2 \geq 0$$

When solved by the familiar simplex method, the solution one obtains is $X_1 = 3$, $X_2 = 1$, with the maximum of the objective function being 5.

This programming problem can easily be converted to a fuzzy linear

one by changing the constraint coefficients from crisp numbers to
T.F.N.s and replacing the inequality signs by the 'contained in' signs
($\subseteq$). Of course, this latter alteration stems from the fact that T.F.N.s
are sets whose supports contain more than one element. We place a
bar($-$) over a number to indicate that it is a T.F.N. and rewrite the
problem with T.F.N.s as

$$\max X_1 + 2X_2 = f(x)$$

subject to
$$\overline{3}X_1 + \overline{5}X_2 \subseteq \overline{14}$$
$$\overline{1}X_1 + \overline{7}X_2 \subseteq \overline{10}$$
$$X_1, X_2 \geq 0$$

This programming problem would then be specified at every $\alpha \in [0, 1]$
and solved at that α after appropriate slack variables are introduced.

Solving the above at $\alpha=0$ establishes $X_1 = 2.76$, $X_2 = .75$ with a max
value of 4.26. This procedure would be repeated for $\alpha=.1, .2, .3...$
1.0. As α increases in magnitude, the max value also increases
reaching its greatest value at $\alpha=1$. In other words, there is a direct
correspondence between α, the level of presumption, and the related
optimal objective function.[20] Most significantly, the $\alpha = 1$ value
establishes the same maximum as the crisp number maximum. This
reveals the crisp number scenario as not only a special case, but as the
extreme special case of fuzzy set mathematics.

It warrants emphasis in this introductory chapter that the possibility
(fuzzy) world is clearly distinct from that of random (or subjective)
probability: First, our fuzzy program is not solved as is a random
one; rather, the method and tools of fuzzy sets are different from those
of random measures. Second, we are able to maximize the objective
function of a fuzzy linear program by finding the applicable values for
different possibility levels (i.e. different α's), whereas with probability
we simply find the mean and then maximize the function. Most
fundamentally, crisp number exactness involves a single possibility
and does not hold in a world subject to behavioral uncertainty.

Fuzzy mathematics is of further importance to economists because
it alerts the theoretician, as well as the applied scientist, to consider
the different levels of possibility which exist. Precise thinking
decision makers must account for these possibilities and would indeed
view the problem differently than that depicted under a crisp number

probability set. The fact is that crisp results tend to overestimate and hence mislead, given the ambiguities at hand. It is actually in a mechanical universe that crisp numbers apply, whereas in the behaviorally uncertain world of the social sciences the numbers are fuzzy.

SOME ADDITIONAL FUZZY CONCEPTS

Multiplication of a Fuzzy Number by an Ordinary Number

$$\forall x \in \mathbf{R}$$
$$\mu_{y \cdot A}(x) = \mu_A(x \cdot y) \quad \text{where } y \in \mathbf{R}$$

or in α−cuts

$$y \cdot A_\alpha = [ya_1 + y\alpha(a_2 - a_1), ya_3 - Y\alpha(a_3 - a_2)]$$

Max−Min Principle

The Max−Min principle proposes that if X, Y are sets in $\mathbf{R}$, where $A \subset X$, $B \subset Y$, then

$$\mu_{A *_B} z = \vee(\mu_A(x) \wedge \mu_B(y))$$
$$z = x^* y$$

where $*$ can be $+$, $-$, $.$, $\div$, $\wedge$, $\vee$. The max−min convolution is employed later and explained further by example at that point.

Extension Principle

The extension principle was initially developed by Zadeh (1965) and later modified by Zadeh (1973), Zadeh et al (1975) and Jain et al (1977). The generally accepted version of the extension principle is presented below.

The extension principle simply extends operations from a fuzzy set A to $f(A)$ as follows

$$\text{Let} \quad A = \frac{\mu_1}{x_1} + \frac{\mu_2}{x_2} + \frac{\mu_3}{x_3} + \frac{\mu_n}{x_n}$$

$$\text{and } f(A) = f\left[\frac{\mu_1}{x_1} + \frac{\mu_2}{x_2} + \frac{\mu_3}{x_3} + \frac{\mu_n}{x_n}\right]$$

$$= \frac{\mu_1}{f(x_1)} + \frac{\mu_2}{f(x_2)} + \frac{\mu_3}{f(x_3)} + \frac{\mu_n}{f(x_n)}$$

Formally, we define the extension principle as follows (Zadeh (1973), Dubois and Prade (1980), Zimmerman (1985)) : Let X be a Cartesian product of universes, $X = X_1, X_2, ..., X_n$ and $A_1, A_2,..., A_n$ be n fuzzy sets in $X_1, X_2, ..., X_n$, respectively. Let f be a mapping from $X_1, X_2,... X_n$ to a universe Y such that $y = f(x_1, x_2,...,x_n)$. Then a fuzzy set B on Y is defined by $B = \{(y, \mu_B(y)) \mid y = f(x_1,...,x_n), (x_1,...,x_n) \in X\}$ such that

$$\mu_B(y) = \mathop{Sup}_{\substack{x_1,...,x_n \\ y=f(x_1,...,x_n)}} \quad \min\{\mu_{A_1} x_1,...,\mu_{A_n}(x_n)\}$$

$$\mu_B(y) = 0 \quad if \quad f^1(y) = 0$$

where $f^{-1}(y)$ is the inverse image of y. When $n=1$, and f is one to one, the extension principle becomes $\mu_B(y) = \mu_A(f^{-1}(y))$, if $f^{-1}(y) \neq 0$. Less formally, the extension principle provides the means for a function f that maps points $x_1,...,x_n$ in the crisp set X to Y. If more than one element of X is mapped into the same element $y \in Y$, by f, the maximum of the membership grades of these elements is selected as the membership grade for y in $f(A)$. If $f^{-1}(y) = 0$, that is, no $x \in X$ is mapped into y, then the membership grade of y in $f(A) = 0$.

SUMMARY

As initially stated, the material presented herein is a brief introduction to fuzzy sets, fuzzy numbers and their arithmetic. The operations provided in Chapter 1 are not exhaustive, but provide an adequate background for the analysis presented in subsequent chapters of this work.[21] We utilize fuzzy logic as our analytical tool in Chapters 2, 3, and 4.

APPENDIX

Zadeh (1978) introduced the concepts of possibility distribution and possibility measure, which are special types of the fuzzy measure proposed by Sugeno (Sugeno, 1974, and with Terano, 1975). Banon (1981) demonstrated that probability measures are a special case of fuzzy measures. We define axiomatically fuzzy measures, possibility measures and probability measures.

Fuzzy Measures

Let f be a function from $P(X)$, the power set of X to $[0,1]$, then f is a fuzzy measure iff:

   I. $f(\varnothing)=0$; $f(X)=1$
  II. $\forall A, B \in P(X)$, if $A \subseteq B$, then $f(A) \leq f(B)$
 III. $\forall i \in \mathbf{N}$, $A_i \in P(X)$ then

$$\lim_{i \to \infty} f(A_i) = f(\lim_{i \to \infty} A_i)$$

Axiom I assigns a 'grade of fuzziness' 0 to an event that is in the empty set and 1 to the whole set. In other words, the 'grade of fuzziness' (fuzzy measure) is concerned with elements that are subjectively guessed to belong to a subset of X. Axiom II is a monotonicity requirement and implies that '$x \in B$' is more certain than '$x \in A$' since $B \geq A$; that is, B is the larger subset. Axiom III is a continuity requirement.

Possibility Measures

A function Π from $P(X)$ to $[0,1]$ is a possibility measure iff:

   I. $\Pi(\varnothing)=0$; $\Pi(X)=1$
  II. if $A \subset B$, then $\Pi(A) \leq \Pi(B)$
 III. $\Pi(U_i\ A_i) = \mathrm{Sup}_i\ \Pi(A_i)$

A possibility measure can be uniquely defined by a possibility distribution function $g: X \longrightarrow [0,1]$ such that $\Pi(A) = \mathrm{Sup}_{x \in A}\ g(X)$, $A \subset X$ where f is defined $\forall x \in X$ by $g(x) = \Pi(\{x\})$. If the set is normalized then $\sup_{x \in X} g(x)=1$.

Probability Measures

The following definition of a probability measure is based on Kolmogoroff (1933). *Pr* is a probability measure iff:

I. $\forall\ A \in P(X),\ Pr\ (A) \in [0,1];\ Pr\ (X) = 1$

II. $Pr\ (A\ \cup\ B) = Pr(A) + Pr(B)$ given that A, B are mutually exclusive

III. $\forall i \in \mathbf{N},\ A_i \in P(X)$ and $\forall i \neq j,\ A_i \cap A_j = \emptyset$, then

$$Pr(\bigcup_{i-1}^{\infty} Ai) = \sum_{i-1}^{\infty} Pr(Ai)$$

Note that *Pr* is clearly a fuzzy measure and while *Pr* and Π are special cases of the fuzzy measure *f*, Π is more general than *Pr* since the former only requires monotonicity, a much weaker condition than the additivity.   Thus, possibility and fuzzy measures generalize the measure.

NOTES

1.   Parts of this chapter borrow heavily from Working Paper 91−22, Texas A & M University, Greenhut and Mansur.

2.   See A. Kandel (1986) for 1000 references on the applications of fuzzy set theory.

3.   For some pioneering applications of fuzzy set theory to economic forecasting, see Chang (1977); Chang et al (1976); and Buckley (1986), where fuzzy set theory is applied to financial analysis.

4.   Since Bernoulli and Laplace, both subjective and objective judgements have been based on the mathematics of probability. However, artificial intelligence researchers, such as Shortliffe (1976) and Szolovits et al (1978), have shown that probabilistic rules are inefficient for analyzing subjective judgements, and often lead to erroneous conclusions.

5.   Distinctions between risk and uncertainty, such as those drawn by F. Knight (1921), do not affect this statement, given the focus of the present chapter. Moreover in the world of classical theory, risk and uncertainty combine to justify what is basically a rental return for those who invest under risky conditions.

6.   We reference exceptions to the traditional view elsewhere in this work.   For completeness, see Greenhut (1956, 1970, 1974), Greenhut et al (1987), and Greenhut−Lane (1989). The majority of our present research is based on the theory and framework presented in the aforementioned works of Greenhut.

7.   In order to maintain simplicity, the pronoun and the female gender will be used alternatively in the generic sense to denote all human beings.

8.   See Zadeh (1978), where the notion of possibility distributions was first introduced. Also see the appendix to this chapter.

9.   'Very' and 'less' constitute only two of the semantical operators that can be used with fuzzy sets. Other vague descriptors, such as 'few', 'many', 'large', will be fully demonstrated as fuzzy sets in Chapter 2 of this work. For a complete and thorough investigation of its meaning, see Zadeh (1988).

10. Zadeh proposed both the concentration and dilation operations as adjectival modifiers to the membership grades. He focused on adjectival hedges such as 'more or less', 'sort of'. Thus 'very tall' is represented by concentration of the fuzzy set A and 'sort of tall' is a dilation of A. We include these hedges for completion. For an extensive treatment, see Smithson (1987).

11. Moreover, the definition of fuzzy numbers represents the distinction between fuzzy sets and fuzzy numbers.

12. Note that our set 'tall' is an example of an S−type fuzzy number due to its resemblance to the shape of the letter 'S'. S−type fuzzy numbers arise from statements such as 'approximately more than 6 feet tall' or as in our interest rate example, 'approximately more than 8 per cent'.

13. By choosing lower and upper bounds (7 per cent, 9 per cent) the manager is imposing a restriction on the fuzzy number. This restriction is based on the manager's experience, knowledge, personality and capabilities, which depicts managerial realities.

14. In this chapter we only present the methodology with examples for solving multiplication, inverse and division of T.F.N.s in $\mathbf{R}+$. Additionally, confidence intervals can used for operations in $\mathbf{R}$. The solutions for T.F.N.s in $\mathbf{R}$ under the above operations are omitted due to space limitations. Detailed presentation of the above operations in $\mathbf{R}$ will be provided when the analysis necessitates their inclusion.

15. Clearly, the solution is not a T.F.N. because of the parabola segments. The type of numbers represented above are termed L−R fuzzy numbers and solved for by non-linear membership grade functions utilizing the method provided by Dubois and Prade (1980). Note that the convexity property is preserved.

16. Kaufmann and Gupta (1988) provide a method for checking divergence of C_α from $A_\alpha(\cdot)B_\alpha$. Kaufmann et al, investigate the divergence of the approximation from the left and right of the T.F.N. and obtain their respective maximum.

17. We demonstrate the maximum divergence principle at length in Chapter 3.

18. Additional operations on T.F.N.s, such as log, exponential and n^{th} power, can be found in Kaufmann and Gupta (1985).

19. The contribution of M.L. Greenhut to this example is greatly appreciated.

20. The solutions st the different αs may require that certain tolerance intervals be specified by the decision maker, see Zimmerman (1985) for some tolerance algorithms.

21. We have utilized the simplest types of fuzzy numbers. Only Tr.F.N. and T.F.N have been presented. Other types of fuzzy numbers exist which are equivalent to the above mentioned numbers in importance. For example L−R fuzzy numbers are utilized when approximations of multiplication, division, or inverse operations are highly divergent from actual answers. For an intuitive explanation of LR fuzzy numbers, see Kaufman and Gupta (1985) or for a more rigorous treatment see Dubois and Prade (1978a, 1978b,1980).

2. Oligopolistic Competition and Fuzzy Logic

The present chapter centers its attention on the oligopolistic decision making process, where the entrepreneur subjectively conjectures rivals' actions within an environment of free entry and exit. The treatment of conjectural uncertainty in neo−classical economics is examined; and, a new and more realistic view of the conjectural uncertainty is generated through the application of fuzzy logic to the theoretical framework of traditional oligopoly theory. The infusion of fuzzy logic into existing theory allows us to reject exact estimates and permits a degree of realism in the theoretical presentation of the conjectural process. The result is a view of oligopolistic competition that is theoretically more realistic and quite unique from standard models.[1]

In this chapter, we lead towards the primary goal of this book; namely, the investigation of the long−run equilibrium in oligopoly markets. We move in that direction by presenting here a view of oligopoly in the short run. Our design is of a well directed purpose: the observance of short run phenomena permits insights into the complexities inherent in and unique to oligopolistic competition. It follows that, we do not seek to prove the existence of a general equilibrium in this chapter.[2]

THE NEO−CLASSICAL VIEW

An oligopoly market is characterized as a market with few firms strategically interdependent with each another, producing either homogeneous or slightly differentiated products. The number of buyers in the market is assumed to be large, with any single buyer being an insignificant part of the total and therefore a price taker. The oligopolistic competitors produce at output levels less than or greater than their least cost outputs. In standard presentations, the negatively sloped demand curve (that is, the average revenue, AR curve) of the oligopolist creates a long−run tangency solution with the average cost (AC) curve to occur to the left of the most efficient production level (in $AC(Q)$). Thus the oligopolistic firm is generally considered to be inefficient in neo−classical economics.

Our point of contention with that standard theory (as with others)[3] lies in the presumption that oligopoly is inherently inefficient. We must therefore trace the development of oligopoly theory within the neo−classical framework in order to provide a basis for comparing our theory with the inefficiency assertion of neo−classical economics. Additionally, we must demonstrate how the evolution of oligopoly theory along traditional lines led to the conceptual bias against it as an analytical tool for use in developing microeconomic theory to new frontiers of knowledge.

A Background Sketch

One concept of oligopoly first appeared in Augustine Cournot's 1838 work. Cournot's contribution to economic science was unique in that it was original; that is, no development in the study of oligopoly was noted prior to this 1838 publication.

The originality of Cournot's work led to the 'canonization' of his famous mineral water example as the foundation upon which neo−classical oligopoly theory developed. It is therefore appropriate to begin the present analysis of neo−classical oligopoly theory by utilizing the simple Cournot paradigm in demonstrating the role of conjectural variations in oligopoly markets. A caveat is needed: the following presentation allows two variations from the original Cournot model as (1) the costs of production for each of the two competitors is conceived to be positive and different rather than at zero value, and (2) we extend Cournot's original two firm model to the n-firm case.

Consider an oligopolistic market with two firms producing identical (homogeneous) products. We refer initially to the two homogeneous producers as firm 1 and firm 2.[4] Both firms possess linear cost functions $c_1(q_1)$ and $c_2(q_2)$, respectively

$$c_i(q_i) = a_i + b_i q_i \ , \ i=1,2.$$

Where
a_i = fixed cost of production for firm i
b_i = marginal cost of production for firm i
q_i = the output produced by firm i.

We eliminate economies or diseconomies of scale by assuming that b_i is constant, and thus independent of the level of output. We assume that the firms' managers have perfect foresight.[5] Each producer is fully aware of the other firm's cost of production and the exact market demand. Market price depends solely on the output of both firms; i.e, the cost of shipping the product is 0. An inverse linear demand equation determines market price, as given by

$$P = A - B(q_1 + q_2)$$

where A = the maximum possible price; that is, at $q_1+q_2=0$, $P=A$. and B = the slope of the total market's AR or price line. The products' homogeneity is reflected by the parameter B, demonstrating the consumers' indifference to either product.

Firm 1's profit function is

$$\Pi_1(q_1,q_2) = P(q_1,q_2)q_1 - C_1(q_1) \tag{1}$$

Similarly, firm 2's profit function is

$$\Pi_2(q_1,q_2) = P(q_1,q_2)q_2 - C_2(q_2) \tag{2}$$

In Equations (1) and (2), outputs and total revenues are oligopolistically determined (dependent upon rival's output), whereas the costs (inputs) are imputed in a purely competitive manner. Thus the conjectural process centers in our model solely on the rivals' outputs, and not on the technical inputs whose prices are assumed to be fixed.

We proceed by taking the derivatives of Π_1 and Π_2 with respect to q_1 and q_2. Π_1 and Π_2 are defined by (1) and (2) respectively and lead to

$$\frac{\partial \Pi_1}{\partial q_1} = \frac{\partial[(A - B(q_1 + q_2))q_1]}{\partial q_1} - \frac{\partial C(q_1)}{\partial q_1} \tag{3}$$

Setting $\partial\Pi_1/\partial q_1 = 0$; that is, at $MR=MC$ or the maximum profit condition, we obtain

$$0 = A - B(q_1 + q_2) + q_1(-B) - b_1$$
$$0 = A - Bq_1 - Bq_2 - Bq_1 - b_1$$
$$0 = A - 2Bq_1 - Bq_2 - b_1$$
$$2Bq_1 = A - b_1 - Bq_2$$

$$q_1 = (\frac{A - b_1 - Bq_2}{2B}).$$

$$q_1 = \frac{1}{2}(\frac{A - b_1}{B} - q_2). \qquad (1^*)$$

Equation 1* indicates that the output produced by firm 1 is a function of the market's total demand conditions, the marginal cost of the firm itself, and the output of the rival. Equation 1* provides firm 1's reaction function.

Similarly, from (2) and following the same procedure as (1) establishes

$$q_2 = \frac{1}{2}(\frac{A - b_2}{B} - q_1). \qquad (2^*)$$

where Equation 2* is firm 2's reaction function. Substituting q_2 from (2*) into (1*) provides

$$q_1{}^* = \frac{1}{3}(\frac{A + b_2 - 2b_1}{B}) \qquad (4)$$

Similarly, substituting q_1 from (1*) into (2*) yields

$$q_2{}^* = \frac{1}{3}(\frac{A + b_1 - 2b_2}{B}). \qquad (5)$$

Let $Q^* = q_1{}^* + q_2{}^*$, where Q^* is the optimal total market output given the constant marginal costs of both firms and the market demand conditions (A and B). At $b_1 = b_2 = b$, where b is a constant, $Q^* = (2/3)(A - b/B)$. Furthermore, at $b_1 = b_2 = 0$, $A = B = 1$, $Q^* = 2/3$, which is the solution of Cournot's original model.

Substituting (4) and (5) into the *AR* expression generates the equilibrium price P^* as

$$P^* = A - B(q_1{}^* + q_2{}^*)$$

$$= A - B(\frac{1}{3}\frac{A + b_2 - 2b_1}{B} + \frac{1}{3}\frac{A + b_1 - 2b_2}{B})$$

$$= A - \frac{1}{3}(2A + b_1 + b_2 - 2b_1 - 2b_2)$$
$$= A - \frac{1}{3}(2A - b_1 - b_2)$$
$$P^* = \frac{1}{3}(A + b_1 + b_2)$$

Thus P^* is a function of the marginal costs of the firms and the maximum market price A. Note that if the marginal costs equal zero, as in the original Cournot model, the market price is $1/3 \, A$. In other words, each firm charges a price equivalent to one third the intercept.

Similarly, our analysis can be extended to the n−firm case where $n \geq 2$ as below

$$q_j^* = \frac{1}{2B}(A - B \sum_{i-j}^{n} q_i - b_j) \tag{6}$$

where q_j^* is the optimum output of firm j, $\sum_{i \neq j}^{n} q_i$ is the sum of the reaction functions of all other firms in market and b_j is firm j's marginal cost of production.

The market price P^* is defined below

$$P^* = A - B \left(\sum_{j-1}^{n} q_j^* \right) \tag{7}$$

where $\sum_{j-1}^{n} q_j^*$ is the sum of all the profit maximizing outputs of oligopolists in the market.

The employment of cost variations, as above, amends the Cournot paradigm to produce a more realistic picture of oligopolistic competition. Other components of the Cournot presentation, however, have not been widely challenged by economists or subsequently modified to more closely reflect the reality of the oligopoly market. Thus the concepts put forth by Cournot continue to color neo−classical thought. We address and critique the Cournot methodology and its subsequent impact on the theory of oligopoly.

The use of simplifying assumptions

Cournot, while being credited as the first scholar to utilize general functional mathematical forms in economic analysis, resorted heavily to the use of simplifying assumptions in his model: specifically, a linear demand function and zero production costs were assumed. Whereas each of these assumptions is not in and of itself untenable or unalterable, their joint use strongly impacted oligopoly theory development. Thus neo—classical oligopoly theory has been plagued with simplifying assumptions ever since its conception; and in turn the oligopoly market has been regarded in the same manner as monopoly or perfect competition — a rather abstract model.

The omission of the opportunity cost of the entrepreneur

Let us accept the use of simplifying assumptions, such as zero production costs. However, Cournot's omission of the sellers' respective opportunity costs cannot be ignored. Each seller in the market has to conjecture and guesstimate his rivals' reactions in order to achieve the equilibrium price and output. The conjectural process entails an extra effort by each seller which requires compensation commensurate with extra efforts expended. The significance of the entrepreneur's role in oligopoly markets and the corresponding entrepreneurial opportunity cost should have been manifest in the mineral water example, more so than in many of the complicated models arising in later stages of the theory's development. In the example with zero production costs, the entrepreneur/owner of the individual spring incurs a hardship via his conjectures about the rival's behavior. This hardship, and the evidence of the existence of an opportunity cost, is highlighted by the fact that the entrepreneurial role consists essentially, in fact solely of predicting the rival's behavior, that is; entrepreneurial inputs, other than ownership of the mineral spring and conjectures as to rival's behavior, are non—existent.

Moreover, traditional economic theory regards economic costs as the sum of the accounting (technical) costs and the opportunity costs of the production factors. Despite this treatment of economic costs, neo—classical oligopoly theory continues to reflect Cournot's omission of the opportunity cost associated with conjectural uncertainty from the cost—revenue relationships. We can surmise that the initial omission of the entrepreneurs' opportunity cost from oligopoly theory has contributed to its continued absence in neo—classical oligopoly theory.[6]

Absence of rational behavior on the part of the entrepreneur

Observe the naivety exhibited by the producers in Cournot's model. Each firm assumes that its rivals' present output level will remain unaltered in the future. Firms' expectations are correct at the equilibrium outputs (q_1^*, q_2^*) alone, and, revision does not take place when entrepreneurial expectations are proven inaccurate.[7] The lack of entrepreneurial response demonstrated in the Cournot model persists in neo−classical theory, where the entrepreneur is viewed as a one−dimensional entity, operating without benefit of the innate and/or acquired knowledge needed to respond to changing market conditions.

Dependence on output as the sole strategic variable and as a consequence the Bertrand response

The Cournot justification for the variability of output rests on the homogeneity of both firms' outputs. As such, the change in the firms' respective outputs leads to price determination through the inverse demand relationships. The validity of this justification was not questioned until 1883, when a mathematical economist, Joseph Bertrand, raised the issue.[8] Bertrand utilized price as the strategic (decision) variable, while maintaining the other assumptions of Cournot. As a result, Bertrand obtained a non−cooperative equilibrium at $P_1^*{=}P_2^*{=}0$, where (P_1^*, P_2^*) represents the non−cooperative equilibrium pair.[9]

The Bertrand response to Cournot had both positive and negative theoretical effects. The use of price conjectures provided significant insights into the behavior of the high inventory cost producer; however, on the other hand, the analysis inhibited a greater understanding of firm behavior in oligopoly markets in that discontinuities arose from the use of price conjectures. Under Bertrand, if one firm changes price to a level that is slightly lower than the rivals' price, the firm captures the entire market (since products are homogeneous). Consequently, the sales of the high pricing firms are reduced to zero and discontinuity results. Such phenomena are rarely observed in the 'real' world. The sales of a high pricing firm are not typically reduced to zero; neither are products nor other relevant economic factors perfectly homogeneous in character. Furthermore, the entrepreneurs of the Bertrand analysis, as well as that of the Cournot analysis, exhibit no regret due to wrong conjectures, nor do they learn from past errors; that is, the behavior of rivals, in the past and in the future, is insignificant.

The portrayal of oligopoly as inherently inefficient

Cournot conceptualized the actions of the oligopolistic competitor, even though the term 'oligopoly' is not mentioned in his work. In fact, Cournot refers only to a market composed of two sellers. Until 1933, the terminology, 'two monopolists' and 'three monopolists' was employed to describe 'duopoly' and 'oligopoly', respectively. [10] Monopoly has been and continues to be viewed as an inefficient market type, thus we surmise that the inefficiency of the monopoly market was imposed on the oligopoly market; that is, since a monopoly is inefficient, two monopolies are also inefficient. The lack of differentiation between monopolies and oligopolies in the early stages of the development of oligopoly theory may have contributed to the existing neo—classical view of oligopoly as an inefficient market type, certainly the preconceptions of inefficiency may have directed researchers away from investigating possible efficiency conditions. [11]

While neo—classical economic theory continues to view oligopoly as an inefficient market type, a developing body of literature in economics has been presenting a different view of oligopoly markets (M.L. Greenhut 1956, 1970, 1978, and with G. Norman, C.S. Hung 1987, and with W. Lane 1989; H. Demsetz, 1959, 1967, 1968, 1972; H. Ohta, 1977; B. Benson 1980,a,b). In his (1970) book, M.L. Greenhut assembled together the fundamentals which proposed a determinate long—run equilibrium for competitive oligopoly markets. The basic premise of that theory is its emphasis on including behavioral uncertainty as part of the classical cost curves of the oligopolistic firm. [12] Our present work is based on the above noted works of Professor Greenhut. We will confirm Greenhut's theory and conclusions through a deterministic (not probabilistic) formulation. Fuzzy sets are utilized to demonstrate human ignorance (uncertainty) via possibilistic distributions, elastic estimates, and purely subjective judgements.

OLIGOPOLY REDEFINED VIA FUZZY SETS

Recall that an oligopoly market is characterized as a market with a large number of consumers and few firms strategically dependent upon one another. The consumer accepts market demand conditions as given, while the oligopolistic competitor guesses and conjectures about rival behavior patterns. These conjectures imply a behavioral uncertainty in the market that is unique to oligopoly. [For purposes of simple exposition and in conformance to the thesis that behavioral uncertainty can be considered as additive to other uncertainties (for example, Greenhut, 1970), we shall henceforth use the term uncertainty in the inclusive sense, except when special emphasis on the behavioral uncertainty facet is desired.] The goods produced in an oligopolistic industry are either homogeneous or slightly differentiated.

Duopoly theorists who examine rivalry in that market oftentimes claim that their results extend to the more than two firm case.[13] In traditional microeconomic literature, 'few' therefore connotates two or more firms. But how many firms are really designated by the word 'few'? The term 'few firms' of course elicits differing numbers for different people, as the linguistic descriptor 'few' is itself subjective.

Classical logic offers specific (crisp) numbers to describe the word 'few'. For example, 'few' can denote 20 firms or 30 firms or a 100 firms. What about the instance of 101 firms? Do the firms cease to be oligopolistic competitors? Does the interdependence among firms break down once an additional firm enters the market? The word 'few' does not constitute a rigid bound for the maximum number of firms in an oligopolistic market. A crisp number cannot capture the elastic word 'few' because 'few' is a vague linguistic descriptor. We must utilize a fuzzy number such as 'approximately 50' or 'approximately between 60 and 70' to describe 'few'. Thus a trapezoidal, triangular fuzzy number or an alternative type of fuzzy number can effectively describe the elasticity of the bounds which apply to the number of firms. Alternatively we can define the number of firms heuristically as a 'small number of firms', where the descriptor small refers to a fuzzy subset of numbers in the set of positive integers.[14]

'Similar products' is another fuzzy linguistic descriptor inferring 'differentiated products', rather than necessarily being a technically determined (objective) reference. What is similar is fundamentally a subjective decision. Products can vary in similarity. Homogeneous or identical products then present a special case of the larger set of 'similar products'.[15] Unrelated products, in turn, serve as a unique special case of the set 'similar products', where the unrelated product has a membership grade zero in the fuzzy subset of 'similar products'.[16]   We conceive additionally of the normal fuzzy set 'similar' to include a member whose product is identical to that of the representative firm and therefore is also given the membership grade 1.[17] All subjectively assigned grades of membership are designated by the representative firm's entrepreneur.

The degree of interdependence among firms is not identical.   The economic landscape is diverse and varied. A firm may be located in closer proximity to the representative firm, henceforth call it F, than another. Firms may be of differing size. The costs at the different sites may vary for each firm. Transportation of products from market peripheries may be affected by long–haul economies afforded to some but not to others.   Pricing strategies may also differ.   Firms may possess dissimilar views of risk, with some having a history of leadership while others are content to follow.   Therefore, only the naive can view the economic landscape as homogeneous and exact. The diversity of the landscape is reflected in the nature of the interdependence among firms; that is, the firm possesses a unique interdependence with every other firm participating in the oligopolistic market.   The   heterogeneity   of   space   precludes   identical interdependence among all firms in the oligopolistic market.

It follows that the entrepreneur or manager of firm F is subject to a vague theoretical understanding of the oligopolistic market. This vagueness or uncertainty clearly exists in the 'real' world,[18] where competitors guesstimate and conjecture about rivals' behavior in a seemingly subjective manner. Yet, these guesstimates and conjectures are not devoid of knowledge.   To the contrary, each entrepreneur's conjecture is the result of a knowledge base, which is itself imprecise or vague. In the short run (and possibly the long run), the oligopolist may not possess sufficient statistical data to obtain probabilistic inferences from observed market behavior. Recall the car example presented in Chapter 1.   Does an analogy exist between our car example and the economic environment of the oligopolist?   The answer is in the affirmative.   The businessman (entrepreneur or manager) who desires to be completely objective throughout the decision making process is totally useless to the firm. Each entrepreneurial decision which is made with absolute objectivity and accuracy is also extremely costly. Simply put, complete accuracy and precision in decision making cannot be acquired at a low price. One fact is that the price incurred may be so great that it counters and nullifies the expected gains from the decision itself.

An oligopolistic competitor has a subjective (vague) knowledge of the firm's market. This knowledge is aided by the market's theoretical description, which is also fuzzy. In effect both the oligopolistic competition theory and practice fall within the realm of 'fuzziness'. Each of the fuzzy descriptors creates a possibility distribution. The term 'oligopoly' generally establishes the set of 'few firms' 'similar products' 'interdependent firms.'

'Similar products':=S^*:	is the fuzzy set of products in the market with each assigned a membership grade to describe the degree of similarity of the product to that of firm F. Let $X_{ij} \in Z$, where i refers to the firm i and j to it's product. Thus we allow a firm to produce more than one similar product.
'Interdependent firms':=I^*:	is the fuzzy set of firms whose membership grades represent the degree of perceived interdependence between a firm and the F firm. Let $X_i \in Z$, where i refers to the firm.
'Few firms':=F^*:	is the fuzzy number of firms where a degree of membership is assigned to the discrete numbers.[19] The membership grade describes the belief of the entrepreneur that $i \in$ (approx n), where $i \in Z$.

We obtain the membership grades of the fuzzy set $O^* \approx$ (oligopolistic market) by the extension principle. This principle extends operations from a fuzzy set A to its image $f(A)$ as follows[20]

$$\text{Let } A = \frac{\mu_1}{x_1}, \frac{\mu_2}{x_2}, \frac{\mu_3}{x_3}..., \frac{\mu_n}{x_n}$$

$$\text{and } f(A) = f\left[\frac{\mu_1}{x_1}, \frac{\mu_2}{x_2}, \frac{\mu_3}{x_3}..., \frac{\mu_n}{x_n}\right]$$

$$= \frac{\mu_1}{f(x_1)}, \frac{\mu_2}{f(x_2)}, \frac{\mu_3}{f(x_3)}..., \frac{\mu_n}{f(x_n)}$$

When more than one element of a set is mapped onto an element of another set, the maximum of the membership grades of the elements in A is accepted as a confidence limit of the membership grade in $f(A)$. This principle is readily illustrated by the following example.

$$\text{Let } S^* = \frac{.8}{X_{11}}, \frac{.9}{X_{12}}, \frac{.7}{X_{21}}, \frac{.6}{X_{31}}, \frac{.7}{X_{32}}, \frac{.2}{X_{41}}, \frac{.1}{X_{51}}, \frac{0}{X_{61}}$$

$$I^* = \frac{.7}{X_1}, \frac{.8}{X_2}, \frac{.9}{X_3}, \frac{.1}{X_4}, \frac{0}{X_5}, \frac{0}{X_6}$$

$$F^* = \frac{1.0}{1}, \frac{1.0}{2}, \frac{.9}{3}, \frac{.8}{4}, \frac{.7}{5}, \frac{.2}{6}$$

Note that in our example the products of all of the firms, with the exception of that of firm 6, are similar to firm F's product. Firms 1 and 3 produce two products each. Via I^*, firms 5 and 6 are not considered to be interdependent with F, but firm 3 is viewed to exhibit a 'strong' interdependence with F. In turn, firms 1 and 2 exhibit a 'semi−strong' interdependence with F, while firm 4 has a 'weak' interdependence with F. It is further the case that F^* is the fuzzy number of firms which reflect the entrepreneur's belief that 'few' means 1 or 2 firms are full members of the same set; 3, 4, 5, or 6 firms carry partial memberships.

Before proceeding further, let us utilize the numerical values of F^* to answer the question posed earlier as to the significance of a new firm entering the market. The question can be restated as 'Is 'few + 1' the same as 'few'?' What is the possibility of 7 firms being few? Note that within the fuzzy math framework, 7 can be the sum of 1 and 6, 2 and 5, or 3 and 4. In membership grades, the combinations are $(1.0 \wedge .2)$ or $(1.0 \wedge .7)$ or $(.9 \wedge .8)$; that is, $\vee((1.0 \wedge .2), (1.0 \wedge .7), (.9 \wedge .8)) =$

$\vee(.2,.7,.8) = .8$. The possibility of 7 firms being few is .8. Accordingly, the statement '7 firms is a few firms' has the possibility $\Pi_F(7) = .8$.

The set O^* consists of the sets S^*, I^*, and F^*. Semantically, the oligopoly market is composed of a few, interdependent firms that produce similar products. Note that the relationship between S^*, I^* and F^* is fuzzy (vague). The logical ($\vee$) does not suffice to explain the relationship among the three sets.[21] Thus we utilize the extension principle.

The solution is obtained by joining the membership grades of a product with that of the interdependent firm producing it and the membership grade of the firm in 'few'. We then obtain the maximum membership grade among all the membership grades to obtain each firm's membership grade in O^*. We demonstrate this procedure below utilizing the membership grades of S^*, I^*, F^*.

Firm 1's membership grade =

$\vee[(.8\wedge.7\wedge1.0), (.8\wedge.7\wedge1.0), (.8\wedge.7\wedge.9),$
$(.8\wedge.7\wedge.8), (.8\wedge.7\wedge.7), (.8\wedge.7\wedge.2),$
$(.9\wedge.7\wedge1.0), (.9\wedge.7\wedge1.0), (.9\wedge.7\wedge.9),$
$(.9\wedge.7\wedge.8), (.9\wedge.7\wedge.7), (.9\wedge.7\wedge.2)]$
$= \vee[.7, .7, .7, .7, .7, .2, .7, .7, .7, .7, .7, .2] = .7$

Each of the individual triplets represents the mapping of a product in S^* onto an element contained in both I^* and f. The first element of each triplet represents the membership grade of the firm's product in S^*. The second element is the membership grade of the firm in I^*. The third element represents the firm's membership grade in f. The minimum membership grade is selected from each mapping via the intersection of the elements (membership grades) in the triplet. If any of the elements contained in the triplet is 0, the membership grade of their intersection is also 0. In other words, an element must exist in each of the possibility distributions, S^*, I^*, f, in order to be in O^*. Each element in S^* has six minimal possibilities which are represented by the minimal grades in each triplet. The highest possibility is then selected as the membership grade of the firm in O^* via the union of the minimal grades of each triplet. This procedure is a direct application of the max$-$min principle and is applicable to all firms as demonstrated below.[22]

Firm 2's membership grade =

$\vee[(.7\wedge.8\wedge1.0), (.7\wedge.8\wedge1.0), (.7\wedge.8\wedge.9),$
$(.7\wedge.8\wedge.8), (.7\wedge.8\wedge.7), (.7\wedge.8\wedge.2)]$
$= \vee[.7, .7, .7, .7, .7, .2] = .7$

Firm 3's membership grade =

$\vee[(.6\wedge.9\wedge1.0), (.6\wedge.9\wedge1.0), (.6\wedge.9\wedge.9),$
$(.6\wedge.9\wedge.8), (.6\wedge.9\wedge.7), (.6\wedge.9\wedge.2),$
$(.7\wedge.9\wedge1.0), (.7\wedge.9\wedge1.0), (.7\wedge.9\wedge.9),$
$(.7\wedge.9\wedge.8), (.7\wedge.9\wedge.7), (.7\wedge.9\wedge.2)]$
$= \vee[.6, .6, .6, .6, .6, .2, .7, .7, .7, .7, .7, .2] = .7$

Firm 4's membership grade =

$\vee[(.2\wedge.1\wedge1.0), (.2\wedge.1\wedge1.0), (.2\wedge.1\wedge.9),$
$(.2\wedge.1\wedge.8), (.2\wedge.1\wedge.7), (.2\wedge.1\wedge.2)]$
$= \vee[.1, .1, .1, .1, .1, .1] = .1$

Firm 5's membership grade =

$\vee[(.1\wedge0\wedge1.0), (.1\wedge0\wedge1.0), (.1\wedge0\wedge.9),$
$(.1\wedge0\wedge.8), (.1\wedge0\wedge.7), (.1\wedge0\wedge.2)]$
$= \vee[0, 0, 0, 0, 0, 0] = 0$

Firm 6's membership grade =

$\vee[(0\wedge0\wedge1.0), (0\wedge0\wedge1.0), (0\wedge0\wedge.9),$
$(0\wedge0\wedge.8), (0\wedge0\wedge.7), (0\wedge0\wedge.2)]$
$= \vee[0, 0, 0, 0, 0, 0] = 0$

Therefore, $O^* = .7/\text{firm 1}, .7/\text{firm 2}, .7/\text{firm 3}, .1/\text{firm 4}, 0/\text{firm 5}, 0/\text{firm 6}$

Deleting firms 5 and 6 from O^* since their respective membership grades are zero, we obtain

$O^* = .7/\text{firm 1}, .7/\text{firm 2}, .7/\text{firm 3}, .1/\text{firm 4}.$

The membership grades indicate the degree of inclusion and the level of conjectural uncertainty attributable to each firm in the market. Thus the entrepreneur of firm F expects firms 1,2,3 to exhibit a relatively strong and equal level of rivalry with firm F. Firm 4 displays a weak level of rivalry in regards to firm F. The operation utilized in the above example can be stated canonically as follows

$$\mu_O.(\text{firm } i) = \wedge(\mu_S.(x_{ij} \wedge \mu_I.(x_i) \wedge \mu_F.(i))$$

For the moment, it warrants mention that other fuzzy variables can be added, for example a 'large' number L^* of consumers, where L^* is a fuzzy number, we have $O^* \triangleq (F^* \wedge S^* \wedge I^* \wedge L^*)$, where $\triangleq$ means 'described by'.

Each oligopolistic market can be defined uniquely in a manner similar to the above.[23] Most importantly, the possibility distribution generated by the set O^* can be used to describe the degree of membership (or the possibility) of a firm's inclusion in the set. The entrepreneur can evaluate the possibility of each firm being an oligopolistic competitor by projecting the firm into the possibility distribution O^*.[24]

The entrepreneur evaluates the fuzziness (the subjective uncertainty) in the set O^* through the derived measure of fuzziness. For example, let $d(O^*) \Leftrightarrow$ measure of fuzziness; that is, the degree (d) measures the uncertainty which the entrepreneur ascribes on the basis of the opportunity that was considered as the best alternative. The rejected activity forms the lost opportunity cost that the selected activity must cover in the long run. Then $d: P(O^*) \rightarrow [0, \infty]^{25}$, which satisfies the following axioms

1) $d(O^*) = 0 \Leftrightarrow O^*$ is a crisp set with zero uncertainty,
   which is also the universal set whose elements are x.

2) $d(O^*)$ has a unique maximum (completely fuzzy, or say
   constantly uncertain) if $\mu_O.(x) = \frac{1}{2}$.

The assignment of a membership grade $= \frac{1}{2}$ to an element indicates that the entrepreneur is uncertain of the element's inclusion in the set. If the membership grade is less than $\frac{1}{2}$, the entrepreneur is inclined to omit the element from the set. Conversely, at a membership grade greater than $\frac{1}{2}$ the entrepreneur is more likely to include the subject element in the set. The membership grade assignment of $\frac{1}{2}$ demonstrates that the entrepreneur is equally uncertain whether to include or exclude the subject element from the set. Thus the uncertainty measure is highest when $\mu_O.(x) = \frac{1}{2}$.

3) $d(O^*) \geq d(O')$ if O' is sharper (crisper) than O^*, and the opposite inequality holds.

4) $d(O^*) = d(O^e) \Rightarrow O^e$ is as fuzzy (or say as uncertain) as O^*.

We suggest the following measure proposed by de Luca et al (1972), which is also identifiably similar to Shannon's well−known entropy.[26]

$$d(O^*) = -K\sum_{i-1}^{n} \mu_O(x_i)\ln(\mu_O(x_i)) + (1-\mu_O(x_i)\ln(1-\mu_O(x_i)) \tag{4}$$

where K is a positive constant and n is the number of elements, or say firms i in O^*. This measure can be demonstrated by the use of the set O^* developed in our previous example.

Recall $O^* = .7/\text{firm 1}$, $.7/\text{firm 2}$, $.7/\text{firm 3}$, $.1/\text{firm 4}$

where the membership grades indicate the degree of competitiveness or, say, reaction grades. Normalize the constant term K in the $d(O^*)$ expression. Substituting reaction grades in the entropy formula (4) generates:

$$d(O^*) = -1[(.7\ln(.7) + .3\ln(.3)) + (.7\ln(.7) + .3\ln(.3)) + (.7\ln(.7) + .3\ln(.3)) + (.1\ln(.1) + .9\ln(.9))]$$
$$\therefore d(O^*) = (.611 + .611 + .611 + .325) = 2.158$$

The value 2.158 represents a measure of the possibilistic entropy (uncertainty or vagueness) contained in the set O^*. The significance of the measure is demonstrated by example. Let θ^* be the value of an alternative oligopolistic industry that the entrepreneur evaluates for possible entry. If $d(\theta^*)$ is greater than 2.158, the level of conjectural uncertainty in θ^* is greater than that contained in O^*. Entry into θ^* therefore requires a greater entrepreneurial energy−investment than that required in O^*. Accordingly, the entrepreneur requires a return commensurate with the energy−investment expended in θ^* which is greater than the return required for participation in O^*. Note that each industry can be defined by the entrepreneur similarly and a measure of fuzziness for the level of uncertainty derived. Next the industries (or markets) would be ranked according to their fuzziness.[27]

The level of uncertainty in an oligopolistic market, contained and described by O^*, indicates to the entrepreneur that greater (less) entrepreneurial efforts or investment are required to obtain an information level commensurate with the uncertainty level in the market. Oligopolistic markets are classified by the differential uncertainties which in turn are represented by O^*, where O^* is not necessarily relevant to other market types. Behavioral uncertainty is unique to oligopolistic markets. Since each oligopolisitic market is uniquely defined by a corresponding O^*, an individual (entrepreneur, owner/manager) may have to work harder (less) in one industry compared to another.[28]

SHORT–RUN OLIGOPOLISTIC COMPETITION AND FUZZY SIGNALS

A short–run model which attempts to capture all of the market aspects or the true heterogeneity of the economic landscape to derive a general (or partial) equilibrium via traditional mathematics must ultimately fail.   The model maker has to delete certain market characteristics; that is, provide simplifying assumptions, in order to derive the equilibrium.   But, the equilibrium obtained may not depict reality if the short–run equilibrium depends on including selected, but not vital market characteristics.[29]

This writer does not profess in any way the ability to formulate a model which can include of all market characteristics.[30]   However, through the use of fuzzy logic, he believes economists can depict a competitive oligopolistic process, one that includes the heterogeneous characteristics of the market, as represented by O^*. Significantly, this O^* defines the oligopolisitic market that the entrepreneur views with the market uncertainty being contained within O^* and is established by $d(O^*)$.

We present a fuzzy deterministic view of the short run in oligopoly markets.   Assume the entrepreneur (firm F) desires to decrease the price of the firm's product in order to gain additional market shares. A decrease in price will expand the customer base and/or induce existing customers to purchase additional units of the product. Firm F expects each market rival in O^* to react differently to the price change.

Recall $O^* = .7/\text{firm 1} , .7/\text{firm 2} , .7/\text{firm 3} , .1/\text{firm 4}$

The reaction of each firm is a function of its perceived interdependence with firm F, its product similarity to that of firm F, and the characteristic of being one of the 'few' firms. Suppose the manager of firm F expects the response set X_e from the market rivals, where $X_e = (.7/x_1 , .7/x_2 , .7/x_3 , .1/x_4)$, with x_i being the response of firm i. The responses may be expressed in a variety of forms. A market rival may respond by changing price, product quality, location, advertising or any combination of the aforementioned. [31] The strength of each expected response is represented by its membership grade in the set X_e. Simply stated, firm F expects each rival to react in accordance with their respective membership grade in O^*. The entrepreneur expects a weak response (membership grade = .1) from firm 4; relatively strong and equal reactions from firms 1, 2 and 3.

Additionally, the entrepreneur may have another expectation set such as Y_e, where Y_e consists of future states that may or may not be independent of the price change. These states, whether resulting from the price change or not, must be accounted for in the decision making process. Thus, the entrepreneur expects a market response set Y_e, where $Y_e = (.6/y_1 , .4/y_2 , .3/y_3)$. The elements of Y are defined below.

$y_1 = $ entry of new firms

$y_2 = $ change in input prices due to changes in output demand or changes in the states of nature, for example, the Iraqi invasion of Kuwait and its subsequent effect on world oil prices.

$y_3 = $ change in market size.

The sets X_e and Y_e represent two expected reaction sets. The first set describes market rivals' possible reactions, while the latter describes parametrical changes in the market itself. [32] Functioning in an oligopolistic market, the entrepreneur conjectures the degree and extent of rivals' reactions to a certain signal (such as a price decrease by the firm) within the heterogeneous space. Such conjectures are in addition to those concerning market uncertainties stemming from the state of the world. The relationship between both expectation sets is described by a fuzzy relationship, such as 'and' or '+', etc. In other words, a vague knowledge rule assigns expected outcomes to the interactions of the two expectation sets. The heterogeneous economic space precludes the assignment of crisp rules (for example the logical 'and' or ordinary addition); these rules do not compensate the entrepreneur for the existing uncertainty in each element. [33]

The entrepreneur utilizes a vague relationship or a knowledge rule that is based on his vague (incomplete) knowledge of all the precise variables affecting the actual responses to his signal. The entrepreneur formulates the knowledge rule semantically as 'if x_i and y_j, then z_t ', where z_t is the entrepreneur's counter response in the next period. The time period simply refers to the time when new evidence/information become available to the entrepreneur or rivals' reactions to the entrepreneur's signal are observed. Note that in our model, the decision period need not be specified. The entrepreneur is required only to estimate rival firms' counter responses over time by a fuzzy number. If a determination of the decision period (duration) becomes necessary, the entrepreneur identifies an approximate expected response time. The entrepreneur assigns partial membership grades to the rivals' response time and correspondingly, the firm's individual response time. It may be the case that the manager of firm F expects firm 1 to respond 6 months from an initial signal time with a conjectured .9 certainty; firm 2 responds in three months from the initial signalling, with a .8 certainty, etc. Each firm is expected to respond in accordance with its own input−output and inventory cost relationships. The response time of the individual firms may be estimated fuzzily or by a fuzzy estimate assigned to the whole set O^*. We define a third set (N_e), where $N_e :=$ approximately $N-$months from the time the signal was sent. N_e is discrete with each month assigned a membership grade. By the max−min principle, we obtain a joint possibility distribution of X_e and N_e. The time adjusted X_e is denoted as $X_e{}'$. Similarly, the set Y_e may be adjusted independently by time and a new set $Y_e{}'$ obtained. The adjusted sets $(X_e{}'$ and $Y_e{}')$ are then utilized to determine the membership grades of Z.

We illustrate the counter response membership assignment process with a numerical example. Let $Z = (z_1, z_2, z_3)$, where z_1, z_2, z_3 are possible responses at the end of the decision period. [34] The entrepreneur subjectively assigns a membership grade indicating the degree of certainty or uncertainty of the occurrence of each element in the X_e and Y_e sets.

Recall $X_e = (.7/x_1 , .7/x_2 , .7/x_3 , .1/x_4)$
and $Y_e = (.6/y_1 , .4/y_2 , .3/y_3)$,

where both x,y are fuzzy sets as defined above.

Let there be a function f (the vague knowledge rule) that maps ordered pairs from X_e, Y_e to Z_e. The elements are described by the following matrix.

$$
\begin{array}{c c c c}
 & y_1 & y_2 & y_3 \\
x_1 & z_1 & z_1 & z_2 \\
x_2 & z_1 & z_3 & z_1 \\
x_3 & z_1 & z_2 & z_3 \\
x_4 & z_3 & z_1 & z_1
\end{array}
$$

The membership grades of the elements in z can be calculated from the extension principle as follows

$$\mu(z_1) = \vee[(.7 \wedge .6),(.7 \wedge .4),(.7 \wedge .6)(.7 \wedge .3),(.7 \wedge .6),(.1 \wedge .4),(.1 \wedge .3)]$$
$$= \vee[.6,.4,.6,.3,.6,.1,.1] = .6$$

$$\mu(z_2) = \vee[(.7 \wedge .3),(.7 \wedge .4)]$$
$$= \vee[.3,.4] = .4$$

$$\mu(z_3) = \vee[(.7 \wedge .4),(.7 \wedge .3),(.1 \wedge .6)]$$
$$= \vee[.4,.3,.1] = .4$$

Clearly z_1 has the highest membership grade. Thus z_1 is the response chosen by the entrepreneur based on his expectations.

Suppose that after transmitting the signal (price change), the entrepreneur observes the sets X_0, Y_0 where X_0, Y_0 are not identical to X_e, Y_e respectively. Note that the observed responses may not be the actual market responses; that is, the signal transmitted by each rival can be a mixture of actions where estimates are not easily or objectively determined. In other words, a response is distorted by discounts, promotional campaigns, increased sales force, reimbursements, or product differentiation (horizontal or vertical). The output signals (responses) of rival firms are also distorted because actual production and exact capacities of rivals may not be disclosed to the entrepreneur. Thus we propose that the entrepreneur in firm F

receives a fuzzy message (X_0) from the market rivals. Additionally, the uncertain states of the world that are observed by the entrepreneur (Y_0) may also be fuzzy or vague, for example, a firm may decide to enter the market on a trial basis by shipping a similar product for the one period under observation.

It is further the case that entry may be temporal or permanent. An entrepreneur can only ascertain (presume) to a certain degree whether an entry is temporary or permanent. Correspondingly, a membership grade would be assigned conveying the entrepreneur's level of presumption as to entry. In substance, the entrepreneur assigns membership grades to X_0, Y_0 in demonstrating the perceived level of certainty or uncertainty that an actual occurrence has taken place. The subjective membership grade that is assigned to each signal observed may also be viewed as describing the firm's recognition of a signal to the basic characteristics of the signal.

The entrepreneur adjusts X^e and Y^e according to X^o, Y^o according to the following rule

$$\mu_{X^A}(x_i) = \vee(\mu_{X^o}(x_i) \wedge \mu_{X^e}(x_i))$$
$$and \ \mu_{Y^A}(y_i) = \vee(\mu_{Y^o}(y_i) \wedge \mu_{Y^e}(y_i))$$

A new (adjusted) z matrix is formed corresponding to the new adjusted values. Note the consistency of this method with Fisher's assertion (1898):

> ...As a matter of fact, no businessman assumes either that his rival's output or price will remain constant any more than a chess player assumes that his opponent will not interfere with his effort to capture a knight. On the contrary, his whole thought is to forecast what move the rival will make in response to one of his own.[35]

A new set O^*_A, the adjusted oligopoly set, is formed based on the adjustment process presented above. In other words, the entrepreneur re−evaluates the initial view of the market in light of the newly acquired information. The information, being itself vague (uncertain), is incorporated into O^* through the max−min principle; and $d(O^*_A)$, the uncertainty measure, is obtained as before. If $d(O^*_A)$ is not consistent with the entrepreneur's desired (acceptable) uncertainty level the entrepreneur may exit the market. The decision to exit the industry may not be based solely on the one–period observation. The profit maximization principle may be sacrificed in the very short run in favor of long–run profit maximization. Rational behavior indicates that a decision to exit the industry, if the decision is based on one period alone, may be an outcome of a special case or circumstance, the circumstance being that the entrepreneur is completely outperformed by the market rivals. In this case, the entrepreneur decides to minimize losses by exiting the market immediately.[36]

Suppose an entrepreneur believes that she is not yet fully attuned to the market. In other words, the entrepreneur realizes that due to lack of experience, the message received (observed) may not be the actual message (accurate interpretation of the message) or the message that an experienced rival would observe. Thus the newcomer has an added uncertainty, one that is centered on the accuracy of her judgement. This type of uncertainty is reduced through time and learning; however, the conjectural uncertainty remains as an indivisible part of the market.

Should adjustment be necessary, the entrepreneur may use one of the following methods to adjust the observed message X_0

1. A dilation or concentration of membership grades in the set X_0.[37]

2. Assignment of fuzzy membership grades in place of the crisp membership grades to the message set X_0.

Let $\mu_{X_0}(x_1) = .8$, the entrepreneur replaces .8 by 'approximately .8'; that is, the fuzzy number .8. The set X_0 becomes a fuzzy set of the second degree.[38]

3. The entrepreneur may create a set x_B, where X_B is the message set the entrepreneur believes to have occurred but did not observe due to market inexperience. A new possibility distribution is obtained through the intersection of X_0 and X_B denote the new set as X_N, where X_N is given below.[39]

$$\mu_{X_N}(x) = \vee(\mu_{X_0}(x) \wedge \mu_{X_B}(x))$$

The new set X_N is then used in the decision process in place of the set X_0.

SUMMARY

Thus far we have demonstrated a new realistic view of short—run competition in oligopoly markets by utilizing a model of signalling that is based on the theoretical definition of oligopoly markets. Throughout this presentation, the market is viewed as a complex environment with the entrepreneur acting as the catalyst for production and pricing decisions. Our entrepreneur is no longer viewed as the naive Bertrand—Cournot competitor but as a complex uncertain human being who reacts to an uncertain environment. The uncertainty in oligopoly is shown to arise not only from the states of nature and time, but also and most importantly, from the interdependence among rivals in a vaguely defined market.

The short run in oligopoly, as we have stressed and illustrated in this chapter, is chaotic and seemingly disordered, this disorder, however, is rooted in an extremely well known pattern, that of the conjectural process. We refrain from depicting a short—run equilibrium in the oligopoly market because our focus and theory is partially based on the traditional assumption that viable firms operate in accordance with their efficient cost curves in the long run. In the case of oligopoly, not only is the viable firm required to be efficient in its technical neo—classical cost imputations, but the entrepreneur must efficiently match her skills with the conjectural uncertainty existing in the market.

We shall contend that the conjectural uncertainty is correctly estimated by all market survivors in the long run. These surviving firms are those whose entrepreneurs go beyond meeting the neo—classical technical efficiency requirements to correctly estimate the true level of uncertainty in their industry. These firms (and hence their owners—managers) are capable of living with and surviving at that level. As Frank Knight (1921) stated, the entrepreneur's role is to minimize the level of uncertainty, not to eliminate it. We add to this the thesis that entrepreneurs make choices among oligopolistic markets based essentially on the perceived level of behavioral uncertainty in a market. The process of choice and imputation of the cost of uncertain behavior is the focus of Chapter 3.

NOTES

1. Parts of this chapter draw heavily from Working Paper 91–22, Texas A & M University, Greenhut and Mansur.
2. A general equilibrium for oligopoly markets will be fully demonstrated in Chapter 4.
3. See page 42 of this chapter.
4. We relax the duopoly and homogeneity in production assumptions later in the analysis. These two assumptions are used solely as a point of departure for later analysis.
5. We also eliminate perfect foresight at a later stage in the analysis. Indeed, all restrictions will be relaxed as we proceed into the realistic (fuzzy) world of oligopolistic competition.
6. The subject of the eawrepreneur's opportunity cost is addressed in Chapters 3 and 4; thus we only note this oddity in this present conception.
7. This component of the Cournot model has received the most criticism. The merits and demerits of the so-called 'no regret criterion' in Cournot are well established in the economic literature.
8. Bertrand also demonstrated that Cournot's solution was inferior to the cooperative (collusive) equilibrium, an equilibrium which Cournot had rejected as a possible solution.
9. Bertrand's use of pricing as the strategic variable was critical to the analysis of the behavior of firms facing high inventory costs. Such firms change price continually to associate demand with production rates as opposed to the use of outputs as the primary decision variable by firms which face low inventory costs. Bertrand's analysis of the high inventory cost producer is considered to be one of his major contributions to oligopoly theory.
10. The term 'oligopoly' first appeared in the work of Schlesinger in his *Theore der Geld und Kredt Wertschaft* (1914, pp. 17, 18, 57). The term was later popularized by Chamberlin (1933). Interestingly, Chamberlin was credited with coining the term 'oligopoly' until 1936, when it was realized that Schlesinger had conceived of the term 19 years earlier.
11. We do not claim that inaccurate terminology contributed solely to the labelling of oligopolies as inefficient. We recognize the generally accepted view that the inefficiency of the oligopoly market arises from the negatively sloped demand curve, via which any tangency solution between the AR, AC curves must occur to the left of the most efficient production level (in $AC(Q)$).
12. Oligopolistic behavioral uncertainty is said to arise from the interdependent actions of oligopolistic firms. This interdependence does not exist in perfect competition where the firm is simply a price taker in the market. With corresponding result, albeit opposite in form, the monopolist is also not subject to interdependent behavior. Having no rivals nor prospective rivals, this seller sets price and output according to classical theory's revenue and cost relationships.
13. See Greenhut, Lee and Mansur (1991) for a refutation of a specific case in spatial economics where the results of a duopolistic model do not extend to the oligopolistic situation.
14. Chamberlin (1962, p. 100) describes oligopoly as the 'small group', which he defines as 'a group of relatively few sellers, perhaps only two'. Chamberlin claims that the interdependence among oligopolistically competitive firms arises from the sellers being 'relatively few in number'. Our analysis demonstrates otherwise.

Interdependence, in conjunction with the other factors, defines the oligopolistic uncertainty.

15. Chamberlin (1962), p. 56−57 states that

> a general class of product is differentiated if any significant basis exists for distinguishing the goods (or services) of one seller from those of another. Such a basis may be real or fancied... Where such differentiation exists, even though it be slight, buyers will be paired with sellers, not by chance and at random (as under pure competition), but according to their preferences... When these two aspects of differentiation are held in mind, it is evident that virtually all products are differentiated, at least slightly...

We believe that our set 'similar' captures the definition of product differentiation that was set forth by Chamberlin.

16. This approach to product differentiation differs significantly from existing approaches, such as Lancaster (1966), Lane (1980), Leland (1977), in that the boundaries of the set 'similar products' are not crisply defined.

17. The condition that at least one product is identical to firm F's is not binding since we can always normalize the set by dividing each membership grade by the maximum membership grade in the set.

18. We define the term 'real world' to mean the economic landscape in general, and the oligopolistic market as viewed by the entrepreneur specifically.

19. Two reasons account for regarding the term 'few firms' as a fuzzy number. First, the descriptor 'few' is a vague descriptor. Second, with free entry and exit into the market, a firm which plans its productive capacity for a given time period must take into account the possibility of new entries or exits even in the immediate future (production period). Because a firm in a geographically separated market (e.g., in a different state or country) may enter a market by shipping its product a little further, up to and including the market where firm F is located, the number 'few' is, therefore, a justifiably fuzzy number.

20. At the cost of seeming repetitive, the extension principle is restated for relevance and significance. This principle will be utilized throughout the remainder of this chapter.

21. An elementary example of fuzzy relationships will suffice at this stage. Suppose the entrepreneur states 'I want to employ someone who is intelligent and efficient'. The word 'and' is a fuzzy connector. It does not mean a simple ordinary ($\land$) but a fuzzy ($\land$). To solve a fuzzy relationship we utilize Zadeh's extension principle where $\mu_{U \land V}(z_i) = \lor \ (\mu_U(u) \land \mu_V(v))$, $U \in$ 'intelligent', $V \in$ 'efficient' and Z is 'employee'.

22. This procedure involves a compensation to the decision maker for the stringent intersection requirement (minimal possibility). While the entrepreneur accepts only the minimal possibility in each mapping, she is compensated for her adherence to this stringent requirement by choosing the highest possibility outcome.

23. The interdependence among rivals in each market differs among markets. The size of the market also varies in terms of the number of firms across the differentiated industries. Moreover, the degree of product similarity is a product specific endowment and is only relevant when firms are in the same market. Clearly n firms may produce m products, where $m \neq n$. Each entrepreneur has to define the market subjectively, but the fuzziness of any competitive decision is, we see, quantifiable under the fuzzy set approach.

24. Zadeh (1978) introduced the concept of possibility distribution and possibility measure. A possibility measure is a function $\Pi : P(X) \rightarrow [0,1]$, where $P(X)$ is the power set of X. Π must satisfy the axioms set forth by Zimmerman (1985), namely

1) $\Pi(\phi) = 0$

2) $A \subseteq B \Rightarrow \Pi(A) \subseteq \Pi(B)$

3) $\Pi(\vee_{i \in I} A_i) = SUP \ \Pi(A_i)$

Once the possibility distribution is normalized, the fuzzy measure becomes a possibility if X is finite.

25. $P(O^*)$ is the power set of O^*, or the set of all the fuzzy subsets of O^*.

26. For other measures of fuzziness, see Klir et al (1988), *Fuzzy Sets, Uncertainty and Information*.

27. Ranking can also be qualitative such as 'less fuzzy', 'more fuzzy', etc. Note that the measure of uncertainty presented above can be thought of as the measure of potential information required in the oligopolistic market. Reduction of the uncertainty in the market is equivalent to acquiring new information.

28. We demonstrate later the process of estimating the impact of uncertainty on the entrepreneurial opportunity cost. It suffices to mention at this stage of the analysis that the entrepreneur is assumed to perceive of this uncertainty as a requirement for additional entrepreneurial inputs.

29. Observe the requirement in the mathematics of chaos that a deterministic pattern can be recognized within a seemingly random behavior if the initial conditions and the objective function are known. This knowledge, we contend, is not achievable and/or imputable. Whereas determinism may exist in seemingly random behavior, we can only observe randomness. True patterns are not identifiable in chaotic phenomenon.

30. The ardent reader may investigate the 'general equilibrium' of G. Debreu (1959). Debreu's analysis, while mathematically sophisticated and relevant to perfectly competitive markets, is based on and facilitated by the use of simplifying assumptions. This widespread practice of economic theoreticians is observed in existing economic models. Simplifying assumptions typically declare certain variables as negligible. While some variables may be negligible in a static one period model, the inclusion of time in a model may cause 'negligible' factors to become significant in the multi–period analysis. Thus, simplifying assumptions may lead to erroneous conclusions.

31. Although only four expected responses are mentioned, our model allows for the inclusion of other responses and nesting. Each market participant in O^* may select one or all of the following strategy sets: price, product quality, location, shipping mode and pricing (f.o.b., uniform or discriminatory). Observe the consistency of this method and assumptions with those of Kahn (1962), p. 55, where he notes that '...complex possibilities emerge when the businessman realizes that neither the outputs not the prices of his competitors will remain constant if he alters his own price'.

32. The set Y_e is identified separately from X_e in order to isolate the uncertainty arising in any market type; and to distinguish it from the conjectural uncertainty that is unique to oligopoly markets.

33. See endnote 13.

34. The set Z may contain more than three elements. Three elements were selected to achieve simplicity in explanation.

35. As quoted in E.H. Chamberlin's *Monopolistic Competition*, 1962, pp. 46,47.

36. We explain and elaborate market entry and exit decisions in Chapters 3 and 4 of this work. For our present purpose, the above intuitive discussion suffices.

37. See Chapter 1 of this work for the explanation of these two concepts.

38. See Dubois and Prade (1980), pp. 62–63.

39. This method benefits in part from a similar model developed by Yager (1980).

3. Fuzzy Opportunity Costs

In Chapter 2, we conceptualized the oligopolistic market and interpreted the complexities therein by employing fuzzy logic as our analytical tool. The conjectural variation process was demonstrated through the quantification of the factors contributing to the entrepreneur's conjectures concerning market rivals' behavior patterns (for example, expectations, prior knowledge, and continual learning). This was done in a realistic manner via fuzzy sets. The present chapter builds on Chapter 2's findings in demonstrating how opportunity cost in oligopoly markets can be estimated. Moreover, it evaluates entrepreneurial investments (efforts and/or expenditures) that are associated with conjecturing and guesstimating the rivals' behavior.

For long−run viability each oligopolist must be compensated fully for the opportunity cost associated with the investment. Thus this chapter must establish how the oligopolist determines the cost of uncertainty, which cost must, to repeat, include (and relate to) the opportunity cost set of the subject entrepreneur. Again we utilize fuzzy sets in the analysis to estimate the entrepreneurial expenditures and to evaluate the required returns. It will be evident that the oligopolistic entrepreneur requires compensation for the cost of uncertainty in addition to the traditional factor rents, the firm and its entrepreneur may earn because of greater skills, location, and the like.

THE ENTREPRENEURIAL ROLE − REVISITED

In classical economic theory, consumer preferences and tastes are identified in utility analysis, purchasing behavior and product price. Differing tastes, incomes, wealth, and the consumer's locale within the economic landscape are recognized as demand determinants; thus consumer diversity is accounted for fully, however, the multi — dimensional nature of the entrepreneur is absent from the theory of the firm. As if by magical decree, neo — classical theory characterizes the entrepreneur as a species totally separate from that of the consumer counterpart, in that the formation of product characteristics and price is devoid of the human aspects of the entrepreneur.

Any brief review of a principles or intermediate economics textbook would illustrate our point since the entrepreneur is glibly defined simply as a gatherer of economic resources and the bearer of risk whose payment (rent) for this role is the profit or losses generated by the enterprise. Personal likes and dislikes, in addition to income constraints, determine the consumer's decision to purchase a product. On the other hand, the entrepreneur's decision to produce this or that product, or several products, is based solely on the marginal equalities of the firm, attributed to market price also and derived fraw factor input costs. The entrepreneur's utility or disutility arising from the participation in one industry compared to another does not enter into the analysis of markets and firms.[1]   Whereas the consumer is individualized from her income expenditures, the entrepreneur is simply merged with the firm; yet, both the consumer and the entrepreneur are 'two sides of the same coin'.

The merger of the entrepreneur with the firm, we conjecture, arose from the Marshallian need to separate demand and supply. The resulting division of the economic process into two groups, households and firms, led to the characterization that the function of the household is consumption and the function of the firm is production; that is, firms are non — consumers. Had the human aspects of the entrepreneur (owner/manager) been considered in the market, the construction of the simple demand and supply paradigms would not have been possible. Consider a market which approximates the purely competitive market, for example, the wheat market. Assume that positive economic profits are observed to exist in the market. As a consequence of profit observation, one thousand farmers enter the market. Traditionally, entry causes the supply curve to shift to the right; that is, supply increases. However, if we adhere to the principle that entrepreneurs (farmers) are human and hence are also consumers of a combination of products, one of which may be wheat, we must also accede that the market demand for wheat is changed because of the increase (1000) in the number of consumers in the market. Since a farmer who produces wheat is likely to obtain the quantities needed for consumption at cost rather than at the market price, the market equilibrium becomes essentially meaningless, especially in purely competitive markets where a large number of firms exist in the market. In other words, the concept of a purely competitive market equilibrium is destabilized once the entrepreneur is considered both as a producer and a consumer. A clear cut distinction between consumers and producers is essential to the workings of the Marshallian analysis. From this, the dehumanization of the entrepreneur evolved.

While the dehumanization of the entrepreneur may be valid in the abstract and unrealistic world of pure competition, the resulting one–dimensional characterization of the entrepreneur is not definitive of the entrepreneur of more realistic market types, such as oligopoly markets. The subjectivity of the conjectural process necessitates consideration of the oligopolistic competitor as a living, thinking organism. Furthermore, as no two individuals are alike, no two entrepreneurs are identical. Consequently, the singular nature of the entrepreneur requires that entrepreneurial utility (disutility) be entered into the profit–maximizing analysis of the firm.[2]

In addition to the inconsistent treatment of the entrepreneur *vis à vis* the consumer, neo–classical economic theory minimizes the significance of the entrepreneurial role within the economic landscape. In purely competitive and monopolistic markets, the entrepreneurial role is restricted to one of gathering economic resources and assuming the risk inherent in each market type. In these markets, the entrepreneur is either a price taker or a price setter, respectively; one who is dependent on market demand, the dictates of marginal costs and revenues, and the risks associated with business ventures. Thus, the entrepreneur assumes a dormant role, composed of mechanical, rote actions which are devoid of instinctive behavior, intuitive abilities, and subjective thought processes.

An analysis of the neo–classical view of the entrepreneurial role as a bearer of risk illustrates our point. Risks can be easily estimated and adjusted by means of objective probabilities. Accepted methodologies of experimentation, the gathering of historical data, and the use of sampling techniques can provide scientific estimates of the risk involved in certain processes. For example, the probability that certain raw materials will be flawed can be estimated objectively through the observation of the quantity of flawed materials occurring in prior batches; subsequently, the laws of probability, distributions, means, variances, confidence intervals, etc. can be applied. In turn, inferences can be rendered as to the probability that a specific number of elements in a sample will be flawed.

It is also the case that methodological risk estimation is not limited to events of a repetitive nature. With initial occurrences, such as the landing of Apollo on the moon, modelling and the simulation of scientific data can be utilized. Thus where data availability and research initiatives exist, an objective probability can be successfully estimated. Therefore, entrepreneurial talent is not essential to the risk estimation process. In fact, the entrepreneur, as depicted in neo−classical economic literature, is ultimately replaceable by a calculating machine (computer) which can provide equivalent or superior performance results to that of the entrepreneur.[3] A machine can produce precise estimates of risk and factor costs; and determine the profit maximizing level of output by equating marginal revenue to marginal cost. The machine operates on precise principles and given the same inputs, the same output decisions are derivable at all times.

While the analytical capacities of computers are consistent, we observe that the entrepreneur's performance is hampered or stimulated by personal traits, biases, preferences, and day to day nuances. Accordingly, the machine acquires the entrepreneurial rent, which is expended on the servicing and programming of the machine. Thus the neo−classically defined entrepreneurial role is explained away.

Corresponding in result to the above, the capitalistic economy can be eliminated as well (in terms of supply) and replaced by a central planning agency or a device that provides objective decisions for the enterprises which operate throughout the economy. Envision in this context an economy that exhibits the following characteristics: the supply side is completely determinable as a calculating machine employs all the factors of production. Prices are flexible; business cycle fluctuations are eliminated, and therefore lay−offs are non−existent; so technology thrives and inflationary or recessionary gaps are relegated to points of historical reference; that is, in short, a Pareto optimal economy evolves, an economy that is perfect in conception and no longer subject to entrepreneurial short—comings. That business world borders on perfection.

However, neither the abstract nor realistic interpretations of economic theory in total maintain the simplistic, naive neo—classical view of the entrepreneur. Elimination of the entrepreneur's role in centrally planned economies, where they are replaced by government managers or machines, has contributed to the failure of these systems, not only in terms of achieving Pareto optimality but also in the provision of basic subsistence products. The collapse of eastern European economies in the face of the continued success of economies which have adhered to 'capitalistic' philosophies provides a living testimonial to the significance of the entrepreneur and the importance of the entrepreneurial role in economic systems.[4]

The role of the entrepreneur extends far beyond the neo—classical definition of gathering and organizing resources and imputing risk. The entrepreneur is an intelligent, reactive, and continuously learning organism operating in an environment of uncertainty. Uncertainty, by its very nature, is the product of variety in existence among all species, where systematic or consistent behavior is not observable at all times. A sole organism is unable to obtain and receive all existing data. Furthermore, it is incapable of processing and assimilating all relevant data to form a deterministic, all inclusive model that describes phenomena. Additionally, time change, whether continuous, discrete or dimensionally relative, enhances the element of uncertainty in the environment as organisms change either in character, constitution and/or reactive behavior.

Correspondingly, the existence of the entrepreneur in an uncertain environment necessitates the inclusion of the environmental uncertainty into the entrepreneurial role. Uncertainty may arise in all market types. In pure competition, monopolistic competition, oligopoly, and monopoly, uncertainty may emanate from imperfect (vague or incomplete) knowledge of the existing market demand, changes in demand conditions, and factor input prices. However, in oligopoly, as demonstrated in Chapter 2, there exists an additional uncertainty, above and beyond those uncertainties occurring in the other market types. This added uncertainty results from the interdependence among rivals, where conjectures and guesstimates are the *modus operandus* of the oligopolistic market participants.

Uncertainty is distinct from risk. Risk is objectively determined while uncertainty is subjectively determined. As Frank Knight (1921), the first economist to distinguish sharply between risk and uncertainty, observed:

> The practical difference between the two categories, risk and uncertainty, is that in the former the distribution of the outcome in a group of instances is known (either through calculation a priori or from statistics of past experience), while in the case of uncertainty this is not true, the reason being in general that it is impossible to form a group of instances, because the situation dealt with is in a high degree unique.

The element of risk in a venture can be estimated by utilizing objective probabilities, whereas uncertainty cannot be objectively determined but only inferred from personal (subjective) experiences, observed (vague) outcomes and imperfect (approximate) knowledge, with varying degrees of ambiguity and subjectivity across the economic landscape. Hence, the functions of gathering economic resources and assuming risk can be assigned to a mechanical device. In contrast, decision making under conditions of uncertainty is beyond the capacities of a machine. Machines require exactness and objectivity; business decisions hinge to a large extent on vague and incomplete knowledge of all relevant existing and initial conditions.

The entrepreneur not only surpasses a calculating machine in analyzing incomplete data, but further excels over machines in predicting futuristic outcomes involving the firm and the market. Without possessing exact knowledge, the entrepreneur tries to consider each relevant future element along with their effects upon each other. Frequently she must rely on, what is simplistically called, a 'gut feeling'. This gut feeling or intuition is an extension and result of the entrepreneur's knowledge, expertise, individual characteristics, and the social and psychological factors which directly or indirectly impact the entrepreneur's environment. These factors form the basis of the decision making process under conditions of uncertainty.[5] Thus, we redefine the entrepreneur as an organizer of the production factors and as the predictor and bearer of the risks and uncertainties associated with and emanating from the business venture.[6]

The inclusion of uncertainty as a fundamental part of the entrepreneurial decision making process was also formalized initially by Frank Knight (1921):

> The adventurer has an opinion as to the outcome, within more or less narrow limits. If he is inclined to make the venture, this opinion is either in expectation of a certain definite gain or a belief in the real probability of a larger one. Outside the limits of the anticipation any other result becomes more and more improbable in his mind as the amount thought of diverges either way.

Notice the similarity between Knight's description of anticipated returns and our earlier presentation of a fuzzy number in Chapters 1 and 2.

Decades before its formal conception, Knight envisioned the concept of fuzziness or vagueness and called for its use to describe uncertain returns. His call for a bounded rationality is echoed by Simon (1982), who wanted an infusion from other sciences, such as psychology and sociology, to shed light on the decision making process under uncertainty. Greenhut (1974) explicitly demonstrates the psychological factors' influence on rationality and derives a model upon which this present work is based. The incorporation of these personal factors into the decision making process forms the basis for our next subject.

RATIONAL ECONOMIC CHOICES AND THE ENTREPRENEURIAL OPPORTUNITY COST

Thus far we have stressed the human factor as a determinant of business decision making. We now impute and incorporate the human factor into the opportunity cost of the entrepreneur. Via this imputation, we demonstrate that the rational man is also an economic man. It will be manifest that decisions perceived as irrational by outsiders, are in fact rational once the entrepreneur's opportunity cost is imputed into the decision making process. This opportunity cost must allude to and incorporate the human aspect of the entrepreneur in addition to the traditional goal of profit maximization.[7]

We utilize a simple plant location example to demonstrate the opportunity cost imputation process. Conceive of an entrepreneur who is awarded a defense contract to produce widgets for the federal government. The contract stipulates that a specific quantity of widgets, Q, is to be produced at a fixed price, P. Payment to the entrepreneur by the government will take place at the end of the production period. The entrepreneur is furnished a listing of sites within the United States that represent potential locations for the manufacturing facility. We perceive of the sites as a finite set X where $X = (x_1, x_2, x_3, ...x_n)$. Traditional set theory would assign a full membership grade to each element in X. However, upon examination of the site listing (the set X), the entrepreneur of our example determines that several of the potential sites are more appealing or desirable from a purely personal viewpoint than others. Therefore, the entrepreneur assigns different membership grades to the various sites. Each membership grade is subjectively assigned according to personal preference. A high membership grade specifies the site as highly desirable; conversely, a low membership grade represents a less desirable location. Thus, the sites are ordered in accordance with the entrepreneur's preferences.

We assume for simplicity that all technical production costs, including shipping costs, are precisely determinable at each site in X. The production costs and shipping costs differ among the sites. In other words, corresponding to X, there is a set C, where $C = (c_1, c_2, c_3, ...c_n)$. The revenues of the firm are identical at all sites; P and Q are contractually specified *a priori*, irrespective of plant locale. $TR = PQ$, the potential profits at site $i \in n$, is π_i, where $\pi_i = TR - C_i$. We define π_i as the firm's technical profits at site i. The terminology 'technical profits' refers to the technical factors or inputs employed at each site specifically, with the opportunity costs covered in full for all the factors of production, excluding the entrepreneurial opportunity cost.[8] The entrepreneurial opportunity cost refers to the alternative employments within the set X. We impute the entrepreneur's opportunity cost into the profit determining equation and obtain a net or economic profit π_i'.

As stated previously, the entrepreneur ranks the sites in X according to personal preference. W.o.l.o.g., assume that the entrepreneur is an avid surfer, who surfs regularly in Hawaii. Let the entrepreneur consider the availability of the surf as the sole personal determinant; that is, other possible factors, such as family ties, climatic preference, alternative hobbies, etc., do not exist.[9] Thus the subject entrepreneur ranks the potential sites via the set X in accordance with accessibility to the surf site in Hawaii.

For simplicity, let X, contain only three sites: Montana, Hawaii, and Oklahoma.

$$X = (1.0/\text{Hawaii}, \ .7/\text{Oklahoma}, \ .5/\text{Montana}).$$

Let the technical profits at the individual sites be

$$\pi_H = \$30000$$
$$\pi_{OK} = \$45000$$
$$\pi_{MN} = \$50000$$

The entrepreneur estimates the personal factor cost (the cost of surfing in Hawaii) given the venture is located at one of the three sites selected. The personal factor costs relate to the direct and indirect costs of surfing in Hawaii. Direct costs consist of travel expenses such as air fare, hotel accommodations, taxi fares, etc. Indirect expenses include such considerations as the availability (or lack of) year round access to the Hawaiian surf; delay time at airports; cost of travel time; etc. The direct costs are estimated with a considerable degree of objectivity; however, exact future estimates are not available; air fares may change, hotel rates may fluctuate, etc.

A fuzzy number may be utilized to describe the direct cost associated with each potential site within extremely narrow bounds; that is, the upper and lower bounds are close in value to the estimated number. For example, let the direct costs from site i be 'approx $6000' as represented by the triplet (5900, 6000, 6200). The band width (distance between 5900 and 6200) is $300 or 5% of the approximated figure. This narrow distribution is based on the entrepreneur's subjective belief in the accuracy of the prediction.

Conversely, estimates of the entrepreneur's indirect costs are totally subjective. The indirect costs are also described by fuzzy (uncertain) numbers with utility or disutility forming the basis for the indirect cost estimates. Consider the example of waiting time in airport terminals. The hours spent in an airport terminal, late at night, at an hour past the normal bedtime, entails a greater level of hardship (disutility) than an equivalent delay during daytime hours.[10] Therefore, the entrepreneur can only approximate (at best) the derived utility or disutility.

The personal factor costs (direct and indirect) are summed for each venture locale. Since direct and indirect costs are estimated by fuzzy numbers, the total personal factor cost is a fuzzy number. Let the costs of the personal factor (surfing) at the three sites be

$$C_H = \text{approx } 5000$$
$$C_{OK} = \text{approx } 20000$$
$$C_{MN} = \text{approx } 25000$$

that is, each of the costs is represented by a fuzzy number.

In order to define the approximateness of the cost guesstimates, the entrepreneur utilizes triplets to describe the fuzzy numbers; that is,

$$C_H = (1000, 5000, 9000)$$
$$C_{OK} = (17000, 20000, 25000)$$
$$C_{MN} = (19000, 25000, 31000)$$

Observe that the first value in each triplet represents the lowest possible value in the entrepreneur's personal cost guesstimate, thus describing the lower bound of the possibility distribution around the middle value (the mode). The third value contained in each triplet is the upper bound of the possibility distribution. In the case of an Hawaiian locale, the entrepreneur believes that the personal factor costs will not be less than $1000 or greater than $9000. Thus the entrepreneur believes with varying degrees of certainty that the cost of surfing in Hawaii will be vaguely around $5000, with $5000 being the element with the highest degree of certainty.

Crisp numbers can be viewed as a special case of fuzzy numbers and written in triplet form as below

$$\pi_H = (30000, 30000, 30000)$$
$$\pi_{OK} = (45000, 45000, 45000)$$
$$\pi_{MN} = (50000, 50000, 50000)$$

Of course, in the case of crisp numbers, the membership grades of the upper bounds, lower bounds, and mode are all equal; that is, the degree of certainty is equal (membership grade of 1). The crisp number can also be described by employing the membership function as below

$$\mu_{30000}(x) = 1 \qquad x = 30000$$
$$= 0 \qquad x \neq 30000$$

The entrepreneur then estimates the net profits, including the personal factor cost, of each alternative site by subtracting the personal factor cost from the technical profits at that site, as below

$$\pi_H{}' = \pi_H - C_H \quad = (30000, 30000, 30000) - (1000, 5000, 9000)$$
$$= (30000 - 9000, 30000 - 5000, 30000 - 1000)$$
$$= (21000, 25000, 29000)$$
$$\pi_{OK}{}' = \pi_{OK} - C_{OK} = (45000, 45000, 45000) - (17000, 20000, 25000)$$
$$= (45000 - 25000, 45000 - 20000, 45000 - 17000)$$
$$= (20000, 25000, 28000)$$
$$\pi_{MN}{}' = \pi_{MN} - C_{MN} = (50000, 50000, 50000) - (19000, 25000, 31000)$$
$$= (19000, 25000, 31000)$$

The derived net profits are therefore triangular fuzzy numbers also, and are accordingly expressed in the triplet form.

In order to rank the net profits from each venture site, the entrepreneur may utilize the following procedure (Kaufman and Gupta, 1988).[11] In the initial step of the ranking procedure, the entrepreneur establishes the ordinary number representation for each fuzzy number. Let $\pi_{(\cdot)} = (\pi_1, \pi_2, \pi_3)$, where π_1, π_2, π_3 are the lower bound, mode, and upper bound, respectively, of the net profits at site $(\cdot)$. We denote the ordinary number representation by $\pi^*_{(\cdot)}$ where

$$\pi^*_{(\cdot)} = \frac{\pi_1 + 2\pi_2 + \pi_3}{4}$$

The ordinary number representations for the three venture sites are given below

$$\pi^*_H = \frac{21000 + 2(25000) + 29000}{4}$$
$$= \frac{21000 + 50000 + 29000}{4}$$
$$= \frac{100000}{4}$$
$$= \$25,000$$

$$\pi_{OK}^* = \frac{20000 + 2(25000) + 28000}{4}$$

$$= \frac{20000 + 50000 + 28000}{4}$$

$$= \frac{98000}{4}$$

$$= \$24500$$

$$\pi_{MN}^* = \frac{19000 + 2(25000) + 31000}{4}$$

$$= \frac{19000 + 50000 + 31000}{4}$$

$$= \frac{100000}{4}$$

$$= \$25000$$

In this example, $\pi_H^* = \pi_{MN}^* = 25000$ and $\pi_{OK}^* = 24500$. Oklahoma is therefore ranked the lowest among the venture sites. According to this criterion, Montana and Hawaii are ranked as quivalents although their respective net profits clearly differ.

When nesting occurs, as in the case of Montana and Hawaii, the entrepreneur utilizes a second criterion, the mode of the net profit distributions for each site, whereby the venture with the highest mode is ranked the highest and, correspondingly, the venture with the lowest mode is ranked the lowest, and so forth. The two modes are equivalent (\$25000); therefore both sites are ranked equal under the second criterion as well as the first. Thus each criterion, the first and second, has failed to establish a different ranking of the fuzzy numbers.

A third criterion is then utilized as the final stage of the procedure, in which the divergence between the lower and upper bounds from the mode in each distribution is measured. The venture site having the lowest divergence is ranked the highest. The procedure is demonstrated below

Recall $\pi_H' = (21000, 25000, 29000)$. Therefore the divergence of π_H' from the mode is

$$= (25000 - 21000) + (29000 - 25000)$$
$$= 4000 + 4000$$
$$= 8000$$

and $\pi_{MN}{}' = (19000, 25000, 31000)$

Accordingly, the divergence of $\pi_{MN}{}'$ from the mode is

$$= (25000 - 19000) + (31000 - 25000)$$
$$= 6000 + 6000$$
$$= 12000$$

Clearly the range in $\pi_{MN}{}'$ is greater than the range in $\pi_{H}{}'$, thus Hawaii is ranked higher than Montana. The total ranking of the three venture sites according to the three criteria (ordinary number representation, mode and divergence) is Hawaii>Montana>Oklahoma.

As a result of the ranking procedure, the entrepreneur locates the manufacturing firm in Hawaii. Outsiders may view this locational decision as irrational since the firm's technical returns will be highest if the plant locates in Montana. However, these critics are unaware of the personal factor that influences the entrepreneur's decision. When the personal factor is accounted for in the determination of locale, the decision become rational as well as economic.

The above analysis can be easily extended to academia where university professors forego seeking the higher salaries of the industrial sector, especially in technical fields, in order to teach at the university level. Professors who opt to teach at research oriented universities can be viewed in a manner similar to that of the entrepreneur who enjoys surfing. The sole difference between the two is the hobby itself; the hobby for the professor is research activities. When the costs associated with participating (or not participating) in research activities is imputed into the employment decision, the decision to accept a lower salary may become rational and economic. The industrial sector, in order to entice scientists from their research endeavors, must compensate them for their lost opportunity cost, either monetarily or in−kind.

In order for procedures to be intuitive and clear, assumptions have been simplified in the construction of our example. Time and locational factors have been abstracted. A single personal−locational−choice factor entered our example, the desire to surf and its fuzzy compensation. We assumed the contractual revenues from sales are certain at all venture sites. Additionally, the effect of time on the venture choice has been ignored.[12]

OLIGOPOLISTIC BEHAVIORAL UNCERTAINTY AND THE ENTREPRENEUR'S OPPORTUNITY COST

We reiterate that the competitive process is affected by the personality of each competitor in the market. This section establishes the oligopolist's determination of the cost of uncertainty, which cost must include (and relate to) the opportunity cost set of the subject entrepreneur. We stress that the oligopolistic entrepreneur requires compensation for the cost of uncertainty in addition to the traditional factor rent the entrepreneur may earn because of greater skill.[13]

Any given choice involves a restricted number of alternatives or investment opportunities due to human limitations in acquiring, processing, and inferencing the data set. Thus we speak only of a bounded rationality.[14] The entrepreneur perceives of a set of options which may pertain to different industries or differing locations within the same industry. This entrepreneur investigates and estimates the amount of periodic payoffs in each industry given the perceived subjective uncertainty applicable to each alternative industry (or location) that is considered. The subjective uncertainty is a product of the various factors affecting the mode of competition under each choice. Any estimation of periodic payoffs stemming from the perceived level of uncertainty is subjective, a subjectivity best modeled by fuzzy numbers.

It is also manifest that the work – investment lifetime may vary among the different options facing a decision maker; nevertheless, similar lifetimes for each project or choice are also permitted in our model.[15] It is also clear that future payments for entrepreneurial inputs which should offset the uncertainty that prevails in a given industry must be discounted to the present; that is, the entrepreneur includes the cost of time in the process of decision making. Moreover, the amount of entrepreneurial energy that is expended because of the existing behavioral uncertainty or work involved in an activity varies from one activity to another. We shall propose that an entrepreneur invests more energy in an industry that carries a higher level of behavioral uncertainty than one with a relatively lower level of behavioral uncertainty.

The energy or work expenditure by the entrepreneur can be conceived of as a disutility, a mental strain or greater computer time.

Regardless of the manner in which we view the expenditure, the entrepreneur will experience differing levels of exertion as determined and required by each activity. Equal energy inputs due to equal uncertainty levels among various ventures are, of course, allowed in our conceptual framework.

The process of estimating the opportunity cost over a period of time requires finding the highest discount rate of return on one's own energy inputs. A model based on ordinary logic assigns crisp numbers to each of the opportunity cost variables, so the decision problem is solved by simply discounting future returns and expenditures to the present. It follows that projects can be quickly ranked from highest to lowest, with the first ranked project being the project with the highest rate of return on the input.

The real world of oligopoly somewhat unfortunately 'in a sense' presents a fuzzy problem. The choice set can nevertheless still be ranked in order of preference, with each project being assigned a grade that describes the level of preference. The periodic payoffs for the entrepreneurial inputs and payoffs are not exact (not crisp), but approximate; that is, fuzzy.[16]

Each periodic entrepreneurial payoff for uncertainty is described by a fuzzy number. The future payoffs are uncertain, especially with respect to the unpredictability of oligopolistic ventures. The periodic energy expenditures are also fuzzy numbers, with the fuzziness accounting for vagueness in the boundaries of the disutility of the entrepreneur. Utility or disutility is subjectively measured. A precise measure − crisp number − cannot describe a disutility in the future. Rather we must use hours of work to describe the disutility while allowing for flexibility in estimating these hours. A fuzzy number is then assigned to the energy expenditure of each period.

Any discount rate is subject to an entrepreneur's preference. This preference is established *a priori*. A project that is preferred to another requires a smaller discounting of payoffs in the preferred project than in the less preferred project. The preference adjusted discount rate is a fuzzy number, all entrepreneurs being uncertain about the true value of a discount rate which itself tends to vary over the years.

The energy expenditures are not discounted in our model[17]. The number of years of entrepreneurship in each project is also fuzzy. The fuzzy lifetime of project A can be represented by $n_A{}^*$, with the estimated lifetime of each alternative project also given as a discrete fuzzy number.

We demonstrate below the methodology for solving the uncertain opportunity cost work−investment problem in oligopoly markets. In step one, the interest rate and lifetimes are crisp while the payoffs and inputs are fuzzy. In step two, all variables are allowed to be fuzzy.

In general, let $F^* = 1.0/A$, $.9/B$, $.85/C$, $.2/D$, where A,B,C, and D are the alternative investment choices. Under our specifications, $A{>}B{>}C{>}D$,[18] where the symbol $>$ serves to indicate preference for being in activity A over B, etc. We shall let $d_A{}^*$, d_A = fuzzy and non−fuzzy discount rate assigned to project A.

$A_i{}^*$, A_i = fuzzy and non−fuzzy payoff respectively, in period i for project A, where $i=1,....n$.

e^*_{Ai} = the fuzzy energy expenditure in hours per period i, $i=1,...n$ in project A.

n^*, n = the discrete fuzzy and non−fuzzy lifetimes of project A respectively.

Utilize now the formula for discounting future payments to the present, as given by

$$PV\ (A,d,n) = \sum_{i-1}^{n} \frac{A_i}{(1 + d)^i} \tag{5}$$

Let $n=3$ yrs, $d_A = 8$ per cent. In terms of fuzzy numbers, we have:

$$A_1{}^* := \approx 30000 = (25000, 30000, 36000)$$
$$A_2{}^* := \approx 40000 = (37000, 40000, 42000)$$
$$A_3{}^* := \approx 45000 = (44000, 45000, 48000)$$

and

$$e^*_{A_1} := \approx 500 \text{ work hours} = (450, 500, 530)$$
$$e^*_{A_2} := \approx 550 \text{ work hours} = (510, 550, 580)$$
$$e^*_{A_3} := \approx 500 \text{ work hours} = (590, 600, 620)$$

$$PV(A_i{}^*,d,n) = \frac{A_1{}^*}{(1 + d)^1} + \frac{A_2{}^*}{(1 + d)^2} + \frac{A_3{}^*}{(1 + d)^3}$$

Recall via (3) the alpha cut relation $A^\alpha = [(a_2 - a_1)\alpha + a_1, a_3 - (a_3 - a_2)\alpha]$. Then without also asterisking the A's so that some visual simplicity is maintained, we have

$$A_1^\alpha = [5000\alpha + 25000, 36000 - 6000\alpha]$$
$$A_2^\alpha = [3000\alpha + 37000, 42000 - 2000\alpha]$$
$$A_3^\alpha = [1000\alpha + 44000, 48000 - 3000\alpha]$$

Discounting by $1/(1 + d)^i$ establishes .93, .86, .79, respectively for $i=1,2,3$. Applying the discounts to the A_i^α's, and aggregating over $i=1,2...3$, yields

$$PV(A)^\alpha = [89830 + 8020\alpha, 107520 - 9670\alpha]$$

For energy (investment) expenditures, we assume, without asterisking the e's for visual simplicity, that

$$e^\alpha_{A_1} = [450 + 50\alpha, 530 - 30\alpha]$$
$$e^\alpha_{A_2} = [510 + 40\alpha, 580 - 30\alpha]$$
$$e^\alpha_{A_3} = [590 + 10\alpha, 620 - 20\alpha]$$

Let $e^\alpha = \sum_{i=1}^{3} e^\alpha_{A_i} = [1550 + 100\alpha, 1730 - 80\alpha]$

Then $PV(A^\alpha) \div e^\alpha = R_A^\alpha$

Applying the rule of $\alpha-$cut division establishes

$$R_A^\alpha = \left[\frac{89830 + 8020\alpha}{1730 - 80\alpha} , \frac{107520 - 9670\alpha}{1550 + 100\alpha} \right]$$

Though r and n are crisp, the outcome is a fuzzy set because the A_i's and e_i's are fuzzy. At

$$\alpha = 0 \quad R_A^\alpha = \left[\frac{89830}{1730} , \frac{107520}{1550} \right] = [51.92, 69.37]$$

$$\alpha = 1 \quad R_A^\alpha = \left[\frac{97850}{1650} , \frac{97850}{1650} \right] = [59.3, 59.3] = 59.3$$

Thus R_A^α can be approximated by the (T.F.N) R_A, where $R_A = [51.92, 59.3, 69.37]$. The same procedure is repeated for B, C, and D, the projects being exclusive.

We suggest below two methods for ranking quotients, the first utilizes approximate fuzzy numbers, the second uses $\alpha-$cuts and confidence intervals.[19]   Either technique will suffice.   The first method is the simplest, with the second being the more precise.

Let us demonstrate the first method by numerical example. Recall the approximate T.F.N., R_A = [51.92, 59.3, 69.37]. Assume that the approximate T.F.N.'s for projects B,C,D are the following

$$R_B = [50, 62, 70]$$
$$R_C = [40, 62, 80]$$
$$R_D = [30, 60, 94]$$

First, we obtain the $R_{(\cdot)}$'s ordinary number representatives. The ordinary number representative of a T.F.N. is obtained as follows

$$\hat{R}_A = \frac{a_1 + 2a_2 + a_3}{4}$$

where a_1 and a_3 are the left and right bounds and a_2 is the mode of the T.F.N. $\hat{R}_A$ is the ordinary number representative of R_A.

Then

$$\hat{R}_A = \frac{51.92 + 2(59.3) + 69.37}{4} = 60$$

$$\hat{R}_B = \frac{50 + 2(62) + 70}{4} = 61$$

$$\hat{R}_C = \frac{40 + 2(62) + 80}{4} = 61$$

$$\hat{R}_D = \frac{30 + 2(60) + 94}{4} = 61$$

Since $\hat{R}_A$ is 60<61, project A is ranked lowest. Projects B,C,D have the same $\hat{R}_B = \hat{R}_C = \hat{R}_D = 61$ although their T.F.N's differ. Since B,C,D form a subclass, the modes of each T.F.N. in the subclass are used to rank the projects. The modes of R_B and R_C are 62 which exceed the mode of R_D (60). Therefore, R_D is ranked less than R_B and R_C in the subclass B,C,D and higher than R_A by the first criterion (ordinary number representation).

Projects B and C have the same numerical representatives and modes, yet their approximate T.F.N.'s are not identical. We go on to the third criterion: the divergence of the bounds from the mode in each of the approximate T.F.N.'s R_B, R_C.

Recall R_B = [50,62,70], R_B's mode = 62, therefore R_B's divergence from the mode = $(62-50) + (70-62) = 20$. R_C = [40,62,80], R_C's mode

= 62; therefore R_C's divergence from its mode = $(62-40)+(94-62 = 22+28 = 50$. The divergence of R_C is greater than the divergence of R_B, then $R_C > R_B$. Thus the projects are ranked $R_C > R_B > R_D > R_A$. This technique can be extended to any number of projects.

The second ranking technique utilizes $\alpha-$cuts and the confidence level principle. First, we obtain the $\alpha-$cuts of the quotients $R_A{}^\alpha$, $R_B{}^\alpha$, $R_C{}^\alpha$, $R_D{}^\alpha$. Since we have already obtained the quotient $R_A{}^\alpha$ in our example, we demonstrate this step with the quotient.

$$\text{Recall } R_A{}^\alpha = \left[\frac{89830 + 8020\alpha}{1730 - 80\alpha} , \frac{10520 - 9670\alpha}{1550 + 100\alpha} \right]$$

The entrepreneur assigns α values, $\alpha \in [0,1]$ to the right hand side of the above expression. The α values may be increased in each computation by .1 or .01 or even .001 increments; i.e, we obtain confidence intervals at α = 0,.1,.2,.3,.4,...,1.0, or α = 0,.01,.02,.03,....,.98,.99,1.0, or α = 0,.001,.002,.003, ...,.999,1.0.

Table 3.1 Confidence Intervals

α	$R_A{}^\alpha$	α	$R_A{}^\alpha$	α	$R_A{}^\alpha$
0	52,69	.4	55,65	.8	58,61
.1	53,68	.5	56,64	.9	59.60
.2	53,67	.6	56,63	1.0	59,59
.3	54,66	.7	57,62		

Table 3.1 shows the confidence intervals with $A \in [0,1]$ where α increases by .1 each time. We provide a sample calculation below. At $\alpha = .6$

$$R_A{}^{.6} = \left[\frac{89830 + 8020(.6)}{1730 - 80(.6)} , \frac{107520 - 9670(.6)}{1550 + 100(.6)} \right]$$

$$= \left[\frac{89830 + 4812}{1730 - 48} , \frac{107520 - 5802}{1550 + 60} \right]$$

$$= \left[\frac{94642}{1682} , \frac{101718}{1610} \right]$$

$$= [56,63]$$

The same computation allows at all αs for all projects.

Note that in the first ranking method, the approx T.F.N. R_A was obtained by setting $\alpha=0$ and $\alpha=1$, the first and last rows in Table 3.1, thus ignoring the $(.1 - .9)$ confidence intervals, which exemplifies why R_A is called an approximate T.F.N..

Following the same procedure for B,C,D we obtain three additional tables, which we union at every $\alpha \in [0,1]$. In other words, we obtain the maximal confidence interval $(\vee(R_A^\alpha, R_B^\alpha, R_C^\alpha, R_D^\alpha))$ at each α. Thus, we obtain our maximal set of confidence intervals at each $\alpha-$cut. For present purposes, we demonstrate how a maximal confidence interval is obtained at one α only.

Let $\alpha = .7$. Recall from Table 1, $R_A^{.7} = [57,62]$, and assume for demonstration purposes the following

$$R_B^{.7} = [52,65], \; R_C^{.7} = [50,90], \; R_D^{.7} = [39,85].$$

The maximal confidence interval at $\alpha=.7$ is obtained below

$$U^{.7} = [57\vee52\vee50\vee39 , 62\vee65\vee90\vee85]$$

$U^{.7} = [57,90]$ where $U^{.7}$ is the maximal confidence interval among all projects at $\alpha=.7$. The same procedure is applied at all α's. A table of the maximal confidence intervals is thus constructed. The procedure for constructing this table is provided in the Appendix to Chapter 3.

Next, we obtain, in absolute values at an $\alpha-$cut, the distances of the confidence interval of each project from the maximal confidence interval at that α and aggregate the distances of each $R_{(\cdot)}^\alpha$. The quotients are then ranked according to the closeness of their confidence intervals to the maximal confidence interval set.

Suppose finally the sums for R_A^α, R_B^α, R_C^α, R_D^α are 1.9, 2.0, 3.0, 4.5, respectively. Then R_D^α is the furthest from the maximal (upper bounds) set, and hence D is ranked the lowest. It follows that $R_A^\alpha > R_B^\alpha > R_C^\alpha > R_D^\alpha$, with Activity B thus appearing to this point in our analysis as the project most likely to establish the opportunity cost for

Activity A.

Similar procedures apply if the discount rate is taken to be fuzzy, and so too the work$-$investment lifetime expenditures. Specifically, let

$$d^* = (d_1, d_2, d_3)$$
$$d^\alpha = [d_1 + (d_2-d_1)\alpha - (d_3-d_2)\alpha + d_3]$$
$$PV(A^*,d^*,n) = \sum_{i-1}^{3} \frac{A_i^\alpha}{(1 (+) d_\alpha^*)i}$$

Suppose 'approximately 8 per cent' is the fuzzy interest rate, where 'approximately 8 per cent' $\approx$ (6 per cent, 8 per cent, 9 per cent); alternatively (approx .08)$\approx$ (.06, .08, .09).

$$d^\alpha = [.06 + .02\alpha , .09 - .01\alpha]$$
$$1 + d^\alpha = [1.06 + .02\alpha , 1.09 - .01\alpha]$$
$$\frac{1}{(1 + d^\alpha)} = \left[\frac{1}{1.09 - .01\alpha} , \frac{1}{1.06 + .02\alpha} \right]$$

Using the same A values as before provides

$$PV(A^*,d^*,n) = \frac{25000 + 5000\alpha}{1.09 - .01\alpha} , \frac{36000 - 6000\alpha}{1.06 + .02\alpha}$$

$$+ \frac{37000 + 3000\alpha}{[1.09 - .01\alpha]^2} , \frac{42000 - 2000\alpha}{[1.06 + .02]^2}$$

$$+ \frac{44000 + 1000\alpha}{[1.09 - .01\alpha]^3} , \frac{48000 - 3000\alpha}{[1.06 + .02\alpha]^3}$$

As indicated, we assume also that the number of years the activity will be pursued is fuzzy. Then n^* are discrete fuzzy numbers. For each year the entrepreneur assigns a membership grade. The fuzzy durations of each project are discrete possibility distributions. Let the number of years in project A be fuzzy so that n^* is approx 2. Given an α level of presumption, we can find the confidence interval.

The solution requires the inclusion of the possibility distribution of $[PV(A^*,d^*, \mid n = n_i) \wedge n^*]$ which in turn creates the joint possibility distribution $PV(A^*,d^*,n^*)$. The procedure involves constructing the possibility distributions for $PV(A_1 \mid n=n_1)$ and $PV(A_1+A_2 \mid n=n_2)$ and

$PV(A_1 + A_2 + A_3 \mid n = n_3)$; they provide the marginal possibility distributions with respect to which the membership grade of n^* is imposed. In other words, we obtain three possibility distributions $\pi_1(x)$, $\pi_2(x)$, $\pi_3(x)$, where $\pi_i(x)$ = possibility distributions of x with i payments discounted to the present, $i=1,....n$. Specifically, assume x_i has the membership grades of .2, .7, .9, in PV_1, PV_2, PV_3, respectively, where

$$PV_i := \underset{i}{\vee} \ PV(A_i \mid n = i)$$

Also let the years (fuzzy) have the membership grades .8, 1, .6. for years, 1, 2, 3. In effect, grades .8, 1, .6 indicate that we are certain the activity will run for 2 years even though it may run for 1 or 3 years. The composite membership grade for x_1 is then given by $\vee(.2 \wedge .8, \ .7 \wedge 1, \ .9 \wedge .6) \Rightarrow \vee(.2, \ .7, \ .6) \Rightarrow .7$, which we define as the possibility measure; stated in canonical form, we have $\mu(x) = \max - \min(\mu_{A^*}(x), \ \mu_{n^*}(n))$. Similarly all elements can be projected into the marginal possibility distributions and the possibility measures found from which to construct the possibility distribution of $PV(A^*, d^*, n^*)$. The same procedure applies of course to the energies expenditure sum when the project's duration is fuzzy.

Quotients resulting from discounts or other divisors may not be fuzzy numbers since the convexity property may disappear with division or multiplication of fuzzy numbers. In any case, we establish the possibility distribution by the max min principle for the division operation and obtain a fuzzy set which can be resolved. Alternatively, the quotients of the fuzzy sets can be solved using a method devised by Minkowski (1903) as division operations are typically resolved by utilizing α-cuts (also see Kaufman et al, 1988).

To compare fuzzy sets, it is necessary to determine the possibilistic mean for each venture; that is, the membership grades are multiplied by the respective elements (finite) and a mean is obtained in the same manner as the probabilistic mean utilizing the possibilistic version of Shannon Entropy if two ventures have the same mean, the venture whose vagueness is less than the other is ranked higher. Whichever method is used, a ranking for all projects is derived.

How does the entrepreneur decide which type of industry to enter. The problem is equivalent to determining the industry that offers the best return on the entrepreneurs personal investment? As suggested earlier, the entrepreneur may use the preference set F^* as the basis for changing the payoff discount rates for each project. The effect is that a preferred project would be discounted by a smaller d than a less preferred project. Or, the entrepreneur may employ the desirability membership grade in recomputing R. Whatever the technique, the selected activity is (by revealed preference) the most preferred, and the next best alternative establishes the opportunity cost that must be covered.

Suppose the fuzzy entrepreneurial rates of return are R_A, R_B, R_C, R_D where $R_{(\cdot)}$ is the fuzzy set obtained for A, B, C, D via the discounting process. One method for including preference in the choice process is to select the highest rate of return for a desirable activity; that is, the project must offer the highest rate of return and also be desirable from the entrepreneur's standpoint. In this context, note that each $R_{(\cdot)}$ is intersected with its desirability membership grade, and the new $R_{(\cdot)}$ is obtained at membership grades no greater than the membership grade of the project's desirability. For example

$$R_A = .2/x_1, .3/x_2, .4/x_3, .9/x_4, .7/x_5$$

The desirability membership degree for A in F^* was assumed to be the highest and equal to 1.0. The intersection of $\mu_F.(A)$ and $\mu_{R_A}(x_i)$ thus does not change the R_A value since this project is unitarily desirable. But let $R_B = .4/Y_1, 1.0/Y_2, 1.0/Y_3, .95/Y_4, .8/Y_5$. Intersecting $\mu_{R_B}(Y_i)$, with $\mu_F.(B)$ where $\mu_F.(B) = .9$ yields R'_B and hence $R'_B = .4/Y_1, .9/Y_2, .9/Y_3, .9/Y_4, .8/Y_5$. Following the same process for each project, the entrepreneur then ranks the adjusted Rs by their means.

Still another alternative warrants mention: the desirability membership grade can be multiplied by each of the membership grades of the fuzzy Rs. Under this process, each $R_{(\cdot)}$ is re-evaluated via the adjusted membership grades. This process is demonstrated next for R_B, the procedure being identical, of course, for all R's.

Let R'_B be the desirability adjusted fuzzy rate of return on project B. Then $R'_B = (.9 \cdot .4)/y_1, (.9 \cdot 1.0)/y_2, (.9 \cdot 1.0)/y_3, (.9 \cdot .95)/y_4, (.9 \cdot .8)/y_5 = .36/Y_1, .9/Y_2, .9/Y_3, .85/Y_4, .72/Y_5$. The desirability of the project is an a priori selection by the decision maker as the joint objective of maximum payoff coterminous with desirability often affects what otherwise would result.

Note finally that the desirability of the project is an *a priori* selection by the decision maker as the goal of maximum payoff coterminous with desirability determines the final decision. Most importantly, fuzziness helps keep in a market in the short run entrepreneurs who are only approaching a crisp return for their talents and funds. What happens to these and other fuzzy entrepreneurs in the long run will be considered in Chapter 4 as we prove the existence there of a determinate long−run equilibrium in oligopolistic markets notwithstanding fuzziness.

Suppose the entrepreneur is considering industry Z. Let the optimal alternative in the selected choice set be A, where A involves a number of years, n^*, while Z involves m^*. Note that the average fuzzy entrepreneurial payoff in A can be obtained through the division of $PV(A^*, r^*, n^*)$ by n^*, and similarly for the average entrepreneurial energy inputs in A. We obtain and then approximate the average periodic payoff per unit of energy input in A by using the extension principle.

For the entrepreneur to survive in A, the average periodic payoff per entrepreneurial energy input must at least be equal to the payoff obtained in Z, *ceteris paribus*.

Let R_A^*. = fuzzy entrepreneurial rate of return in project A.
R_Z^* = fuzzy entrepreneurial rate of return in project Z.
S_A^*. = average energy expenditure in A.
S_Z^* = average energy expenditure in Z.
n^* = lifetime of A.
m^* = lifetime of Z.

Fuzziness is allowed to apply to rates of return, discount rates, energy inputs, and the number of years in each industry.[20] The highest rate of return is not the sole determinant of the entrepreneurial opportunity cost and of whether the entrepreneur stays or exits the market. The number of years involved in each project and the level of energy expenditure are also determinants affecting entrepreneurial entry and exit decisions.

Short−run market behavior is dominated by fuzzy estimates. Actual realized outcomes of oligopolistic competition act as a feedback fuzzy control mechanism. Objective data narrow the range of an approximate number or redefine the range completely. Short−run market behavior is dominated by fuzzy estimates of rivals' conjectured and actual behavior.

Objective data which are acquired *a posteriori* serve as a signal affecting the fuzzy outcomes of future decisions, including for the immediately following period. Market competitive evidence indicating an opportunity cost that is not contained in the entrepreneur's opportunity cost set may cause the entrepreneur to exit the industry. Short—run losses may be tolerated in view of entrepreneurial rent and long—run normal profits. Whether or not a narrowing or redefinition occurs, the entrepreneur acquires knowledge which reduces personal uncertainty; behavioral uncertainty, however, is never eliminated completely.

Then $\quad n^* S_A^* \cdot R_A^* = m^* S_Z^* \cdot R_Z^*$

Let $\quad S_A^* \cdot R_A^* = r$ and $S_Z^* \cdot R_Z^* = r^*$

$\therefore r = (m^*/n^*)r^*$

where r is the periodic payoff required by the entrepreneur to stay in the industry. We impute r as a fuzzy set without starring it.

Once the choices are ranked, the entrepreneur finds the best alternative; that is, the alternative which offers the highest payoff to energy ratio. This alternative is Z. As mentioned previously, the problem facing the entrepreneur considering work—investment in A is not a problem of simply comparing rates of return. The entrepreneurial input in industry A may or may not be the optimal input. Furthermore, participation in industry A may involve a greater number of years than the optimal alternative employment and vice versa. The number of years in A may be more or less than the alternative employment depending upon personal demands, institutional factors, the nature of the industry or a combination of the aforementioned factors.

Evidently a comparison between energy inputs in A and Z (the optimal alternative employment) is necessary in order to impute the opportunity cost of the entrepreneur for bearing the cost of oligopolistic behavioral uncertainty.

It is imperative at this stage in the development of our theory to recognize the significance of the entrepreneur's energy imputations. Recall that the horizontal axis of the traditional cost diagram measures output over time; that is, Q/t. Whenever we speak of output, we employ a flow concept, not a stock concept. Q is measured over a period of time, such as a year, month, day, etc. Now, the optimal energy inputs in A are the energies required (in addition to all traditional costs) to produce the most technically efficient level of output in the long run. In other words the energies are measured in relation to Q^*, the neo−classical minimum cost output level.[21] These energy inputs are aimed basically at covering the oligopolistic behavioral uncertainty which reflects the conjectures and guesstimates of all rivals in the oligopolistic market.[22]

Suppose the entrepreneurial energy inputs at Q^* are S, but the entrepreneur prefers only to input $S'<S$. The reason for the entrepreneurial preference lies in the very mix and preferences of the reactive species (the entrepreneur). Assume now for simplicity in concluding our concept of opportunity cost that all variants are non−fuzzy; that is, crisp. Moreover, our entrepreneur has to charge a higher rate of return for personal energies than other entrepreneurs who impute S into their cost functions to arrive at Q^*. The subject entrepreneur thus becomes a high cost producer and market competition forces him to exit.

Suppose the entrepreneur prefers to expend $S''>S$. Then again the entrepreneur is not meeting personal opportunity cost in A since more energies are being expended than those required to attain Q^*. This individual exits that industry (market) as it is realized that industry A fails to provide the efficient entrepreneurial allocation that is required.[23]

Entrepreneurs who survive in the long run are therefore those who expend S energies and recover the opportunity cost in full required by their expenditures. However, as stated earlier, employment (investment) in A may involve a different number of years than in Z. Let the rate of return on Z for the behavioral uncertainty in Z be R_0, where R_0 is the optimal rate of return in the best alternative employment, and where Z involves m years while A involves n years. If $n=m$, then the rate of return in A must at least equal R_0 for the entrepreneurs employment in A to be justified. Let the rate of return in A be R; that is, if $m=n$, $R=R_0$ and there is no reason for the entrepreneur to exit industry A since the individual's personal opportunity cost is being met completely.

Suppose A requires $n>m$ years of employment. The entrepreneur's required return in A must be adjusted to account for the different length of time of A *vis à vis* Z. Since R_0 is an absolute rate of return on energy—investment expenditures, the R_0 is adjusted for the n years duration of A in the following manner

$$R = \frac{mR_0}{n}$$

The entrepreneur imputes R according to this transformation. However, since $R_0 > R$ and $n > m$, the entrepreneur must take into account that at the end of m years a greater lump sum mR_0 is on hand than mR; this excess can be invested up to n years, while activity A is being continued up to the nth year. The final result is that Z is still more profitable than A. Of course, a discounting process is performed on the extra mR_0 payoffs up to the nth year, the related R being evaluated in the context of R_0.[24]

For example, let $m=15$ years, $n=20$ years, where m,n are the durations of employment in activities Z and A respectively. Denote, as above, employment Z's rate of return as R_0 and employment A's required rate of return by R. The entrepreneur requires a yearly rate of return $R = 15/20\ R_0$. Clearly $R = \frac{3}{4}R_0$. Since $R_0 > R$, the employment in Z, *vis à vis* A, involves an added yearly rate of return equal to $R_0 - R$ over the duration of the Z employment (15 years). This differential in the rate of return ($\frac{1}{4}R_0$) translates to an additional yearly return on investment in the Z employment. The compilation of this yearly additional return in Z, relative to A, provides the entrepreneur a lump sum at the end of the 15 year employment in Z. This lump sum is not available from the initial 15 years of employment in A. The lump sum may be employed (invested) over the 5 year differential (the 20 years of employment in A — the 15 years of employment in Z) to generate its own income stream. Employment in Z when compared to employment in A, therefore involves an added return given $R < R_0$ and $m > n$. Accordingly, the entrepreneur discounts the additional income stream from venture A and adjusts R_0 upward. This adjustment is relevant only when comparing investment A to Z with $n > m$. The adjusted rate of return for investment in Z is denoted by R_0', where R_0' includes the shadow price of the additional 5 years of employment in A. Thus the required rate of return in A is $\frac{3}{4}R_0'$.

Given $n < m$, the entrepreneur will not receive R_0 in the period n to m years if R_0 is simply imputed as a rate of return for the S energy expenditures. Rather, the entrepreneur must impute an $R = mR_0/n$, where R is now greater than R_0 since $(m/n) > 1$. Furthermore the R is adjusted for the investment opportunities that the lump sum extra obtained over the n years from the employment in A will provide. This lump sum extra should be considered as being is invested over the $(m - n)$ years, so that adjustments to R would be required to effect a lost opportunity rate r which simply compensates the entrepreneur in full for the lost opportunity cost. Any extra receipts beyond that amount serve as windfalls (a surplus).

In sum, the entrepreneur derives R, the optimal rate of return per unit energy expenditure. R is a factor in the opportunity cost of the entrepreneur for accepting employment in A rather than in Z. However, R is not the only factor that determines the opportunity cost of the entrepreneur for accepting the market uncertainty. The energy – investment expenditures level S is also a factor since R is an absolute rate of return on energy. In order for the entrepreneur's opportunity cost to be imputed, we must allocate $S \cdot R$ at Q^* as the required return on the entrepreneur's optimal energy expenditures. In particular, $r = SR$. It is this r that is ascribed onto the neo – classical cost curves as the opportunity cost attributable to the behavioral uncertainty in the oligopolistic industry.

Heuristic crisp imputations have been used over the last pages, w.o.l.o.g., in order to demonstrate the imputation of r at an elementary – intuitive level. Under fuzziness, derived results are generalized in demonstrating sets of possible values compared to crisp values. Most importantly our prior analysis regarded 'similar products' as the general case in oligopoly markets, with homogeneity in production being allowed as a special case. Several assumptions will henceforth be used in deriving the equilibrium, as we demonstrate in Chapter 4, that all viable market participants produce at their technical (neo – classical) least – cost curves in the long run. Firms producing a homogeneous product are assumed to have identical minimum (technical) average costs. Firms producing 'similar products' are conceived to be subject to different long – run average cost of production curves. It is manifest that these long – run average cost curves may vary among producers of 'similar products' because the product characteristics differ. But even slight product differentiation involves an added (behavior – uncertain) cost to the oligopolistic competitor. Such special costs, that is to say variational cost inclusions, will be seen to facilitate the analysis rather than make it more difficult when fuzziness is recognized to exist and fuzzy set mathematics is utilized.[25]

APPENDIX

The procedure for ranking quotients via α-cuts is presented below by means of a numerical example.[26] Assume that there are three quotients Q_e^α, Q_f^α, Q_g^α. The numerators and the denominators of Q_e^α, Q_f^α, Q_g^α are described by the symbols N_e^α, N_f^α, N_g^α and D_e^α, D_f^α, D_g^α respectively. The numerators represent entrepreneurial returns. The denominators are the entrepreneurial investments. The numerators and denominators are given in final form; that is, after all returns are discounted and all venture specific investments are summed. The numerical values specified below are hypothetical and do not bear on the outcome of the analysis presented in Chapter 3, except to clarify the methodology employed in the analysis.

Let
$$N_e^\alpha = 50 + 10\alpha, \ 80 - 20\alpha$$
$$N_f^\alpha = 40 + 20\alpha, \ 70 - 10\alpha$$
$$N_g^\alpha = 60 + 30\alpha, \ 100 - 10\alpha$$

and
$$D_e^\alpha = 10 + 2\alpha, \ 16 - 4\alpha$$
$$D_f^\alpha = 8 + 3\alpha, \ 13 - 2\alpha$$
$$D_g^\alpha = 14 + 5\alpha, \ 20 - 1\alpha$$

$$Q_e^\alpha = N_e^\alpha : D_e^\alpha = \frac{50 + 10\alpha}{16 - 4\alpha}, \ \frac{80 - 20\alpha}{10 + 2\alpha}$$

$$Q_f^\alpha = N_f^\alpha : D_f^\alpha = \frac{40 + 20\alpha}{13 - 2\alpha}, \ \frac{70 - 10\alpha}{8 + 3\alpha}$$

$$Q_g^\alpha = N_g^\alpha : D_g^\alpha = \frac{60 + 30\alpha}{20 - 1\alpha}, \ \frac{100 - 10\alpha}{14 + 5\alpha}$$

The calculations for $Q_e^{.7}$, $Q_f^{.7}$, $Q_g^{.7}$; that is, the quotients at $\alpha = .7$ is detailed below.

$$Q_e^{.7} = \frac{50 + 10(.7)}{16 - 4(.7)}, \ \frac{80 - 20(.7)}{10 + 2(.7)} = \frac{57}{13.2}, \ \frac{66}{11.4} = 4.32, 5.79$$

$$Q_f^{.7} = \frac{40 + 20(.7)}{13 - 2(.7)}, \ \frac{70 - 10(.7)}{8 + 3(.7)} = \frac{34}{11.6}, \ \frac{63}{10.1} = 4.66, \ 6.24$$

$$Q_g^{.7} = \frac{60+30(.7)}{20-1(.7)} \ , \ \frac{100-10(.7)}{14+5(.7)} = \frac{81}{19.3} \ , \ \frac{93}{17.5} = 4.20 \ , \ 5.31$$

The above calculation is repeated at every α, with α=.1,.2,.3...,1.0 for the three quotients. The numerical values for Q_e^{α}, Q_f^{α}, Q_g^{α} are given in α−cuts for α=0,.1,.2,... 1.0 by the first four columns in Table 3.2. The highest lower and upper bounds of the α−cuts are selected from the three quotients and recorded in the fifth column of Table 3.2. In other words, the union of the lower bounds of Q_e^{α}, Q_f^{α}, Q_g^{α} at each α is obtained and recorded in column 5. The union of the upper bounds of the quotients at each α is obtained also and recorded in column 5. Column 5 therefore contains the union or upper bound of the three quotients at each α; that is, $\vee_{e,f,g}Q_{(\cdot)}^{\alpha}$. The union operation at α=.2 is demonstrated as

$$3.42\vee3.49\vee3.33 \ , \ 7.31\vee7.91\vee6.53 = 3.49, 7.91$$

Table 3.2   The lower and upper bound α−cuts

α	Q_e^{α}	Q_f^{α}	Q_g^{α}	$\vee Q_{(\cdot)}^{\alpha}$
0	3.13, 8	3.08, 8.75	3, 7.14	3.13, 8.75
.1	3.27, 7.65	3.28, 8.31	3.17, 6.83	3.28, 8.31
.2	3.42, 7.31	3.49, 7.91	3.33, 6.53	3.49, 7.91
.3	3.58, 6.98	3.71, 7.53	3.50, 6.26	3.71, 7.53
.4	3.75, 6.67	3.93, 7.17	3.67, 6.00	3.93, 7.17
.5	3.93, 6.36	4.17, 6.84	3.85, 5.76	4.17, 6.84
.6	4.12, 6.07	4.41, 6.53	4.02, 5.53	4.41, 6.53
.7	4.32, 5.79	4.66, 6.24	4.20, 5.31	4.66, 6.24
.8	4.53, 5.52	4.91, 5.96	4.38, 5.11	4.91, 5.96
.9	4.76, 5.25	5.18, 5.70	4.55, 4.92	5.18, 5.70
1.0	5, 5	5.45, 5.45	4.74, 4.74	5.46, 5.46

This operation is repeated for $\alpha=0,.1,...1.0$ to construct column 5 in Table 3.2.

The divergence or absolute distance of each quotient's $\alpha-$cut from the upper bound quotient $(\vee_{efg}Q_{(\cdot)}{}^{\alpha})$ at the same α value is obtained. This process is demonstrated below for $Q_e^{(.7)}$.

At $\alpha=.7$, $Q_e^{(.7)}=4.32,5.79$, $\vee_{efg}Q_{(\cdot)}{}^{(.7)}=4.66,6.24$

Let $d(Q_e^{(.7)},\vee_{efg}Q_{(\cdot)}{}^{(.7)}):=$ the absolute distance between Q_e and the upper bound at $\alpha=.7$

$$d(Q_e^{(.7)},\vee_{efg}Q_{(\cdot)}{}^{(.7)}) = |4.66-4.32| + |6.24-5.79|$$
$$= .34 + .45$$
$$= .79$$

The computation of the distances of Q_e^{α}, Q_f^{α}, Q_g^{α} from $\vee_{efg}Q_{(\cdot)}{}^{\alpha}$ is provided in Table 3.3.

Table 3.3 Divergence for the upper bound

α	$d(Q_e^{\alpha}, \vee Q_{(\cdot)}{}^{\alpha})$	$d(Q_f^{\alpha}, \vee Q_{(\cdot)}{}^{\alpha})$	$d(Q_g^{\alpha}, \vee Q_{(\cdot)}{}^{\alpha})$
0	.75	.05	1.74
.1	.67	0	1.59
.2	.67	0	1.54
.3	.68	0	1.48
.4	.68	0	1.43
.5	.72	0	1.40
.6	.75	0	1.39
.7	.79	0	1.39
.8	.82	0	1.38
.9	.87	0	1.41
1.0	.92	.02	1.44
Totals	8.32	.07	16.19

The distance of each quotient from the upper bound is obtained by summing the $\alpha-$cut distances as shown in the last row of Table 3.3. The quotient with the least total distance (divergence) from the upper bound is ranked highest and so forth. In this example $d(Q_e^{\alpha})=8.32$, $d(Q_f^{\alpha})=.07$, and $d(Q_g^{\alpha})=16.19$. Thus $Q_f > Q_e > Q_g$.

NOTES

1. M.L. Greenhut and M.R. Colberg, 'Factors in the Location of Florida Industry' (Tallahassee; Florida State Studies, No. 36, 1962) and M.L. Greenhut, *A Theory of the Firm in Economic Space* (1974, Appendix B, pg. 376), document and prove that the entrepreneur's personal considerations significantly affect plant and firm location.

2. We do not seek to re-invent the wheel by redefining the entrepreneur; rather, our intent is simply to view this unique factor of production in a realistic manner. We are not singular in this claim. Greenhut (1970, et al 1987, with Lane 1989) and others stress the human side of the entrepreneur.

3. Both machines and government managers perform equally well as substitutes for entrepreneurial services.

4. The nascent free market/mixed market economies of eastern Europe are currently undergoing the painful process of entrepreneurial cultivation. After decades of suppressing free market tendencies and destroying entrepreneurial advancement, the governments of these previously centrally controlled economies are under the illusion that as a consequence of governmental free market policies alone, entrepreneurs will easily emerge and exhibit the same competency level as that of Western entrepreneurs. We contend that entrepreneurial emergence may be easily witnessed as policy changes, however, the competency of the emerging entrepreneurial class will not reach parity with its Western counterparts for years to come or even decades. Observe the case of India and Japan. In *Free to Choose*, Milton Friedman notes that while the Japanese economy has risen to a level of semi-world leadership industrially, the Indian economy while possessing greater economic resources in terms of land and labor, continues to be classified as a third world economy. Friedman attributes the disparate growth trends between the two countries to the absence of an entrepreneurial enhancing ideology in India.

5. The writings of Wald, Luce-Riffa, Harwicz, Savage, Greenhut and Simon, among others, have stressed the difference between decision making under conditions of risk, certainty and uncertainty.

6. In defining the firm, R.H. Coase (1937) p. 351, distinguished between initiative (enterprise) and management:

    > Initiative means forecasting and operates through the price mechanism by the making of new contracts. Management proper merely reacts to price changes, rearranging the factors of production under its control.

    Coase determines that the businessman normally combines both functions.

7. The present analysis is based in part on the thesis established by M.L. Greenhut (1956, 1970, 1974).

8. The technical costs and profits can be fuzzy if we assume imperfect knowledge. However, since we will elaborate on the fuzzy estimates of costs in subsequent parts of this work, we assume, for the moment, that technical costs are precisely determinable and thus estimated by crisp numbers.

9. Although other personal factors are assumed to be non-existent in our presentation, our formulation does not preclude the inclusion of additional personal determinants. The assumption of a single personal factor is utilized solely to maintain mathematical simplicity and clarity; other personal factors may be included in the above formulation in the same manner.

10. Traditional economic theory assumes that the twenty−four hours of the day can be partitioned into leisure and work hours. While we do not debate this assumption, we reject outright the assertion made by Becker (1971) and others, that leisure hours have the identical monetary per hour value as working hours. In actuality, certain hours of the day hold greater value than the hourly wage rate earned by a worker, while others hold less value. For example, observe Greenhut (1981) pp. 169−177, where the hours spent in physician waiting rooms were costed and became a determinant of the physician fees. Clearly, the disutility incurred from waiting to see a physician when one is sick and/or in pain, is not identical to the disutility incurred from standing in line to purchase a ticket to a football game, provided one is healthy. Therefore, each hour in the 24-hour day does not have the same shadow price as proposed in the Becker analysis.

11. To maintain the simplicity of our intuitive example, only the above ranking technique is demonstrated. In subsequent sections of this chapter, alternative ranking techniques are designed and explained.

12. The goal of simplicity in presentation does not weaken our model. All of the variables can be estimated subjectively and incorporated into the model without any loss at all.

13. It may appear that we are alluding to a new concept (the uncertainty cost); however, in actuality, we are simply investigating the well-known doctrine of opportunity cost. Even before the time of Ricardo, opportunity cost (that is, the cost of alternatives foregone) was identified in economic treatises. Ibn Khaldoun in his celebrated 14th century magnum opus (1544), states that the entrepreneur who travels further than others in search of new and unique products demands and receives a higher payoff for his additional entrepreneurial inputs (both capital and personal). This conception, as indicated by the date of his writing, is approximately 500 years old.

14. We are in this respect in agreement with the work of Simon (1957).

15. An entrepreneur who desires early retirement, as opposed to a late retirement, usually enters into short-term ventures unless the long-range venture provides adequate compensation for the inconvenience of working additional years.

16. Furthermore, because the calculation involves utilities and disutilities from work, fuzzy numbers capture the elastic bounds of utility measures in addition to the vagueness of future predictions.

17. Economists typically discount earnings to demonstrate the time value of money. There is no standard practice for discounting disutilities or energies. Of course, the entrepreneur may place a value on energies expended during one's prime years that is less than the value of energies expended later in life. This concept is not alien to economic theory. In a skewed manner, such concept captures the essence of Modigliani's life cycle hypothesis where yearly consumption ascends to a peak, then decreases as one grows older. Higher discount rates are therefore assigned symmetrically among projects in the later years of life relative to the earlier years.

Our model's generality allows for the acceptance of such discounting of energy inputs.

18. If the highest grade is less than 1.0, the fuzzy set is normalized by dividing each membership grade by the highest membership grade in the fuzzy set.

19. The ranking of fuzzy sets is more involved than that of ordinary set rankings; however, the methods are similar. For a detailed analysis of fuzzy set ranking, see Kaufman et al 1988.

20. The fuzzy values allow for a range of possible values in lieu of a crisp singular value for each variable. Furthermore, the conjectured imputations can vary in the short run within the fuzzy subset without causing the appearance of drastic measures in the entrepreneur's behavior. Unless the observed outcome is completely outside the fuzzy set, re-evaluations are not needed; only the presumption level adjusts.

21. Output is technically determined. Therefore, Q^* is considered to be a crisp number. Recall that a crisp number is a special case of the fuzzy number. Therefore, Q^* can be conceived of as the minimum neo−classical cost output at a presumption level of 1.

22. See Greenhut (1970) for a detailed analysis of the effects of energy inputs, project lifetimes and payoffs as variants in oligopolistic behavior.

23. At this juncture we distinguish between the owner/manager and the hired manager. Agency cost theory suggests that the agent (manager) possesses behavioral preferences dissimilar from those of the entrepreneur. The agent may require luxury goods as an indirect compensation, in addition to the payoff. Our theory maintains that only the long-run efficient entrepreneur (manager) survives. High cost producers eventually exit the market.

24. Adjustments to R_0 become unnecessary with the realistic assumption that the entrepreneur choosing among oligopolistic ventures sets the employment time identical to the investment n in all projects. Furthermore, the fuzzy n allows for elasticity in the imputation process, as m can be included in n at a high or low degree of membership.

25. The entrepreneur who chooses to enter the pharmaceutical industry, *vis à vis* the food industry, accepts a high level of uncertainty in comparison to other industries. The higher the level of uncertainty within an industry, the higher the level of energy the entrepreneur is forced to expend in managing his uncertainty and vice versa.

26. This ranking procedure is outline in Kaufman et al (1988) pp. 212−219.

4. The Long–Run Competitive Oligopoly Equilibrium

We have represented human ignorance (uncertainty) by possibilistic distributions, elastic estimates, and purely subjective judgements. Most importantly, the entrepreneur is shown and treated not as an adding machine, but as a thinking, uncertain, reactive organism. Each entrepreneur in the oligopolistic markets must conjecture and guesstimate the actions and reactions of rivals. This conjectural behavior created an added risk (uncertainty) that is unique to oligopolistic markets. This oligopolistic uncertainty can be quantified through the use of fuzzy sets.

In this chapter we subsume the fuzzily quantified oligopolistic behavioral uncertainty cost within the neo–classical long–run cost, revenue framework. Then we derive a stable long–run equilibrium that is allocatively and technically efficient. The opportunity cost of the entrepreneur is imputed in the cost function of the firm, first by treating the fuzzy opportunity cost as a fixed cost and then as a variable cost. These approaches will be shown to be equivalent in establishing the existence of a well defined long–run equilibrium in each competitive oligopolistic market of a free enterprise economy. This long–run equilibrium will be established in two stages. In the first stage, long–run market participants will be viewed as imputing the correct fuzzy set r in their cost functions. In the second stage, an element in r is selected by all market rivals that establishes the crisp equilibrium.[1]

Consider the existence of a generic or basic (numeraire) product which commands a market price $\tilde{P}$. Let consumers compensate the producer for any additional utility derived from a differentiated product. Added product characteristics that continue to prevail in the long run can be considered to be beneficial characteristics; as such they command an additional cost and hence higher price. Harmful or negative characteristics are eliminated in the long run.

Let θ be the number of additional characteristics that distinguish a product from the generic or standard product. θ may, for example, represent reduced waiting time in receiving the good or service; or it may represent lower transportation costs, improved color, desirable options, etc. Define $\partial(\theta)$ as the entrepreneur's fuzzy (uncertain) estimate of the utility gain to the consumer of a differentiated product. This consumer pays a price $\hat{P}$ for the θ improved−differentiated product, where $\hat{P} = \tilde{P} + \partial(\theta)$. This ∂ is a monotonically increasing function of θ, given that the differentiated product is within the characteristic space of the set 'similar products'.[2] Moreover, $\partial(\theta)$ is a fuzzy number indicating the possibility distribution, or say the approximateness of the estimate. We divide $\hat{P}$ by $\tilde{P}$ and obtain

$$\frac{\hat{P}}{\tilde{P}} = 1 + Z, \; where \; Z = \frac{\partial(\theta)}{\tilde{P}}$$

$$\therefore \hat{P} = (1 + Z)\tilde{P}$$

The *AR* of the θ differentiating firm is therefore a $(1+Z)$ transformation of the *AR* of the numeraire producer.

THE IMPUTATION OF r AS A FIXED COST IMPUTATION

Regard the behavioral−uncertain opportunity cost r as a fixed cost; that is, r is independent of the output level. It is imputed through an operator, α_i, which relates the optimal technical output of firm i to that of the marginal firm or to any other firm in the market; that is, $\alpha2 = Q^*_2/Q^*_1$, with firm 1 being the referenced numeraire firm. For simplicity and w.o.l.o.g., assume that only two firms exist in the market. Firm 1 produces Q_1 of the numeraire product; firm 2 produces Q_2 of the differentiated product. Firm 2 perceives an added opportunity cost that is commensurate with the degree of product differentiation. Departure from homogeneity in production generates an added behavioral uncertainty because the actions and reactions of market rivals are no longer restricted to price and/or output. Actions and reactions may involve retaliatory product differentiation. Therefore, a producer who offers added advantages to the firm's product *vis à vis* the generic product is required to add on an extra cost in the firm's cost curves, over and above the cost of homogeneous products; that is, there is an implicit extra cost in conjecturing the rival reactions to product differentiation.

The neo−classical (technical) cost functions of the oligopoly market rivals are crisp; that is, objectively determined. Each market participant knows with certainty the technical costs required to produce the firm's output, thus all technical costs estimates are crisply determined by the entrepreneur or the engineers and/or accountants of the firm. Risks associated with production costs such as material flaws, machine breakdown, strikes, etc. are all objectively determined and imputed into the cost functions of each market rival.[3]

In the long run, the differentiating entrepreneur includes the cost of the added uncertainty in calculating the total opportunity cost to be charged to the firm. Any entrepreneur offering θ added characteristics requires additional compensation commensurate with the entrepreneur's energy expenditures in conjecturing rival reactions. We transform r by $(1+Z)$ to compensate the product differentiating firm for the added market uncertainty. It therefore follows that firm 2 imputes $(1+Z)r$ in place of r.[4] Most vitally for purposes of simplicity, and again w.o.l.o.g., we assume that the numeraire firm ignores whatever conjectural uncertainty would otherwise attribute to firm 2's differentiated product.

The adjusted cost curves for the two firms, inclusive of the product differentiation costs, are accordingly

$$\overline{AC}_1 = AC_1(Q_1) + r/Q_1 \tag{1}$$

$$\overline{AC}_2 = AC_2(\theta, Q_2) + [Q^*_2/Q^*_1 \cdot r/Q_2](1 + Z) \tag{2}$$

In Eq. (2), $AC_2(\theta, Q_2)$ represents the average cost of producing Q_2 of the differentiated product with θ characteristics. The opportunity cost imputation is an extension (differentiated product oligopoly) of the Greenhut−Lane (1989) methodology with r and $1+Z$ being fuzzy.

Differentiating (1) and (2) with respect to Q_1 and Q_2 at the optimal−least technical cost outputs and recognizing that

$$\frac{dAC_1(Q_1)}{dQ_1} \Big|_{Q_1=Q_1^*} = 0$$

$$\text{and } \frac{dAC_2(\theta, Q_2)}{dQ_2} \bigg|_{Q_2 - Q_2^*} = 0$$

for (1) and (2) respectively[5] establishes

$$\frac{d\overline{AC}_1}{dQ_1} \bigg|_{Q_1 - Q_1^*} = \frac{-r}{(Q_1^*)^2} \tag{1a}$$

$$\frac{d\overline{AC}_2}{dQ_2} \bigg|_{Q_1 - Q_1^*} = \frac{(-r - Zr)}{Q_1^* Q_2^*} \tag{2a}$$

In order for a long−run oligopolistic equilibrium to exist, a tangency must occur between the r adjusted average cost curves and the average revenue curves (or say the respective demand curves) for each firm's product. Zero economic profit signifies full compensation for (a) the technical production costs, (b) the basic oligopolistic uncertainty in the market, and (c) the extra uncertainty stemming from the product differentiation. In contrast, positive or negative economic profits would be destabilizing.

Consider now the average revenue function of the numeraire firm. This firm 1's long−run equilibrium output is given as Q_1^*. Let $Q_1^*/Q^* = \beta_1$, where β_1 represents the ratio of the firm's output to the output of the total market at the respective lowest production cost level. The demand for the generic product at Q_1 is therefore a function of the market's total output Q^*. In turn, $AR_1 = \tilde{P}(Q^*)$, when expressed in terms of Q_1^* and β_1, becomes $AR_1 = \tilde{P}(Q_1^*/\beta_1)$. Taking the slope of AR_1 at output Q_1^* produces

$$\frac{dAR_1}{dQ_1} = \frac{d\tilde{P}(Q_1^*/\beta_1)}{dQ_1} = \tilde{P}'(Q^*)/\beta_1 = \frac{Q^*}{Q_1^*} \tilde{P}'(Q^*) \tag{3}$$

Firm 2's demand is not a simple function of total market output; rather, it is also a function of its product differentiation. We accordingly have

$$AR_2 = \hat{P}(Q^*, \theta) = (1+Z)(\tilde{P}(Q^*))$$

$$\frac{dAR_2}{dQ_2} = (1+Z)\tilde{P}'(Q_2^*)/\beta_2 = (1+Z)\frac{Q^*}{Q_2^*} \tilde{P}'(Q^*)$$

The slopes of $\overline{AC}_1$ and AR_1 are equal at their point of tangency.

This establishes

$$\frac{Q^*}{Q_1^*} \, \tilde{P}'(Q^*) = \frac{-r}{(Q_1^*)^2} \qquad (4)$$

or

$$Q^* Q_1^* \, \tilde{P}'(Q^*) = r \qquad (5)$$

Rearranging (5) in order to recognize firms 2's sales proportion *vis à vis* that of firm 1 generates

$$\frac{Q^*}{Q_2^*} \, \tilde{P}'(Q^*) = \frac{-r}{Q_1^* Q_2^*} \qquad (6)$$

Then multiplying (6) by $(1+Z)$ yields

$$\frac{Q^*}{Q_2^*} \, \hat{P}'(Q^*) = \frac{-r(1+Z)}{Q_1^* Q_2^*} \qquad (7)$$

Equation (7) provides the tangency solution for firm 2, from which it follows that when one firm is in stable equilibrium, equilibrium also holds for the other firm(s).

Our results demonstrate a zero profit equilibrium $(AR_i(Q_i^*) = \overline{AC}_i(Q_i^*)$, such that the profit maximizing output must be at $MR_i(Q_i^*) = MC_i(Q_i^*)$. Observe further that $MC_i(Q_i^*)$ refers to the technical (crisp) marginal cost of producing Q_i^*. The imputation of the fuzzy opportunity cost r as a fixed cost affects only the total and average costs of the firm. In other words, the imputation of r as a fixed cost has no bearing on the technical marginal costs of the firm. Thus, the equality of the oligopolist's technical marginal cost with the firm's marginal revenue determines the profit maximizing output level of the firm. $MC_i(Q_i)$ is a crisp function (objectively determined), that is, not fuzzy; therefore, $MC_i(Q_i^*)$ is a crisp number. A set of possible AR's may be tangent to the fuzzy adjusted AC's at Q_i^*, which results in a fuzzy set of prices for each firm in the oligopoly market. However, only one $AR_i(Q_i^*)$ may be tangent to $\overline{AC}_i(Q_i^*)$ (the zero profit condition at Q_i^*) whose corresponding $MR_i(Q_i^*) = MC_i(Q_i^*)$(the technical profit maximizing condition at Q_i^*). The entrepreneur selects a crisp r from the fuzzy set r to maximize profits and establish the $\overline{AC}_i/AR_i$ tangency (the zero profit condition) at Q_i^*. An explanation of the crisp r selection is provided in the appendix to this chapter.

In summary, the zero profit equilibrium is established through the imputation of the fuzzy r. However, only a crisp r brings forth the profit maximization condition and establishes a unique, stable, long−run equilibrium that is technically and allocatively efficient. We demonstrate the equilibrium for firm 1, inclusive of the fuzzy r, in Figure 4.1. In Figure 4.1, the alternative MRs (illustrated by broken

Figure 4.1   Firm 1's equilibrium.   The solid $\overline{AC}_1$ and AR_1 demonstrate the choice of the entrepreneur as determined by the profit maximizing condition.

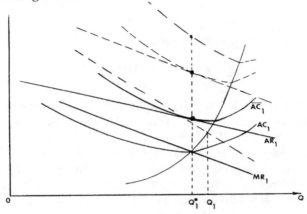

Figure 4.2   The crisp equilibrium for firms 1,2

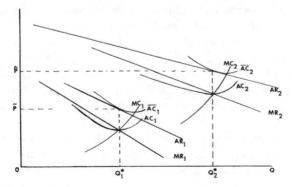

lines) establish either the profit maximizing condition at $Q_1 \neq Q_1^*$ or the zero profit condition at $Q_1 = Q_1^*$. However, only a single MR (solid line) simultaneously establishes profit maximization and zero profit conditions at Q_i^*. The crisp equilibrium for firms 1,2 is demonstrated in Figure 4.2.

The Significance of the *r* Imputation

Economic theory traditionally defines the long run as a period of time in which all production costs are variable. However, consider a market where entry or exit apply because of the prevalence of positive or negative economic profits. It is counter—intuitive and unrealistic to assume that recent market entrants will impute all costs as variable. Consequently, an intermediate run may arise with some, but not all, of the market participants complying with the theoretical distinction between the short and long run. In the words of Alfred Marshall:[6]

> ...there is no hard and sharp line of division between 'long' and 'short' periods. Nature has drawn no such lines in the economic conditions of actual life; and in dealing with practical problems they are not wanted.'

Note that the semantics long and short are vague (fuzzy) descriptors; their boundaries cannot be sharply defined conceptually. However if fuzzy sets are utilized, we can define the long run and the short run as fuzzy sets with the number of years or periods in each set assigned a membership grade. Assignments by the theorist or the entrepreneur of different membership grades to the number of years in the sets 'long run' and 'short run' lend precision and realism to these vague concepts.

If a set 'long' is employed, similar in shape to the set 'tall' presented in Chapter 1, Figure 1.1, the true meaning of the word 'long' is captured by assigning partial membership grades to certain periods and full membership grades to later periods.[7] The later periods coincide with the 'very long run' (Chapter 1, Figure 1.2) or alternatively are in the extremum of the set long, as in Chapter 1, Figure 1.1.

The fuzzy sets 'long run' and 'short run' may merge (intersect) at the lower and upper set boundaries, respectively. Accordingly, we perceive of the fuzzy r imputation to occur within the intersection of the fuzzy sets 'long' and 'short'. The fuzzy r imputation, by which the entrepreneur approximates (but does not necessarily achieve) the profit maximizing condition, is perceived to occur at the early stages of the long run and the final stages of the short run; that is the intermediate run. The crisp r selection and imputation occurs in periods outside of this intersection and in the long−run set alone. Hence, the zero profit maximization conditions and profit maximization are simultaneously satisfied only in the long run.

The imputation of r, we know, involves existence of a full set of values that conform to the various membership degrees (belief) of the entrepreneur. The range of the set r can be narrow or wide, which is to say that the degree of width does not affect the subject equilibrium. However the market rival who imputes a crisp element in the set r will cause other rivals to impute the same element of r in order to arrive at the firms' respective tangencies and profit maximizing output levels. Deviations from this equilibrium in output and/or price will destabilize the equilibrium. Entry or exit, rationalization of firm size, or further product differentiation may occur.

A price level greater than the price required by the crisp equilibrium rejects the zero profit condition. Although the entrepreneur's compensation for her conjectural opportunity cost may be within the market's fuzzy r, the firm is technically inefficient due to the marginal equality at $Q_i > Q_i^*$. This inefficiency will be noted by insiders (those in the firm's employ) as well as outsiders (market rivals or prospective rivals), and as a result entry occurs. On the other hand, at prices lower than the equilibrium price, the entrepreneur does not recover the opportunity cost associated with the market's level of conjectural uncertainty. Ultimately this entrepreneur either exits, rationalizes the firm's size to a level commensurate with the recovered opportunity cost, or reduces the firm's product differentiation.[8]

As $Z \rightarrow 0$, $\hat{P} = \tilde{P}$, and we obtain a unique, technically and allocatively efficient long−run equilibrium for the homogeneous and similar product scenarios.[9] The crisp r imputed equilibrium in the homogeneous product scenario is graphically presented in Figure 4.3.

Figure 4.3 The fixed, crisp r imputation — the homogeneous product scenario

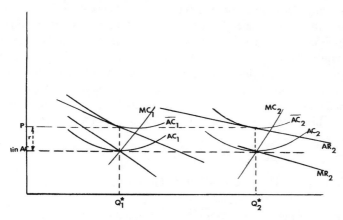

Changes in the State of Nature

If market uncertainties other than the oligopolistic behavioral uncertainties, arise from changes in the state of the world, such as war, earthquakes, etc., the market demand parameters and technical costs may become uncertain. The entrepreneur then estimates subjectively, through the use of fuzzy numbers, the approximate (uncertain) effects of this change on the firms' technical costs, demand conditions, and possibly its applicable r. All costs and revenues become fuzzy; approximateness replaces exact estimates. In other words, Q_i^*, the minimum technical cost output, becomes a fuzzy set where each element in the set is assigned a subjective membership grade by the entrepreneur. The technical production cost function becomes fuzzy and the minimum technical cost production capacity become indeterminable; that is, the entrepreneur is unable to precisely determine a crisp Q_i^*.

Inability to determine a crisp Q_i^* implies deviations from the crisp equilibrium. The consequences of such deviations is that a unique and stable equilibrium does not hold *a priori*. However, the deviations from the crisp equilibrium are within a range determined by the fuzzily estimated uncertainty. Once the uncertainty state is removed, the market returns to a crisp equilibrium. The *ex post* crisp equilibrium may either identify with or differ from the *ex ante* crisp equilibrium. In other words, alterations in the state of nature may temporarily or permanently affect the oligopoly market parameters (production cost, market demand, and the level of conjectural uncertainty) and thus define an identical or different *ex post* oligopolistic equilibrium, respectively. If the *ex post* equilibrium differs from the *ex ante* equilibrium, adjustments (entry or exit, rationalization and/or product differentiation) will occur until the *ex post* viable firms are fully compensated for their technical and conjectural costs.

THE VARIABLE COST r IMPUTATION

The fixed cost analysis demonstrates the means by which the producer imputes his opportunity cost for bearing the conjectural behavioral uncertainty in the oligopolistic market. The opportunity cost imputed as a fixed cost r is independent of the level of output. What, however, is the result of imputing oligopolistic behavioral uncertainty as a variable cost?

Pursuant to that question, let us now allow the entrepreneur to impute the cost of behavioral uncertainty in accordance with the firm's output at any moment in time.

The basis for the adaptation of the variable cost imputation is twofold: All costs are treated as variable in the long run. Not withstanding the fact that the opportunity cost of which we speak is unique and distinct from all other costs, we see no reason to preclude it from conforming to the other factor costs in the imputation process. This condition does not contradict the thesis stressed in Greenhut (1970, 1974) nor in Greenhut and Lane (1987) which emphasizes that the behavioral uncertainty cost is a residual to be viewed in the same pattern as a Ricardian rental for supra−marginal land (or the firm). In still other words, r may, of course, be viewed equally as a fixed or variable residual cost, and imputed accordingly.[10]   Additionally, while r represents the true opportunity cost of the entrepreneur, at output levels greater (less) than the optimum technical output Q_i^*, the entrepreneur must incur a greater (lower) opportunity cost than r.

Therefore, the treatment of the opportunity cost as a variable cost is justified. Moreover, we perceive of a personal preference in Greenhut (1970, 1974) for the variable imputation of the lost opportunity cost over that of the fixed cost but a pragmatic surrender to the standard graphics; that is, of the two approaches '[the] variable input treatment, though in many respects the more precise, is the more difficult to depict'.[11] We agree that the variable imputation is the more precise while also being equivalent to the fixed imputation.

Pursuant to the above, let r' be the fuzzy variable oligopolistic opportunity cost of the entrepreneur, where $r'(Q_i)$ is a function of the firm's output. Utilizing next the model's assumptions that were provided previously, with the exception of imputing r' in the place of r, define $r'=r(Q_i/Q_i^*)$, $i=1,2$; that is, the variable uncertainty cost is a monotonically increasing linear function of r. Manifestly in $r'=r(Q_i/Q_i^*)$, $i=1,2$, both Q_i and Q_i^* are crisp; nevertheless, the previous computation of r as the fuzzy opportunity cost in the alternative employment still holds.

At $Q_i<Q_i^*$, the entrepreneur of firm i inputs less energy (entrepreneurial investment) than that which applies to the optimal input level, and receives $r'<r$. At $Q_i=Q_i^*$, $r'=r$. At $Q_i>Q_i^*$, $r'>r$. An entrepreneur who receives less than r is neither utilizing the firm's basic capacity, nor is this entrepreneur able to receive the full opportunity cost as represented by r. Consequently, the entrepreneur who receives less than r is in a sense wasteful. Conversely, an expansion beyond Q_i^* requires investment levels beyond the optimal plant size as well as entrepreneurial inputs beyond those the entrepreneur considers optimal. Thus the entrepreneur personally and technically becomes a high cost producer and exits the market. Because of the uncertainty factor, this entrepreneur has more incentive than any neo−classical counterpart, and also greater incentive than the entrepreneur of the previous analysis to produce at Q_i^*. Deviation from Q_i^* is both technically and entrepreneurially inefficient.

The differentiating firm (firm 2) imputes (Q_2^*/Q_1^*) (r'/Q_2) adjusted by $(1+Z)$ to compensate for the additional conjectural behavior arising from product differentiation. To recognize this firm's perspective, let AC_i' be the variable adjusted AC curve for firm i, $i=1,2$.

$$\text{AC}_1' = AC_1(Q_1) + r'/Q_1 \qquad (8)$$

$$AC_2' = AC_2(\theta, Q_2) + (Q_2^*/Q_1^*. \ r'/Q_2)(1+Z) \tag{9}$$

Note that

$$r'/Q^1 \ \Big|_{\ Q_1-Q_1^*} = Q_2^*/Q_1^*. \ r'/dQ_2 \ \Big|_{\ Q_2-Q_2^*}.$$

that is, at $Q_1=Q_1^*$, $Q_2=Q_2^*$; then there is no product differentiation, the minimum adjusted average costs are equal for both firms; that is, all market rivals share the same level of technical efficiency. $AC_2'(Q_2^*)$is greater than $AC_1'(Q_1^*)$ according to the degree of product differentiation (technical and conjectural costs).

Derivatives of (8),(9), w.r.t. the firms' respective outputs at their optimal technical levels (Q_1^*, Q_2^*), produces zero slopes at $AC_1'(Q_1^*)$ and $AC_2'(\theta, Q_2^*)$. The adjusted cost curves are the mirror images of their neo−classical counterparts. Therefore, each firm faces a set of fuzzy adjusted average cost curves, with each curve corresponding to the entrepreneurial level of belief.

Clearly, any variable adjustment of the *AC* curves must involve a similar adjustment of the *MC* curves. We obtain the adjusted marginal costs of the firms from their adjusted total cost functions $TC_1'(Q_1)$, $TC_2'(\theta, Q_2)$

$$TC_1' = TC_1(Q_1) + r' \tag{10}$$

$$TC_2' \ (\theta, Q_2) = TC_2(\theta, Q_2) + r' \ \frac{Q_2^*}{Q_1^*}(1+Z) \tag{11}$$

Taking the derivative of (10) w.r.t. Q_1 provides

$$\partial TC_1'/\partial Q_1 = \frac{\partial TC_1(Q_1)}{\partial Q_1} + \frac{\partial Q_1}{\partial Q_1}.\frac{r}{Q_1^*}$$

and therefore

$$MC_i'(Q_i) = MC_1(Q_1) + \frac{r}{Q_1^*} \tag{12}$$

Similarly, taking the derivative of (11) w.r.t. Q_2 provides

$$\partial TC_2'(\theta Q_2)/\partial\theta Q_2 = \frac{\partial TC_2(\theta, Q_2)}{\partial Q_2} + \frac{\partial}{\partial Q_2}[\frac{Q_2^*}{Q_1^*}.\frac{Q_2}{Q_2^*}r](1+Z)$$

and therefore

$$MC_2'(\theta,Q_2) = MC_2(\theta,Q_2) + \frac{Q_2^*}{Q_1^*} \cdot \frac{\partial Q_2}{\partial Q_2} \cdot \frac{r}{Q_2^*}(1+Z)$$

which simplifies to

$$MC_2'(\theta,Q_2) = MC_2(\theta,Q_2) + \frac{r}{Q_1^*}(1+Z) \tag{13}$$

From Equations (8),(9),(12),(13), $MC_1'(Q_1^*) = AC_1'(Q_1^*)$ and $MC_2'(\theta,Q_2^*) = AC_2'(\theta,Q_2^*)$. Corresponding result holds at Q_1^*, Q_2^*, as $Z \to 0$; that is, the homogeneous product scenario, $MC_1'(Q_1^*) = AC_1'(Q_1^*) = MC_2'(Q_2^*) = AC_2'(Q_2^*)$.

It is manifest that both the average and marginal costs become fuzzy when adjusted by r', in contrast to the fixed r imputation, where the adjusted average costs are fuzzy but the marginal costs remain crisp. Thus exact mirror images of the technical costs are obtained under the variable imputation at various levels of presumption, as determined by the uncertainty in the fuzzy sets r and $(1+Z)r$.

The variable imputation for firm 1 is given in Figure 4.4. The r' adjusted AC and MC curves are represented by broken lines, and the technical costs are drawn with solid lines. For visual simplicity we assume r to contain three values only, subject to three corresponding presumption levels.

Figure 4.4 The fuzzy average and marginal costs of firm 1

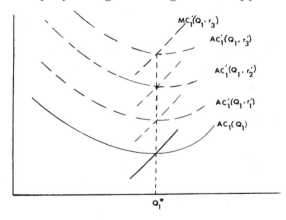

Figure 4.4 indicates that the entrepreneur of firm i knows with certainty the technical costs of production. At Q_1^*, Q_2^* respectively, $MC_1(Q_1^*) = AC_1(Q_1^*)$ and $MC_2(\theta,Q_2^*) = AC_2(\theta,Q_2^*)$. For production to occur at Q_i^*, the technical marginal equalities must be satisfied; that is, at Q_1^*, Q_2^*, $MR_1(Q_1^*) = MC_1(Q_1^*)$ and $MR_2(\theta,Q_2^*) = MC_2(\theta,Q_2^*)$, where $MR_i(\cdot)$ is firm i's actual marginal revenue. Production at $Q_i \neq Q_i^*$ is technically inefficient and is therefore rejected as a possible output decision.   Even though the entrepreneur of firm i may be overcompensated for the fuzzy opportunity cost, the technical inefficiency may cause others to enter the market, thereby destabilizing any solution that may exist at $Q_i \neq Q_i^*$.   Technical efficiencies must be fully met in order for a stable equilibrium to exist.

Additionally at Q_1^*, Q_2^*, the entrepreneurs of firms 1 and 2 must be fully compensated for their lost opportunity costs r and $(1+z)r$, respectively.   Otherwise the entrepreneur who fails to receive full compensation for all conjectured costs becomes a high cost producer and exits the market. On the other hand, the entrepreneur who is overcompensated for the conjectured opportunity costs receives positive economic profits.   One result of positive profits is either that other firms are induced to enter the market or existing firms perceive of an opportunity to further differentiate their products and/or expand their capacity output.   In order for a stable equilibrium to occur, each of the individual entrepreneur's lost opportunity costs due to the oligopolistic behavioral uncertainty must be fully met; that is to say, each viable firm's variably adjusted AC must equal the actual AR at Q_i^*.   In such equilibrium, prices must fully compensate the viable firms for their technical and conjectural costs.   Therefore an equilibrium can exist only at Q_i^*, where $MC_i(Q_i^*) = MR_i(Q_i^*)$ and $AC_i'(Q_i^*) = AR(Q_i^*)$.

Recall in this same context that the entrepreneur's opportunity costs are imputed through fuzzy numbers. However, the technical marginal and average costs are crisp.   Two conditions must be met simultaneously in order for the equilibrium to exist in the long−run oligopoly market: Each firm's respective average revenue must equal the variably adjusted average cost at Q_i^*. Moreover, at Q_i^*, the technical marginal cost/marginal revenue equality must also be satisfied.   Several marginal revenue curves may equal MC at Q_i^*; only one marginal revenue (MR_i) curve will however, also include an AR/AC' equality at Q_i^* being equal to the firm's technical marginal cost. Corresponding to this $MR_i(Q_i^*)$ is the requirement of one and only one relevant average revenue curve, that is, the average revenue curve at which $MR_i(Q_i^*) = MC_i(Q_i^*)$.[12] Since one AR alone is relevant for each firm, only one adjusted AC is selected from the fuzzy set of adjusted AC's to obtain the AC'/AR equality. Despite the fuzziness in r, which generates a fuzzy set AC', the entrepreneur is guided by the technical cost relationships to a crisp equilibrium at Q_i^*.[13] At (Q_1^*, Q_2^*), $MC_1(Q_1^*) = MR_1(Q_1^*)$, $MC_2(\theta, Q_2^*) = MR_2(\theta, Q_2^*)$. In addition, the average revenue curves of each firm must intersect the adjusted average and marginal cost curves at (Q_1^*, Q_2^*) respectively; that is,

$$AR_1(Q_1^*) = MC_1'(Q_1^*) = AC_1'(Q_1^*) \text{ and}$$
$$AR_2(\theta Q_2^*) = MC_2'(\theta Q_2^*) = AC_2'(Q_1^*)$$

Therefore when firm 1 produces Q_1^*, and attains the long−run equilibrium, firm 2 will also be at equilibrium. Firms 1,2 technical and conjectural costs are fully met at Q_1^* and Q_2^* respectively. The fixed cost and variable cost approaches produce equivalent final results; that is, both attain the basic equilibrium.

Figure 4.5 Equivalence of the fixed and variable imputations for firm 1

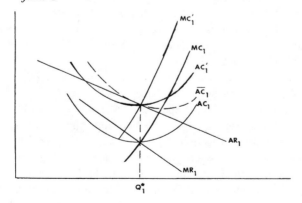

Figure 4.5 demonstrates this equivalence in imputations for firm 1. Figure 4.6 utilizes the variable cost imputation to demonstrate the crisp general equilibrium for both firms.

*Figure 4.6 The (crisp) general equilibrium for firms 1,2 under the
        variable imputation*

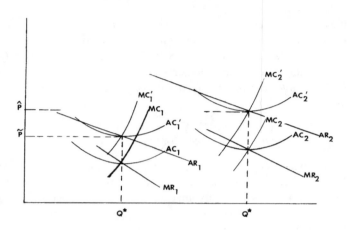

It is clear from Figure 4.6 that $MR_1(Q_1^*) = MC_1(Q_1^*)$ $\overline{AC}_1(Q_1^*) = AC'(Q_1^*)$. However, returning to Figure 4.5, recall that tangency exists between $\overline{AC}_1$ and AR_1 at $Q = Q_1^*$ (as previously demonstrated mathematically and graphically), whereas AR_1 crosses AC_1' alone at the outputs Q_1^* and possibly crosses AC at a point such as M. Of course at Q_1^*, the entrepreneur's opportunity cost and technical efficiency requirements are fully met.

Can an equilibrium exist at outputs between M and Q_1^* as a result of a possible tangency between a steeper AR_1 and AC_1'? The answer to this question is in the negative. A tangency at M does not compensate the entrepreneur for the lost opportunity cost since $r'<r$, and hence the firm is technically inefficient. Exit (or entry by an outsider) will occur. Tangency points at output levels slightly greater than M, but less than Q_1^*, are also unstable because $r'<r$ and the firm's output is not technically efficient. The same general results hold for $r'>r$ tangencies. As in the fixed cost imputation, a stable crisp, unique, technically and allocatively efficient long−run equilibrium is obtained. The variable cost adjustment leads to equilibrium at Q_1^*.

Lastly, as $Z \rightarrow 0$, $MC_1'(Q_1^*) = MC_2'(Q_2^*)$, and $AC_1'(Q_1^*) = AC_2'(Q_2^*)$ $= MC_1'(Q_1^*) = MC_2'(Q_2^*) = P^{\hat{}} = \tilde{P}$. In other words, the homogeneous product equilibrium is obtained, as depicted in Figure 4.7.

Figure 4.7 The Homogeneous Product Equilibrium

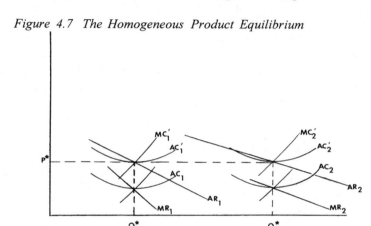

THE MARGINAL COST ADJUSTMENT AND THE ENTREPRENEUR'S INDIVIDUAL PROFIT MAXIMIZING OUTPUT LEVEL

Equations (12) and (13) indicate that $MC_1'Q_1^*) = MC_1(Q_1^*) + r/Q_1^*$ and $MC_2'\theta,Q_2) = MC_2(\theta,Q_2^*) + r/Q_1^* (1+z)$, respectively. Also Q_i^* is the technical profit maximizing and the zero profit level of output. However, the entrepreneurs' individual profit maximizing condition is not included in the above formulation. Our results demonstrate that $MR_1(Q_1^*) = MC_1(Q_1^*)$, $MR_2(\theta,Q_2^*) = MC_2(\theta,Q_2^*)$, $AR_1(Q_1^*) = AC_1'(Q_1^*)$ $AR_2(\theta,Q_2^*) = AC_2'(Q_2^*)$, and the entrepreneurs' $MC_i'(\cdot) \neq MR_i(\cdot)$. Clearly, in order for this equilibrium to be consistent with our underlying thesis, the technical profit maximizing condition must be satisfied; that is, $MC_i'(\cdot) = MR_i'(\cdot)$. Then since $MC_i'(\cdot) = AC_i'(\cdot) = AR_i(\cdot)$, one may conclude that under the variable imputation, the zero profit output is not equivalent to the maximum profit output. In still other words, since the actual average revenue curves of the firm are negatively sloped, the marginal revenues must lie below their respective average revenue curves for all output levels; and, because the marginal costs are positively sloped (increasing in Q_i), profit maximization would appear to require at an output level smaller than Q_i^*, the most technically efficient output level. On the other hand, we stress that the zero and maximal profit point (inclusive of the entrepreneur's conjectural costs) is a concurrent one at the same output level Q_i^*. Our reasoning will become clear as the thesis that follows unfolds. We demonstrate the equilibrium for the homogeneous product case and then the equilibrium when the products are differentiated.

THE HOMOGENEOUS PRODUCT EQUILIBRIUM

Recall from the fixed cost imputation that $MR(Q_i^*) = MC(Q_i^*)$. Also, we have established that $MC_i'(Q_i^*) = MC_i(Q_i^*) + r/Q_i^*$. A marginal equality must therefore set $MR_i'(Q_i^*) = MC_i'(Q_i^*)$, where $MR_i'(Q_i^*)$ denotes the marginal revenue viewed by the oligopolist who is imputing r'. Clearly $MR_i'(Q_i^*) \neq MR_i(Q_i^*)$, with the latter being the actual marginal revenue previously utilized to describe the fixed cost imputation; moreover, $MR'(Q_i^*){>}MR(Q_i^*)$ since $MC'(Q_i^*){>}MC(Q_i^*)$; and in fact $MR'(Q_i^*) = MR(Q_i^*) + r/Q_i^* = AR(Q_i^*)$. Thus, $MC'(Q_i^*) = MR'(Q_i^*) = AR(Q_i^*) = AC'(Q_i^*)$.[14]

Let P^* be the price at Q_i^*, where $P^* = MC'(Q_i^*) = MR'(Q_i^*) = AR(Q_i^*)$ $= AC'(Q_i^*)$. Each firm in the market at (P^*,Q_i^*) is producing at its technical least−cost output, and is fully compensated for all factor inputs including the entrepreneur's conjectural opportunity cost. The price P^* prohibits any market rival from charging $P{>}P^*$ for the following reasons: First, $P{>}P^*$ is inconsistent with the market demand conditions at Q_i^*, since at P the oligopolist will produce output $Q_i{<}Q_i^*$, an inefficient level of production for firm i. This inefficiency causes entry and replacement of the over−pricer by an efficient firm. Second, at (P,Q_i^*) the over−pricer will be undersold (replaced) by market rivals (new market entrants) as that subject firm exits the market. Third, at $(P,Q_i{>}Q_i^*)$, which is the least likely scenario, inefficiency occurs and entry by an efficient producer, in conjunction with market demand, again forces the excessive size firm to exit the market.[15] Thus P^* is the sole equilibrating market price.

In actuality, P^* causes all oligopolists to view their respective demand curves at $Q_i \neq Q_i^*$ as being irrelevant. What is relevant alone is P^*. Therefore, P^* can be viewed in the long run (or say conjectured) by all market rivals as a horizontal demand curve. We stress however that the conjectured horizontal demand curve is not the market demand.

Only the foolhardy will price at $P \neq P^*$ according to this reasoning.[16] At Q_i^*, $AR(Q_i^*)=MR'(Q_i^*)$. An oligopolist who attempts to produce beyond Q_i^* will suffer a loss since all factor costs will not be met. This entrepreneur exits or rationalizes the firm's size. The resulting equilibrium at Q_i^* is a stable, technically and allocatively efficient equilibrium.[17]   Figure 4.8 depicts the variable imputation for firm 1.

Figure 4.8   The variable imputation for firm 1

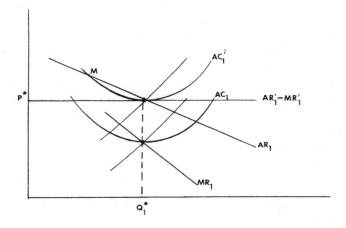

A proponent of the fixed cost imputation would argue that a variable imputation is problematic in regards to the possibility that outsiders (non−market rivals and possible entrants) and insiders (engineers, accountants; that is, company employees) may view the return on the oligopolistic uncertainty as a positive profit and decide to enter the market, thus destabilizing the existing equilibrium. Our response to this postulation is two−fold:

1. Outsiders who enter will immediately realize that their previous

conception of a positive economic profit is, in actuality, a return for the existing entrepreneur's lost opportunity cost.[18] Entrants who cannot bear the market uncertainty become inefficient producers, as asserted above and in Greenhut's works; they ultimately exit the market thereby causing the return of the original market participants to the long−run equilibrium. Furthermore, we reiterate our contention that each oligopolistic market has a unique level of uncertainty. This uniqueness qualifies only certain entrepreneurs to exist in the long run: namely, those whose lost opportunity costs are at a minimum and are fully met by the market's equilibrium rate of return.

2. It has been argued that an entrepreneur who adjusts the firm's marginal costs and revenues in accordance with r may induce those in the firm's employment, for example, accountants, engineers, etc., to believe that the marginal relationships are inflated or that the firm is operating inefficiently. Thus the employees may leave the firm and enter the market as rivals. These insiders, even though possessing the technical knowledge required for production, lack the essential ingredient for long−run survival in the oligopolistic market; that is, the insight of the entrepreneur as to the precise level of uncertainty intrinsic to the subject market. Insiders, as well as the outsiders, may, accordingly, commit the 'sin' of ignoring the importance of the market's precise and unique uncertainty level. Its effect on the long−run equilibrium will be short−lived, as the exit of those who fail to appreciate the relevant degree of uncertainty in the market is imminent. In short, ignorance of knowledge (the entrepreneur's) is weakness.

THE DIFFERENTIATED 'SIMILAR' PRODUCT SCENARIO

Recall that firm 1 (the basic numeraire product firm) receives $\tilde{P}$ and firm 2 (the θ differentiating firm) receives $\hat{P}$ per unit of product sold. The entrepreneur of firm 1 views a market demand for the firm's product as perfectly inelastic; that is, any deviation from $\tilde{P}$ causes the firm and the entrepreneur to be inefficient. A price $P_1 > \tilde{P}$ results in product differentiation and/or expansion of plant size by market rivals; or entry by outsiders as well as insiders. At $P_1 > \tilde{P}$, the entrepreneur is compensated insufficiently for the technical and conjectural production costs. Similarly for firm 2, any deviation from the product price (inclusive of θ and all technical and conjectural costs) causes market rivals to enter this market and replace firm 2. Thus firm 2's entrepreneur perceives of a horizontal (that is perfectly elastic) demand curve at $\hat{P}, Q_2$. The arguments presented in the homogeneous product scenario also hold in the 'similar' (differentiated) product case. Additionally, the threat of possible product differentiations by rivals to counter any deviations from the equilibrium price is also present. Thus, every long−run viable oligopolist must perceive of a perfectly elastic demand curve for the firm's output. This perfectly elastic demand curve is necessitated and brought forth by the entrepreneur's correct variable imputation of the conjectural cost. The entrepreneur's viewed or conjectured AR_i is tangent to $AC_i'(\cdot)$. At Q_i^*, both the conjectured AR and actual AR are equal.

Let $AR_1'(Q_i^*), AR_2'(\theta, Q_i^*)$, be the conjectured AR curves for firms 1 and 2, respectively. Also $AR_i'(\cdot) = MR_i'(\cdot) = AR_i(\cdot)$ at Q_i^*. The long−run equilibrium via the variable imputation is established for firms 1,2, at Q_1^*, Q_2^* by the equalities, I and II, stated below

$$MC_1'(Q_1^*) = MR_1'(Q_1^*) = AC_1'(Q_1^*) = AR_1'(Q_1^*) = AR_1(Q_1^*),$$
$$\text{and } MC_1(Q_1^*) = MR_1(Q_1^*) \qquad \qquad \text{I}$$

$$MC_2'(\theta, Q_2^*) = MR_2'(\theta, Q_2^*) = AC_2'(\theta, Q_2^*) = AR_2'(\theta, Q_2^*)$$
$$= AR_2(\theta, Q_2^*), MC_2(\theta, Q_2^*) = MR_2(\theta, Q_2^*) \qquad \qquad \text{II}$$

ADDENDUM

One final case warrants investigation. If $r \rightarrow 0$, what impact applies to the oligopoly market equilibrium that was obtained above. Can the fuzzy r or crisp r be zero? What effect, if any, does the null r have on our equilibrium? Before this question is answered, let us recount the analysis presented in Chapter 2. It was established there that the fuzzy set O^* obtains from the fuzzy sets I^*, F^*, S^*, where

O^* represents the set of oligopolistic rivals;
I^* represents the set 'interdependent firms';
F^* represents the set 'few firms'; and

S^* represents the set 'similar products.'

Based on the set O^*, the level of conjectural uncertainty and in turn the calculation of the entrepreneur's opportunity cost r that is attributable to the oligopolistic market's level of conjectural uncertainty are derived.

In order for the set r to be empty; that is, $\forall x \in \mathbf{R}$, $\mu_r(x)=0$, one of the sets I^*, F^*, S^* must also be empty. Neo−classical theory has traditionally viewed I^* to arise from F^* and S^*, however, as demonstrated in Chapter 2, in order to obtain a precise definition of the oligopoly market, I^* must be investigated separately from and utilized in conjunction with S^* and F^*, for example, a market may consist of a few firms producing similar products with the individual firm's trading space being geographically separated from the market of the other firms.[19]

The entrepreneur may view I^* as empty; so that all of the potential member firms in I^* are assigned a zero membership grade. The entrepreneur thus perceives these firms as not significantly impacting her firm's (henceforth call it F) product pricing, output, or product characteristics. Firm F is, in short, independent of the other firms despite the fact that there are few firms producing somewhat similar products in the market.

The set O^*, resulting from I^* (empty), S^*, F^*, is an empty set; all the elements in O^* have zero membership grades. Hence, the O^* set does not represent an oligopoly market. Since O^* does not contain a single market rival, r is also empty because the conjectural uncertainty arising from the interdependence of firms in the market does not exist.

As $r \rightarrow 0$, the oligopoly market becomes a monopolistically competitive market with the latter being a special case of the former. Correspondingly, not a single characteristic of the equilibrium is applicable to monopolistic competition. In fact, the monopolistically competitive equilibrium is non-optimal and unstable. The non-optimality is due to tangencies between market firms' technical AC and respective AR in the decreasing section of the AC curves; hence, there is an under-utilization of resources which characterizes the market's inefficiency.

The instability of the equilibrium in a monopolistically competitive market also arises from the removal of trade barriers and from technological advances that break geographic market barriers. Lower shipping costs within a nation or a pacified cooperative political climate among nations destabilizes the equilibrium by allowing entry of the distant firm into a market area that was formerly protected. In addition to the above, product loyalties may shift with time thus reshaping the perceived security of firms as to their protected markets.[20]   Under any scenario, monopolistic competition and the 'Chamberlinian' tangency depicts only a restricted and incomplete oligopoly market and thus the equilibrium (inclusive of the r imputation) therein.

SUMMARY

This chapter imputed the fuzzily quantified oligopolistic behavioral uncertainty cost to the neo-classical long-run cost revenue framework in deriving a stable long-run equilibrium in oligopolistic markets. This equilibrium is technically and allocatively efficient; moreover, it is unique to oligopoly markets.   The intermediate-run oligopoly equilibrium is shown as fuzzy.   Viable firms approximate profit maximization and are adopted by consumers and in effect their respective industries.   In the long run, these same oligopolistic competitors adapt themselves and their firms to their industries, with a crisp determinate long-run equilibrium eventuating.   At this equilibrium, both the technical and personal opportunity costs (inclusive of the oligopolistic conjectural uncertainty cost) are compensated for fully. The adapting process of the long-run viable firms to the market's realities gains reward for them in a profit maximizing crisp, stable, and technically allocatively efficient equilibrium.   In the words of the ancient Chinese philosopher, Lao Tsu[21], which relate to our viable oligopolistic entrepreneur: 'Knowing ignorance is strength'.

APPENDIX

The process of the crisp r selection for firm 1 is demonstrated by means of an example.   Let r (fuzzy) consist of three elements w.o.l.o.g. r_1, r_1, r_3, where $r_1 < r_1 < r_3$, and whose membership grades are .5, .6, .7 respectively. From Equation (1) recall that

$$\overline{AC}_1 = AC_1(Q_1) + \frac{r}{Q_1}$$

When (1) is re-written in terms of α-cuts (the entrepreneur's levels of presumption) the fuzzy r is replaced by the elements r_1, r_1, r_3 at .5, .6, .7.

$$\overline{AC}_1^{\alpha} = AC_1(Q_1) + \frac{r^{\alpha}}{Q_1}$$

$AC_1(Q_1)$ is firm 1's technical (neo-classical) long-run average cost of producing Q_1. $AC_1(Q_1)$ is objectively determined (crisp). $\overline{AC}_1^{\alpha}(Q_1)$ is a fuzzy function since the argument r is fuzzy. At .5, .6, .7 we obtain

$$\overline{AC}_1^{(.5)} = AC_1(Q_1) + \frac{r_1}{Q_1}$$

$$\overline{AC}_1^{(.6)} = AC_1(Q_1) + \frac{r_2}{Q_1}$$

$$\overline{AC}_1^{(.7)} = AC_1(Q_1) + \frac{r_3}{Q_1}$$

Since $r_1 < r_1 < r_3$ then $\overline{AC}_1^{(.5)} < \overline{AC}_1^{(.6)} < \overline{AC}_1^{(.7)}$. In other words, the manager of firm 1 envisions three adjusted cost curves at the presumption levels .5, .6, .7 as shown in Figure 4.9.

Entry and exit causes the firm's demand curve (AR_1) to rotate; that is, the slope of (AR_1) changes. The slope of the firm's TR function alters accordingly. Thus corresponding to every demand curve, a marginal revenue curve is observed by the entrepreneur which reflects the slope of the TR function. Simply put, an MR corresponds to each AR that arises from the entry or exit of rivals in the market.

In order to obtain a zero profit output, the firm's demand curve must be tangent to $\overline{AC}_1^{\alpha}(Q_1)$; that is, it must be tangent to one of the three adjusted ACs. The levels of output that result from this tangency and profit maximizing requirement may or may not be the most efficient (minimum technical cost) output level Q_1^*. While $AC_1^{(.5)}(Q_1^*) = AR(Q_1^*)$ and $MR_1(Q_1) = MC_1(Q_1)$ may occur, it is rejected as a possible equilibrium solution since $Q_1 \neq Q_1^*$ and firm 1 is technically inefficient at $Q_1 \neq Q_1^*$. The entrepreneur who adheres to this tangency solution at a .5 presumption level is only approximating the profit maximization level of output and is therefore inefficient.

Figure 4.9 $\overline{AC}_1^\alpha$ *at .5, .6, .7 Presumption Levels*

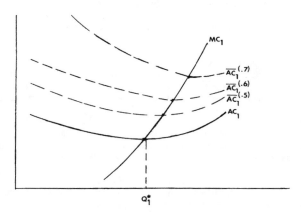

Entry or exit continues until a tangency occurs at $AC_1^{(.7)}(Q_1^*) = AR(Q_1^*)$, with $MR_1(Q_1^*)=MC_1(Q_1^*)$, and Q_1^* providing the minimum technical cost output of firm 1. At this Q_1^*, r_3 is imputed and the zero profit output coincides with the technically efficient profit maximizing output. No further entry or exit and/or other market adjustments take place. The resulting equilibrium is stable, with the firm being technically and allocatively efficient.

NOTES

1. Parts of this chapter borrow heavily from Working Paper 91−21, Texas A & M University, M.L. Greenhut and Y. Mansur.
2. See Chapter 2 for the treatment of the set 'similar' as a fuzzy set.
3. We elaborated on the distinction between risk and uncertainty in Chapter 3 of this work. We will deal with market uncertainties (those other than the oligopolistic conjectural uncertainty) through subjective (fuzzy) estimates in the forthcoming analysis. For the present however, we assume that market uncertainties do not exist.

4.   Freedom of entry and exit in the oligopolistic market applies to the long run when the opportunity cost of the entrepreneur in the market is not met fully and the market product is homogeneous.   However, product differentiation can be viewed as a substitute for entry and exit when the latter actions are too costly.   An entrepreneur who foresees an opportunity cost of $(1+Z)r$, $Z\neq0$, differentiates the firm's product by θ to obtain the additional Zr. In the long run, producers who are unable to obtain Zr through product differentiation exit the market.   Thus, our model embodies the very nature of competition in that entry, exit and product differentiation are allowed.

5.   The average cost, inclusive of θ product differentiation, must also be minimal at the least cost technical output; that is, the differentiated product follows the same neo-classical cost relationships as the numeraire product.

6.   (1910), 6th edition, p. 378.

7.   'Tall' refers to people; 'long' refers to objects.   Heights are represented on the horizontal axis of the figure depicting the set 'tall'.   In comparison, the number of years are designated on the horizontal axis in the graphical representation of the set 'long'. The semantical use of the term 'short', however, unlike 'long', can be applied to both people and objects. The set 'short' may be viewed as a flattened Z or simply a mirror image of the set long.

8.   Both our theory and analysis allow for free entry or exit, as in Greenhut (1970,1974). The entrepreneur who does not receive r at $Q_i^{\,*}$ may expand or contract the firm's technical capacity (plant size) to produce at $Q_i{>}Q_i^{\,*}$ or $Q_i{<}Q_i^{\,*}$, respectively. Rationalization of plant size necessitates the adjustment of the energy expenditures such that the entrepreneur's return is consistent with that of the market r.   As a substitute for, and in conjunction with the free entry and exit mechanism and/or rationalization, the entrepreneur may opt to increase or decrease the differentiating characteristics of the firm's product.   Of course, in the homogeneous product case, only the first two adjustments are available to the entrepreneur of this market type.

9.   Greenhut (1970, 1974), Greenhut et al (1987) and Greenhut and Lane (1989) have demonstrated the long-run equilibrium for the homogeneous product oligopoly.

10.   Acceptance of our results hinges on the viability of the fixed cost imputation.

11.   See Greenhut (1970, 1974) p. 87.

12.   The argument θ is excluded from this equality in order to maintain notational simplicity.

13.   Appendix to Chapter 4 demonstrates this principle for the fixed r imputation and is also applicable to the argument presented above.

14.   The use of subscripts in the cost revenue relationships is not necessary since we already established and demonstrated that the traditional (technical) cost relationships are equal in the long run for all market firms; that is, technical efficiency is a characteristic shared equally by all of the market participants in the long run.

15.   By an efficient producer, we refer to the producer whose opportunity cost is consistent with the market's r, and who is able to produce at $AC(Q_i^{\,*})$, while being fully compensated by P^{*}.   Of course, rather than exit, an excessive size firm may reduce the total capacity of the firm (call it rationalizing to its optimal size).   Then as others move in or out of the market, it ultimately proves to be a viable firm.

16.   Collusion is not permitted in our model.

17.   Note that a broken AR does not arise in our model.   The actual market AR remains intact while the conjectured AR exists only in the mind's eye of the entrepreneur. Thus, the argument presented by Sweezy and others as to taxing oligopolies does not apply to our formulation.   Each oligopolist is producing at $MR_i(Q_i^{\,*}){=}MC_i(Q_i^{\,*})$; i.e., the actual MR and technical MC equality. A production tax will create inefficiency by raising the MC, MC' and AC, AC' curves above P^{*} by the amount of the tax.

18. Free entry and exit is intrinsic to our theory.
19. Geographic separation may be due to natural or artificial barriers. Natural separation may be a result of distance such that the total shipping and production costs from another firm's plant to the market extremity of firm F (the representative firm) is greater than F's maximum possible price at its market's extremum. Artificial separation may be due to trade barriers erected to protect an infant industry (firm F), as a retaliatory measure, or as a consequence of political disputes, or for a host of other motivations, all resulting in the establishment of commercial policies that prohibit trade among two nations.
20. E.H. Chamberlin (1962) considered loyalty a factor in the separation of markets and as an exhibition of a degree of monopoly.
21. Quoted in G. Klir and T. Folger,(1988).

5. From Fuzzy Math to Chaos Theory and the Long Run

The long−run equilibrium of oligopoly markets was established in Chapter 4 by static analysis. Significantly, it can also be established and proven by use of a fuzzy r tracked along the dynamic path that is followed to its long−run equilibrium. We shall, in this chapter, allow the membership grade and its argument in the fuzzy r to vary over a discrete space−time period where the path of motion is controlled by a state equation based on the entrepreneur's 'beliefs'. The attributes of the fuzzy math approach will, therefore, be viewed directly. It will be further manifest that the fuzzy−math system of thought is a natural counterpart to the 'real−life' role of the entrepreneur in the oligopoly market setting. Last, but not least, let it be emphasized that the dynamic path taken in reaching the oligopoly long−run equilibrium is a chaotic one.

Although the dynamical map employed in this chapter involves a rather simple, deterministic mathematical relationship, the path that it follows is quite complex; yet within its chaotic form lies the determinism pre−ordered by the long−run equilibrium. Phrased more pointedly, the crisp long−run equilibrium that eventuates is shown to be dynamically stable and deterministically tractable.[1]

The long−run equilibrium of oligopoly markets was previously shown to require imputing the oligopolist's opportunity cost onto the traditional economists' cost and revenue functions. The cost relates to the conjectural−uncertain nature of oligopolistic competition. Moreover, this cost dovetails directly with the entrepreneur's optimal personal investment(s). Full compensation for the oligopolist's business activities, including his/her conjectural−related−opportunity cost is a basic requirement for any stable long−run equilibrium. Otherwise the short−run inefficiencies which prevail before all market adjustments have taken place (including the entry/exit, rationalizing of size, product differentiation process) would continue forever. As was emphasized in Chapter 4, the imputed opportunity cost serves as the vehicle which elicits the efficient long–run allocation of resources, and with that the stable, technically and allocatively efficient process that defines the subject oligopoly markets.[2]

THE DYNAMIC PATH TO EQUILIBRIUM

Newton, in the first edition of the *Principia*, proposed that sufficient knowledge of a phenomenon enables one to determine its past and future outcomes, whereas incomplete knowledge of the phenomenon is the cause of what many scholars consider to be random occurrences. He invented a deterministic differential equation in deriving Kepler's law from the concept of gravity. A differential equation, according to Newton, is:

> ...an instantaneous relation between position, velocity, and acceleration, which is supposed to hold through the motion. Integrating, or solving, the equation, means to deduce from this relation the actual trajectory which will be followed and the motion thereon (Ekeland 1988, p. 21).

Poincaré, the father of many mathematical disciplines including topology, showed that all of Newton's quantitative results were wrong; and he proved that quantitative analysis of dynamical systems provided no significant insights into the trajectory. 'To Poincaré, global understanding of the gross behavior of all solutions of the system was more important than the local behavior of the particular' (Devaney 1987, p. vii).[3] Almost a hundred years later, in Ruelle et al (1971), also Roux et al (1983), and Swinney et al (1985), Poincaré's method and observations were put in practice. Ruelle et al argued that more can be learned about certain types of fluid flow turbulence by understanding the long–run behavior of their time paths. Then Roux et al and Swinney et al documented the existence of the seemingly random turbulence that arises from purely deterministic systems in nature.

Interest in the qualitative analysis of dynamical systems resulted, giving birth in turn to chaos theory: a mathematical subdiscipline which will presently be defined and whose principals will be utilized to explain the dynamic path of competitive oligopoly markets to their long–run equilibrium. In doing this, we shall utilize a discrete, deterministic, belief–based–state–equation which describes the time path of the subject (competitive) oligopoly markets. Our reasons for choosing a discrete (not continuous) time approach relate to the fact that although change is continuous over time, and so is a formal view of it, individuals observe, evaluate, and make their decisions at discrete intervals (the beginning or the end of a time interval, depending on one's focaawpoint). In still other words, decision makers view change as being continuous over time, but think of it in discrete terms. It is further our contention that sound business decisions are never continuous but discrete; in effect, a planning or decision period is required by the decisionmaker (planner) to assimilate all existing–available data within a coherent decision space.

We elect accordingly to denote the dynamics of the oligopoly market by a deterministic system equation. The equation is deterministic in that given the state of the system at time t, we are able to specify its state at $t+1$. A non–deterministic system is characterized by the inability to determine the $t+1$ state of the system exactly, no matter how specific one's knowledge is of the input and the system's state at time t. Such non–deterministic systems include a stochastic element which would be introduced as an input parameter or as a separate variable. Its stochastic property generates a set of probability distributions at points along the dynamic path of the system. Significant insight may be gained by introducing uncertainty (the stochastic property) into an otherwise deterministic system; however, the decision maker is assumed to know exactly the system's probability distribution in order to effect the required estimates. Yet this exact knowledge of the probability distributions of the random variables in the system is itself a special condition. 'In real life this condition is rarely (if ever) satisfied' (Negoita 1979, p. 33). Therefore, whether we assume the dynamic system to be deterministic or indeterminate, either assumption requires exact knowledge of the inputs or (when random) their distributions. In the words of Albert Einstein, 'So far as the laws of mathematics refer to reality, they are not certain. And so far as they are certain, they do not refer to reality' (quoted in Kosko 1992, p. 263, from *Geometrie und Erfahrurng*).

Our belief—based system utilizes the condition of inexact knowledge in inputs and distributions of the outputs. The subjective belief of the entrepreneur which stems from a knowledge base (for example expertise in an oligopoly industry) is quantified into the inputs at time t. This belief (as we will presently show) generates a time path in which periodic patterns are evidenced in the midst of a seemingly chaotic dynamical system. The state of the system at time t is deterministic in the sense that no randomness applies at any time in the state equation. Furthermore, the state equation is based upon, and determined by the uncertainty surrounding the entrepreneurial input.

OUR BASIC MODEL

Discrete dynamical systems can be obtained easily via simple iterative processes. For example, consider the function $f(X_t) = aX_t$, where X_t is the firm's output at time t, a is some tuning parameter which describes the strength of the dependence of the output in the next period on the present period's output, and $f(X_t) = X_{t+1}$ is the next period's output. Thus the output of the next period is functionally dependent on the present period's output. The tuning parameter can take any value over $[0, \infty]$; that is, the production level in the next period is either positive or zero regardless of the present level of output; also, because output is a physical quantity, it cannot be negative. The output in the successive periods can be described by applying an X_0, the initial output level, which w.o.l.o.g. is assumed to start at zero time, and some $a \in [0, \infty]$ to establish the equation. By calculating aX_0, X_1 obtains. Similarly, x_1 is then applied to obtain X_2, and so forth. The total process involves iterating the function n times, $n \geq 1$. The process can be described as

$$X_1 = AX_0$$
$$X_2 = AX_1 = a(AX_0) = a^2 \cdot X_0$$
$$X_3 = aX_2 = a(a(AX_0)) = a^3X_0$$
$$\cdot$$
$$\cdot$$
$$\cdot$$
$$X_n = a^nX_0$$

or $f^n(X_0) = f(f(f- - - -f(X_0)))$ with the superscript n indicating the number of iterations or the time period.

Let the iterative sequence of $f(X_t)$ be referred to as the orbit of X_t; and further refer to the function that generates this sequence as the map of X_t. Then, $f(\overline{X}_t) = \overline{X}_t$, where $\overline{X}_t$ is the output level at the previous period, $\overline{X}$ is called a fixed (equilibrium) point on the map. In the present example the fixed point occurs at $X_0 = 0$ where $X_1 = a(0) = 0$, that is $X_0 = X_1 = X_2 = X_3 \ldots X_n = 0$. A periodic fixed point occurs at $f^n(\overline{X}_t) = \overline{X}_t$, that is, if we are at some period n, the map has returned us to $\overline{X}_t$. Obviously our map has a fixed point at $\overline{X} = 0$ for all periods. This means that if the industry initially produces zero ($t = 0$), it will also produce zero in the future and the system will be stable.

One gains further insight into the system by investigating the parameter a. Since output is always ≥ 0, then a cannot be negative. If $a = 0$, then dynamics do not apply; that is, the system is static. At $a < 1$, $X_0 > 0$ and the economist can surmise that the level of output decreases at an exponential rate such that, after n mappings (n being sufficiently large), the output level approaches zero. If $a>1$ the output level grows exponentially to ∞. The identity map ($a = 1$), $f(X_t) = X_t$ generates an infinite set of fixed points: $X_0 = X_1 = X_2 \ldots = X_n$ for any initial output level. This is why a is called a tuning parameter, obviously regulating the growth, constancy, or death of the system.

We now enter an element of uncertainty in the present simple example. Suppose the entrepreneur is uncertain of the output level at $t = 0$ (cannot determine precisely the initial output level). Based on the entrepreneur's subjective belief, a fuzzy number applies to X_0. So X_0 is a fuzzy set, with different belief levels (possibilities) assigned to the elements in X_0. By the extension principle, the same possibilities are ascribed to $X_1 = \{\alpha X_{om}\}_{m=1,\ldots M}$, where M is the number of elements in X_0. Therefore, vagueness (uncertainty) about a period's output is mapped onto the next period's output level, and so forth.

Alternatively, suppose the entrepreneur is uncertain about a; that is, the vagueness surrounds the next period output, while the present output is fully determined: though given a crisp X_0, a is fuzzy, and X_{t+1} etc. are also fuzzy. In this case, the map is a fuzzifying map because its argument is crisp. Every image may have a different belief (possibility) distribution from the previous image of the map since the membership grades of the fuzzily defined parameter (a) may not be identical to those of a^2, a^3 ..., a^n.[4]

The example given above is naive (unrealistic) since output growth, constancy, or death depends only on the previous period's output: Costs, revenues, feed back, discontinuities due to natural disasters etc., have all been excluded from the basic equation in the system. However, when either X_t or a, or both are fuzzified (made uncertain), the system's equation becomes much more realistic than it was previously. Of course, the realism arises from the quantification of the humanistic belief–factor (uncertainty, the approximate or incomplete knowledge) which underlies all business decisions, especially when applied to an oligopolist environment as we have shown in Chapters 2, 3, and 4.

Having presented the general characteristics of our model, we can now turn to the task of constructing the model, its specifications, its path, its behavior and results.

Denote the fuzzy uncertainty range that an entrepreneur will accept as $\mu_t(r_t) \in [0,1]$ where r_t serves to suggest the net revenues required for the crisp uncertainty that will actually exist and the μ_t provides a membership grade extending from the lowest to the highest membership the entrepreneurs will contemplate (that is, accept). We can denote the fuzzy opportunity cost r by $\tilde{r}$, where $\tilde{r}$ would be the accepted return given the uncertainty.[5] The crisp r_t selection is such that the zero surplus and maximum profits are satisfied completely by its imputation in the neo–classical cost and revenue functions.

The oligopolist market entropy (uncertainty) measure changes in time due to changes in the interdependence levels among market firms, product differentiation, or new entry into the oligopoly market. This entropy change, which we assume to be observed and evaluated at discrete intervals by the entrepreneur, also motivates a change in the entrepreneur's belief that r_t is the appropriate selection for the next period $t+1$. The strength of belief (μ_{t+1}) is brought forth by the change in μ_t, which then dictates the selection of $r_{t+1} \in \tilde{r}$, and which corresponds to μ_{t+1} at the time $t+1$. If two elements in $\tilde{r}$ correspond to μ_{t+1}, the element whose absolute distance from r_t is the smallest, is selected.[6]

The subject dynamical relationship is canonically described by (1) and (2)

$$\Delta\mu_t = \mu_t(1 - \mu_t) \tag{1}$$

$$\mu_{t+1} = k(\Delta\mu_t) \tag{2}$$

where (1) describes the change in μ_t as a nonlinear function of the strength of one's belief and the corresponding strength of one's disbelief; then (2) describes the strength of the entrepreneur's belief over the successive periods of time as a linear function of the change in the strength of the belief in the previous period. The parameter k in (2) is an exogenous variable which describes the rate of change of entropy in a market. The value of k is a monotonically increasing function of the rate of change in entropy; that is, if the change in market entropy is high, the k value will be high and vice versa. The full significance of k will be shown presently in a separate section of this chapter. For our immediate purposes it suffices to state that k is a non−negative real number; a condition imposed by the requirement that μ_{t+1} (and all membership grades) be non−negative at all times. (Recall, Chapter 1.)

Clearly, the relationships (1) and (2) simplify to the quadratic equation

$$\mu_{t+1} = k\mu_t(1 - \mu_t) \tag{3}$$

which join the linguistic−mathematically translated−belief rules into one mathematical relationship: the strength of the belief (or possibility) in the successive period $(t+1)$ is a function of the strength of belief (μ_t) and the strength of disbelief (μ_{t-1}) which prevailed in the previous period.

Equation (3) is the state equation in the dynamical view of long−run oligopoly markets, where μ_0 and k, respectively, the strength of belief and the rate of change in entropy specific to a market, dictate the orbit of the long−run equilibrium map. This equation is well known to students of dynamical systems as the ecology equation. Biologists have utilized the ecology (logistic) equation to describe population changes. Economists, on the other hand, have used the ecology equation to illustrate the mathematics of chaos, as in Baumol et al (1989) and Butler (1990). Unlike biologists, however, economists have been unable (to the best of my knowledge) to provide an economic interpretation of this (the ecology) equation. (Also, see Butler 1990.)

The logistic function's dynamics will appear to be simple at first glance; but this simplicity is deceiving. We shall demonstrate that (with no random element existing either in the variables or the parameter) the elementary and rather standard appearing non−linear difference equation, though deterministic, exhibits a highly complex time path which may appear to be random to the untrained observer. In fact, the quadratic map demonstrates all of the fundamental characteristics of chaos[7], which we define below.[8]

A DEFINITION OF CHAOS

A function that maps a set to itself is called a chaotic map on the set if

(1) The map exhibits sensitive dependence on initial conditions. Canonically stated, $f: C{\to}C$, $\exists\varepsilon>0$, $\exists x\in C$, and any neighborhood of x, N_x, $\exists y\in N$, $n>0$ s.t. $|f^n(x) - f^n(y)|>\varepsilon$.

In less formal verbiage, suppose our set C is a metric interval, then we select a point $x\in C$ and apply the map to it; this yields $f^n(x)$ after n iterations, $n\geq0$, however, if we select an arbitrarily small interval $(x - \varepsilon, x + \varepsilon)$ around x_0 and apply the map n times to a point y in this interval, then $|f^n(x) - f^n(y)|>\varepsilon$ so that the nth mapping of y no longer resembles that of x. For example, a billiard player who ever so slightly changes the striking angle of the billiard ball from his/her original intention, let us say by ε, causes the trajectory of the ball to deviate from the alternative trajectory by more than ε after n bounces off the sides of the billiard table. Thus, a small error in the calculation of the initial input leads to huge errors in long−run results. Just as weather forecasters cannot predict the weather far into the future, macroeconomists cannot provide accurate predictions concerning the economy's position in the long run if their map is sensitively dependent on initial conditions.

(2) After n iterations the map can move an arbitrarily small interval in C, close to any other given point in C. That is, $f: C{\to}C$ is called a topologically transitive map, if for any pair of open sets, $U,V{\subset}C$, $\exists n>0$, s.t. $f^n(U){\cap}V \neq 0$. Thus the orbit of the map comes close to

covering all of the points in C.

A chaotic map is therefore sensitive to initial conditions and unpredictable (from (1) and (2), respectively). An untrained observer of a phenomenon may mistakenly view its path as random. But in the midst of this unpredictability lies an element of regularity; that is, dense periodic points.

(3) Arbitrarily close to any point given in C lies a periodic point; that is, periodic points are dense in C. A subset is viewed as dense if its closure (union with its limit points) is the whole set.

Example $(0,1)$ is dense in $[0,1]$. Periodic points are $f^n(x) = x$, $n>0$. Thus, there exists patterns of regularity under the cloud of unpredictability.

We adopt the following example of a chaotic map from Devaney (1987, p. 50). Consider the map $f: C^1 \rightarrow C^1$ where C^1 is the unit circle and f is defined by $f(\theta) = 2\theta$, where θ is an angle measured in radians. Any point on the circle is defined by $\theta + 2k\pi$ where k is an integer and $f(\theta + 2k\pi) = f(\theta)$. Note that $f^1 (\theta + \epsilon) = 2(\theta + \epsilon) = 2\theta + 2\epsilon$, then $|f^1(\theta + \epsilon) - f^1(\theta)| = |2\epsilon| > \epsilon$. Thus, according to (1), the map exhibits sensitive dependence on its initial conditions. Also, f is topologically transitive, since if we take any small arc U in C^1, it grows under f^n to cover the whole circle and every other arc in the circle. Furthermore, periodic points exist, that is $f^n(\theta^*) = 2^n(\theta^*) = \theta^* + 2k\pi$; that is, θ^* is a periodic point of period n. Then $2^n(\theta^*) = \theta^* + 2k\pi$

$$\theta^*(2^n - 1) = 2k\pi$$
$$\theta^* = \frac{2k\pi}{2^n-1} \ , \ 0 \le l \le 2^n$$

Let $n = 2$, then $k = 0,1,2,3,4$

and
$$\theta^* = 0, \frac{2\pi}{4-1} \ , \ \frac{4\pi}{4-1} \ , \ \frac{6\pi}{4-1} \ , \ \frac{8\pi}{4-1}$$

Similarly $n = 3$, $k = 0,1,2,3,4,5,6,7,8$

and
$$\theta^* = 0, \frac{2\pi}{8-1} \ , \ \frac{4\pi}{8-1} \ , \ \frac{6\pi}{8-1} \ , \ \frac{8\pi}{8-1}, \ldots, \frac{16\pi}{8-1}$$

Therefore as n grows, every point on the circle lies close to a periodic point and the number of periodic points increases. The focus of the researcher is to determine these periodic points.

THE PHASE DIAGRAM

We next utilize the phase diagram of the map f in order to analyze the orbits of the function at $t = 1, 2, 3, ..., n$. The phase diagram plots μ_t on the horizontal and $f(\mu_t)$ on the vertical axes. The map is an inverted parabola whose intercepts occur at $\mu_t = 0,1$ and the maximum $\mu_{t+1} = k/4$ occurs at $\mu_t = .5$. Using the phase diagram, draw a ray (a line starting at $(0,0)$) whose slope is 1, that is, at a 45° angle. Since the 45° ray is the diagonal of a square, any point thereon represents an equilibrium (fixed) point between the horizontal and vertical coordinates (μ_t and $f(\mu_t)$). This equality means that whenever the map (the inverted parabola) crosses the 45° ray, an equilibrium is obtained; that is, $\mu_t = f(\mu_t)$ for two successive iterations, μ_t and μ_{t+1}. Since the belief level can also be viewed as a possibility measure in the possibility distribution $\tilde{r}$, the entrepreneur selects a crisp r from $\tilde{r}$ based upon μ_{t+1} (the possibility measure of the next period); and imputes the crisp r into the technical costs at time $t+1$. The resulting equilibrium and price in an oligopoly market at period t is identical to the equilibrium and price in the successive period $t+1$.

Other types of equilibria may also be shown by the phase diagram. Cycles or oscillatory patterns representing an equality between μ_t and the nth iterate of $f(\mu_t)$, where n is an integer greater than 1, may also appear indicating an equilibrium in the oligopoly market. This equilibrium type is called a periodic or eventually periodic equilibrium.

A periodic equilibrium occurs when $\mu_0 = \mu_n$. Thus $r_0 = r_n$, and given our long−run assumptions the initial oligopoly market equilibrium recurs periodically with n being the interval length. That is, the equilibrium return in an oligopoly market at period $t = 0$ is equal to the equilibrium return n periods in the future. Thus $P_0 = P_n$, $n>1$.[9] This periodic equilibrium re−occurs every nth period if the market entropy maintains its rate of change as measured by k.[10] The repeated periodic equilibrium is in general a set of short run equilibria, albeit in constant cost industries or in industries whose long−run costs swing up and down periodically, the system at hand might be the long—run equilibrium path.

The eventual periodic equilibrium occurs when μ_0, the initial uncertainty belief level, is never repeated; rather an iterate of it at time i (the belief level or membership grade at time i) changes to the belief level at time $i+n$. For example, let $i = 1$ and $n = 2$, then $\mu_1 = \mu_3 = \mu_5 = \mu_7 = \ldots$. When this equilibrium occurs in an oligopoly market, *a* receipts pattern or cycle begins at $R_i \neq R_0$ and is repeated after every n time interval, and depending on the entropy rate of change in each market the periodicity may vary in length from one oligopoly industry to another. Note that if two oligopolistic industries at $t = 0$ possess identical initial membership grades and identical neoclassical costs, their equilibria may not be identical because their entropies or the entropy rate of change for each industry are different. In other words, similarity in technical cost among geographically distinct or separated oligopoly markets, does not necessarily motivate their dynamic equilibria to follow the same orbit. That is, the uncertainty (correspondingly the opportunity cost) and its rate of change in each market are, in general, never identical in the heterogeneous economic space.[11]

It warrants mention at this point that computer advances have enabled depiction of time paths on a phase diagram which never replicates itself perfectly although the paths come very close to each other and never leave a fixed region. These periodic orbits are called strange attractors. The term attractor arises from the observation that paths tend to occur over and over again within a region and never diverge from it. They are called 'strange', which is a misnomer since there is nothing strange about strange attractors, the reason being that as the number of iterations increases, the orbits of the map within the attractor come closer and closer to each other without duplicating themselves.[12] If this type of equilibrium occurs in an oligopoly market, the equilibrium price will fluctuate within a fixed range over time.[13]

ENTROPY

According to the second law of thermodynamics, the entropy of a physical system either increases or remains constant.[14]   While physicists can isolate and test their systems under laboratory type idealizations, economists must analyze phenomena within an environment of change.   We will show presently that change enhances, rather than hinders, the following analysis. We demonstrate below that the oligopoly market entropy follows precisely the second law of thermodynamics.

An oligopoly market is a physical system encased within the demographic boundaries of the physical market. In this system, both an objective (random) entropy and a subjective (fuzzy) entropy exist. The objective entropy is accounted for in our definition of neo−classical costs.[15]   The subjective entropy is the amount of fuzziness in O^* measured in Chapter 2 by Shannon's measure. The amount of fuzziness in O^* remains either constant in the long run as shown in our static analysis (Chapter 4) or increases, as we demonstrate presently. The constancy of entropy is due to both the internal factors (personality traits and desires as well as the efficiencies of the entrepreneurial personal investments) and external factors (institutions, other markets) being fixed or constant; that is, a *ceteris paribus* assumption. However, if the external factors such as politically motivated business−related policies do change, the $d(O^*)$ must also change. This change in external parameters either increases the entropy in O^* or holds it constant through changes in I^*, F^*, S^*, the internal system parameters.

Due to the spatial context and encasement of a market, the markets' entropies respond differently to internal and/or external parametrical changes. Exit by inefficient producers tends to lead to replacement by efficient firms whose entropy is compatible with that of the market. However, the uncertainty that is generated by a firm(s)'s departure is compounded by new entrants whose business policies and practices are not as well known as those of their predecessors.

Our theory originates from a spatial view of the oligopoly market (or any market for that matter) where the firms' locations dictate not only the traditionally recognized factors, such as transportation costs, market size (of the firm itself and the cluster of firms in the market), but additionally the uncertainty level (entropy) intrinsic to each market.   The physical economic space establishes the boundaries within which the oligopoly industries are contained.

In a market of few sellers producing similar products, who initially are dispersed over the economic landscape, a lower entropy will apply than that in a similar market where the sellers are centralized. Agglomeration increases the interdependence of sellers in O^* which in turn increases $d(O^*)$ and thus, the required rate of return on the entrepreneurial investments. Of course, the size of each firm enters into the decision of whether to agglomerate or deglomerate. A small size firm, though producing a similar product, may opt to locate at a distance from the market firms cluster in order to reduce its own entropy. Thus the firm transfers a portion of the entropy cost to shipping costs. As the long−run efficiency requirements prevail, the firm becomes an inefficient producer and therefore exits the market.

An entrepreneur who views the entropy level as incompatible with his/her personally preferred entropy level and optimal investment rate (possibly due to extreme concentration of sellers at a market region) may opt to lower this interdependence and ultimately entropy by locating at an extreme end or close to an extreme quartile of the market, given that the traditional factors such as shipping costs, demand and relocation costs allow this move.[16] Thus the personal entropy is transferred into a spatial dispersement of sellers. This transfer of entropy is similar to energy transfer into heat (a form of energy) in physical systems thereby not decreasing the entropy but simply transforming it into a distance parameter which too is costly.

Some Additional Background on Chaos Theory

Some further background about chaos theory is, however, needed at this point. Historically, it is notable that, via difference and differential equations, time paths were generated. By making x a function of a parameter a and an initial state x_0, specifically $x_1 = ax_0$, we previously noted that $x_2 = ax_1 = a^2x_0$ with a negative a therefore yielding an oscillatory time path. This oscillation reminds one of Samuelson's multiplier−accelerator model (1939). But as Baumol and Benhabib observed (1989), the extreme sensitivity to the parameter values made model formulation difficult; in fact, let this writer propose the word fortuitous. One may therefore ask, how can pure chaos theory really apply to equilibria in oligopoly markets? The answer lies of course in specifying a uniquely precise set of parameters. More on this in a few moments.

For the immediate present, let us return to some additional history of chaos theory, while also inserting selected simplistic, additional explanations about the diagrams which help explain it. Four paths were generally recognized to obtain, two that were oscillatory, one being explosive (that is, its cycles increased in magnitude) and one which converged to fixed equilibrium values; the alternative other set, as one might guess, included non−oscillatory paths which were respectively explosive and stable. Beyond linear equations, nonlinear models were found to yield permanent−stable wanderers. Most importantly, if not singularly important for the purposes of this book, is the fact that chaos and randomness are so similar that many tests of randomness cannot distinguish the one from the other. By an infinitesimally small change in the parameter value, the qualitative character of a chaotic path may be so altered as never to return to a previous point, and hence to appear as if sets of random shocks had taken place. It should be clear that whatever is this chaos, forecasting would appear to be veritably impossible. But this is exactly why chaos and oligopoly theory are intermixed, or shall we say this is why they are inextricable facets of each other. The appearance of strictly fortuitous events is basically gained only as a short−run glimpse; rather, the fact is that chaos models involve a law unto the lawlessness that otherwise seems to prevail. It is in this context that we would, for example, suggest the possibility of a potentially good governmental anti−recessionary economic policy (for example, advancing payments on government insurance refund checks in order to induce greater consumer spending) having bad results, with the bad results occurring because by the time the checks are distributed inflationary forces may have already taken hold. We have here a simple example which reminds us of a dynamic chaos model that is responding to a random shock.

It warrants a related background statement that, depending on the type of state equation, the applicable hill diagram (that is, the phase curve or the map) may be single or multi−peaked. Some single peaked curves, as in Figure 1 below, may lie entirely below the critical 45°. The 45° line of course provides equilibrium points since the $t+1$ value equals the t value, as in the intersection point of a Keynesian cross diagram where $C + I + G + E$ function (whose total is viewed along the vertical axis) equals the GNP value (designated along the *Ox* axis). Clearly if the $C + I + G + E$ function is above (or is below) the 45° at a certain GNP value, then the next period's GNP moves to a greater (lower) value, and ultimately the stable equilibrium GNP value obtains where the $C + I + G + E$ line intersects the 45° line.

Figure 5.1   A chaotic phase diagram $f(\mu_t)$ is plotted at k = .5, 1.5, 2.5, 3.4

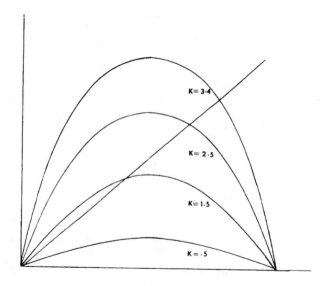

In contrast to the Keynesian cross, a chaos hill curve which is above the 45° line at certain points moves the trajectory from its zero starting point to sets of values that, at first, are only slightly above the 45° line, and then more so, and then still more so, but then are ultimately less and less above it or below, and then back to greater and greater and lower and lower values, ad infinitum. The time path typically oscillates, as in a cobweb pattern around an equilibrium point. Oscillations of this kind, essentially short−run equilibria, are simply sketched in Figure 5.2.

Returning to Figure 5.1, it should be obvious that if k is less than 1, the phase diagram is below the 45° throughout. If k is between the values 1 and 2, the slope of the phase curve is positive as it intersects the 45° line. For k values between 2 and 3, the slope of the intersection point is negative but less than unity in absolute values.

Figure 5.2 The oscillatory time path

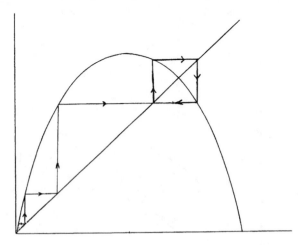

For $k>3$ but <4 the slope at the intersection point is less than -1. The last two cases are of particular interest in oligopoly theory.

Some reasons which apply to the previous statement are these: It can be shown that the subject time path, given a negative slope at the intersection point, is oscillatory. When the slope is greater than unity in absolute value, the oscillations will be explosive. In effect, the rates of return exceed (or fall so much below) the desired uncertainty ranges as to promote excessive entry (exit) and to violate the results of Chapter 4. It can also be shown that for values slightly less than 3, there will be cobweb time paths whose oscillations converge to a stable equilibrium point. Some values establish stable limit cycles; in fact, we previously mentioned two period long cycles; that is, 1, 2, then 1, 2, with the limit stable cycle values, when reached, being the same. Some values generate cycles of four period lengths, such that we reach in time a high point then a low point, then a still higher point and next a still lower point, then back to the original high, low points, and next to the still higher high and still lower low points, over and over again. Most probably, these are short—run equilibria as stated previously, albeit they could relate to different long—run equilibria for industries whose basic costs increase, decrease, etc. from one long run to another with corresponding changes taking place in uncertainty ranges (that is, in the membership grades μ_t). At certain values of k (for example, = 3) there is no stable equilibrium except in the sense that a two period cycle exists with period z_n, let us say, equalling z_{n-2} equalling z_{n-4} etc. There can exist, in other words, controlling values of k that establish an uncountable number of beginning points which in turn generate paths that never repeat any former pattern. One can call this system a aperiodic chaos.

THE SIGNIFICANCE OF k IN OLIGOPOLY MARKETS

As we previously observed, the graphs of $f(\mu_t)$ at different k values (different rates of change in the oligopoly market entropy) were plotted in Figure 5.1 above. Note that the shape of $f(\mu_t)$ and the location of the equilibria depend on the value of the parameter (k). Herein lies the true significance of (k) the entropy change rate of an oligopoly market. The parameter k, as given in Equations (2) and (3), or below in Equation (4), is an exogenous variable which describes the rate of change of entropy in a market. This k is a monotonically increasing function of the rate of change in entropy; that is, if the change in market entropy is high, so will be the k value and vice versa. Example: an oligopolistic industry whose entropy is relatively stable, applies a $0<k<1$, such as $k = .5$ in Figure 5.1; then the only equilibrium occurs at $\mu^*_t = 0$ and the minimum r_t in $\tilde{r}$ is imputed at all times. In other words, since the entropy change is relatively small, the entrepreneurs in exchange for a low membership range of uncertainty, would accept the minimum crisp r in the fuzzy opportunity cost.[17] Furthermore, the k value determines whether the equilibrium is stable, weakly stable or unstable. Let μ^*_t be the membership grade at which an equilibrium exists; that is, $\mu^*_t = f(\mu^*_t)$, then we have

$$\mu_t^* = k \cdot \mu_t^*(1 - \mu_t^*) \tag{4}$$

At $\mu_t^* = 0$, $f(\mu_t^*) = 0 = f^2(\mu_t^*) = f^3(\mu_t^*) = \ldots = f^n(\mu_t^*)$ thus, $\mu_t^* = 0$ is a fixed point of the map.

To obtain other fixed points, that is, when $\mu_t^* > 0$, (4) can be solved as below

$$\mu_t^* = k\mu_t^* - k\mu_t^{*2} \qquad \text{(from 4)}$$

Divide by μ_t^*, and rearrange as below

$$1 = k - k\mu_t^*$$
$$\mu_t^* = \frac{k-1}{k}, \tag{5}$$

Where (5) represents the set of all fixed points of the map, given that $\mu_t^* > 0$.[18] Note from (5) that the equilibrium membership grade (strength of belief or possibility of $r_t \in \tilde{r}$ is totally dependent on the entropy change rate (k) and the subject entrepreneur's accepted range of uncertainty for a related industry.

The value of the absolute slope of the map near the fixed point is required in order to determine whether the fixed point is an attractor (stable) or a repellor. An attracting fixed point is what economists describe as a stable equilibrium point. A fixed point is called an attractor when nearby points converge to it through repeated iterations; that is, the map converges to the fixed point. Describing a fixed point as a repellor (unstable equilibrium) implies the converse; that is, starting from points close to the equilibrium point, the map diverges (guides the time path away) from the equilibrium point. If the absolute slope of the map near the fixed point is less than one, the fixed point is attracting; if the absolute slope of the map near the fixed point is greater than one, the fixed point is a repelling one. Intuitively, the incidence angle of the map on the 45° ray (if an intersection exists), as measured by the absolute slope of the map at a point very close to the fixed point (say a distance h from the point, where h tends to zero at the limit), determines whether the periodic time path near the fixed point diverges from or converges to the fixed point. The slope of the map can be derived rather easily by the derivative of (4), as given by (6).

$$\frac{\partial f(\mu_t)}{\partial \mu_t} = k - 2\mu_t \cdot k \qquad (6)$$

Now, at μ_t^*, $f(\mu_t^*) = \mu_t^*$ so from (5) we know

$$\mu_t^* = \frac{k-1}{k} \ , \ 0<\mu_t^*<1, \ K>1$$

therefore (6) becomes

$$
\begin{aligned}
f'(\mu_t^*) &= k-2\ \frac{k-1}{k}\ \cdot k \\
f'(\mu_t^*) &= k-2k+2 \\
f'(\mu_t^*) &= -k+2 \\
f'(\mu_t^*) &= 2-k \\
|f'(\mu_t^*)| &= |2-k|
\end{aligned}
\qquad (7)
$$

where (7) determines whether the fixed point is stable or not, with the stability or instability of the fixed point hinging on k. Note that if k exceeds 2, then the slope of the map is negative at the map's intersection point with the 45° line. This means that the intersection point (equilibrium) occurs on the declining side of the hill. From the theory of difference equations, if $k>2$, the equilibrium will be oscillatory: $f(\mu_t)$ rises and then falls with iterations. The oscillations may be implosive (convergent) if the absolute value of the slope of the map is less than unity; and explosive (divergent) when the absolute slope of the map is greater than 1. Thus the entropy change rate in a market determines whether a dynamical long—run equilibrium will exist in an oligopoly market at a point in time or not; and it also determines the value of the belief level (possibility measure); and, of course, it also determines the r_t in $\tilde{r}$ which corresponds to the possibility measure μ_t^*; and finally it determines whether the equilibrium will be stable or not.[19]

It warrants specific recall at this time that at $0<k<1$, and $\mu_t \in [0,1]$, the only stable fixed point exists at $\mu_t^*=0$. This result is easily seen from Figure 5.1 where the map lies entirely below the 45° line. Furthermore, we can demonstrate mathematically that $\mu_t=0$ is the only fixed point of the map when k is greater than 0 and less than 1. The proof that $\mu_t^*=0$, given $0<k<1$, is straightforward from the state equation, repeated below

$$f(\mu_t) = k\mu_t(1 - \mu_t)$$

Suppose $\mu^*_t = 0$, then $f(\mu^*_t) = 0$ $\forall k$; that is, $\mu^*_t = f(\mu^*_t) = 0$; it follows that $\mu^*_t = 0$ is a fixed point. The proof that no other $\mu_t \in [0,1]$ is a fixed point when $0 < k < 1$ is more complicated but still relatively simple. Let $\mu^*_t \neq 0$, $\mu^*_t = f(\mu^*_t) = k\mu^*_t(1 - \mu^*_t)$ and $0 < k < 1$; that is μ^*_t is a fixed point given that k (the entropy change rate) is greater than 0 but less than one. Then from (5), $\mu^*_t = k - 1/k$, which implies that $\forall$ $0 < k < 1$, μ^*_t must be less than zero (a negative value) which contradicts both the principles of fuzzy logic and the specifications of our model. It also follows that the only fixed point for $0 < k < 1$ is $\mu^*_t = 0$.

Let us next determine whether the fixed point $\mu^*_t = 0$, with $0 < k < 1$ is stable or not. We shall do this by obtaining the slope of μ_{t+1} w.r.t. μ_t.

Recall $\qquad \mu_{t+1} = k\mu_t(1 - \mu_t), \quad \dfrac{\partial \mu_{t+1}}{\partial \mu_t} = k(1 - 2\mu_t)$

At $\qquad \mu_t = 0$ and $0 < k < 1$, $\quad \dfrac{\partial \mu_{t+1}}{\partial \mu_t} = k(1 - 0) = k < 1$.

Thus $\mu^*_t = 0$, for all $0 < k < 1$ is indeed a stable fixed point (a convergent equilibrium). This signifies that an oligopolistic industry which undergoes very small changes in entropy is intrinsically stable in the long run. From (3), $\mu^*_t = \mu^*_t(1 - \mu^*_t)$ at $k = 1$ with μ^*_t being the fixed point of the map. Then, $\mu^*_t = \mu^*_t - \mu^{*2}_t \Rightarrow \mu^*_t = 0$ at $k = 1$. The slope of the state equation is $k(1 - 2\mu^*_t)$, which simplifies to 1 at $k = 1$, $\mu^*_t = 0$; that is, $f(0) = 0$. It can be shown by graphical analysis that the fixed point ($\mu^*_t = 0$) is weakly attracting. To do so, let us draw a diagram similar to Figure 5.1 with $k = 1$. At $\mu^*_t = 0$ and $k = 1$, the μ^*_{t+1} map is tangent to the 45° ray at 0. Consider a point on the horizontal axis $\mu_0 = \mu^*_t + \varepsilon$ where ε is a positive number, and the draw a vertical line from μ_0. Let this line reflect off the map μ_{t+1}. We can readily observe that the height of μ_0 (that is, the image of μ_0), namely μ_1, is less than μ_0. Next we draw a horizontal from μ_t and reflect this line off of the 45° ray downward until it reaches the μ_{t+1} map; after this, we reflect it horizontally to the 45° ray and continue the process. It will be observed that $\mu_0 > \mu_1 > \mu_2 \ldots \mu_n$. Manifestly, the membership grade decreases with each iteration, such that $| \mu_n - \mu_0 | < \varepsilon$, $n \geq 1$, and therefore the equilibrium is convergent at $k = 1$. Oligopolists who experience an entropy change rate of $k = 1$ and choose the minimum uncertainty membership grade will receive the least acceptable returns; therefore in the process, they adhere to the long–run equilibrium that was established in Chapter 4. However, should the firms deviate slightly from this equilibrium, due to an error in judgement, they will nevertheless gradually move towards this equilibrium as a consequence of being fearful of possible entry by outsiders.

We must next investigate the fixed points at $1 < k < 4$. Initially, let us observe, that the map at $1 < k < 4$ has two fixed points: one at $\mu_t^* = 0$ and the other at $\mu_t^* = k - 1 / k$. At $\mu_t^* = 0$, $f'(0) = k > 1$; therefore, $\mu_t^* = 0$ is a repelling fixed point. It follows that, oligopoly industries which experience a change of entropy of $k > 1$ and accept the minimum uncertainty return will be in an unstable long–run equilibrium position; this result applies because the entrepreneurs always will have an incentive to require a return greater than the minimum return, in which case, they will not stay at the long–run equilibrium position but will continue to move further and further away from it. This kind of oligopoly industry is best represented by those industries which are artificially forced (by legislative action or government policy) to accept a minimum (and in effect, an incompatible) return for the prevailing market uncertainty. The consequence is a forced, regulated, and unstable equilibrium. However, $\mu_t^* = k - 1/k$ and $0 < \mu_t^* < 1$, proves to be attracting for all $1 < k < 3$ (from Equation (7), $|f'(\mu_t^*)| = |2 - k| < 1$ when $1 < k < 2$, $k = 2$, $2 < k < 3$).[20] The fixed points at $1 < k < 3$ are, therefore, dynamically stable (attractors). Oligopoly markets which undergo entropy change rates of $1 < k < 3$ will be at a stable equilibrium in the long run, the equilibria not being identical for all oligopoly markets. Thus the dynamics of the map at $1 < k < 3$ are straightforward with all the complex behavior occurring between $3 \leq k < 4$.

The dynamics of $3 \leq k < 4$ is chaotic. At $k = 3$, $|(2 - k)| = |(-1)| = 1$; that is to say, $\mu_t^* | k = 3$ is neither repelling nor attracting, but is simply a weak fixed point. In fact, the map is about to undergo a bifurcation as we shall explain below, in its second iteration $f^2(\mu_t)$: for the moment it suffices to say that as k increases ever so slightly past 3, two fixed periodic points (two steady states) occur.[21] We can best appreciate the occurrence of a bifurcation in the map by initially glancing at the graph of $f^2(\mu_t)$ against μ_t in Figures 5.2a, 5.2b, 5.2d below. Then consider the following

Figure 5.2a The μ_{t+2} k<3. At k<3 a slight hump appears in the μ_{t+2} function. The equilibrium point is stable.

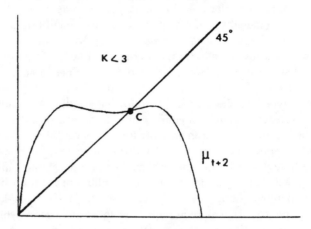

The second iterate of the map, $(f^2(\mu_t))$, contains μ_t^4, a membership grade that is raised to the power 4, therefore, two maximas (a double hump) must occur. This is shown mathematically below

$$f^2(\mu_t) = f(f(\mu_t))$$
$$\mu_{t+2} = f(k\mu_t(1-\mu_t))$$
$$\mu_{t+2} = k(k\mu_t(1-\mu_t))(1-(1-k\mu_t(1-\mu_t))) \qquad (8)$$

At k<3, a slight hump appears in the μ_{t+2}/μ_t graph as shown in 5.2a. In 5.2a, the map of μ_{t+2}, the second iterate of μ_0, intersects the 45° line from above given that k<3. The intersection point (C) is the fixed (equilibrium) point; that is, at C, $\mu_t^* = f(\mu_t^*) = f(f(\mu_t^*))$ ... or $\mu_t^* = \mu_{t+1}^* = \mu_{t+2}^*$ ... The equilibrium point (C) is stable since the absolute slope of the μ_{t+1} map is $|(2-k)| < 1.$[22] Also, since the slope of μ_{t+1} is $(2-k)$, where 2<k<3, then the slope is negative; that is, the time path of μ_{t+1} is oscillatory but stable; it converges to C after n iterations. Note that a slight double hump appears in 5.2a due to the μ_t^4, (the membership grade raised to the power 4) argument in μ_{t+2}. Recall that $\mu_{t+2} = k\mu_{t+1}(1 - \mu_{t+1}) = k(k\mu_t(1 - \mu_t))(1 - k(\mu_t(1 - \mu_t)))$, thus μ_{t+2} has two peaks (maxima) instead of one, as in the case of the quadratic map μ_{t+1}. This double hump becomes more definite as the value of k increases (as we presently show in 5.2b and 5.2d). Thus, not only is k a fine tuner for μ_{t+1}/μ_t but also for the $\mu_{t+2}/\mu_t, \ldots \mu_{t+n}/\mu_t$ graphs. (Note further that μ_{t+n}/μ_t contains n maximas or n humps as a result of the argument μ_t^n in μ_{t+n}/μ_t.)

Figure 5.2b The μ_{t+2} function at $k = 3$. μ_{t+2} is tangent to the ray at $k = 3$, slope $= 1$

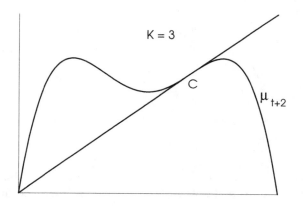

In 5.2b, the map of μ_{t+2} is redrawn against μ_t with the added distinction that k increases to 3; that is, $k = 3$. Note that an increase in k causes the double hump to be more sharply defined in 5.2b than it is in 5.2a. Also, μ_{t+2} is now tangent to the 45° line at C because the slope of μ_{t+2} at C is 1 which is also the slope of the 45° line. Observe that at C, since the absolute slope of μ_{t+2} is exactly 1, the μ_{t+2}/μ_t map is neither repelling nor attracting. (Recall that a repelling (divergent) equilibrium has an absolute slope that is greater than 1; while an attracting equilibrium has an absolute slope that is less than 1.) In fact, the equilibrium at C, with $k = 3$, is weakly stable; that is, the time path takes a long time to converge to the equilibrium as demonstrated

in the sketch below where the graphs of μ_{t+1} and μ_{t+2} are plotted against μ_t.

Figure 5.2c   The μ_{t+1} and μ_{t+2} functions at k = 3

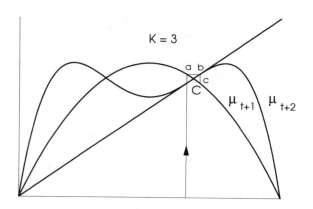

Starting from an initial μ_0 = .6, draw a vertical line which bounces off the μ_{t+1}/μ_t map at a where $f(\mu_t = .6) = .72$. Continue the line to b on the 45° ray and then down to C where $f(\mu_t = .72) = .6048$ intersecting the 45°line at μ_t = .6048 and back to μ_{t+1} where $f(\mu_t = .6048) = .71705$ and so forth. Note that the equilibrium point (C) occurs at $\mu_t = k-1/k = 3-1/3 = 2/3 = .66666 \ldots$. Also, observe that the value of μ_t increases slightly as its corresponding $f(\mu_t)$ decreases and so forth slowly and so forth toward the equilibrium at C, where $\mu_t^* = \mu_{t+1}^* - .66666 \ldots$ That is, the time path converges slowly to C and only achieves the equilibrium at the limit. Thus, C is a weakly stable equilibrium at k = 3.

In 5.2d, k is greater than 3, and the hump that was almost negligible in 5.2a has been further sharpened. Note that the μ_{t+2}/μ_2 map now dips below the 45° line. Thus, μ_{t+2}/μ_t intersects the ray at points A and B. Since the slope of the 45° ray is 1, the horizontal and vertical coordinates of any point on it will be equal; that is, the sides of a square whose corner is on the ray will, of course, be equal. Furthermore, since A and B represent intersections of the μ_{t+2}/μ_t map with the 45° ray, then A and B are corners of the squares whose sides

Figure 5.2d The μ_{t+2} function at $k > 3$. Bifurcation occurs; that is, two new cross points appear (A,B).

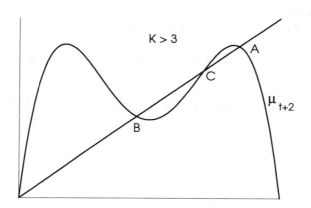

are μ_t^* and μ_{t+2}^*. So at A, $\mu_t^* = \mu_{t+2}^*$ but not $\mu_t^* = \mu_{t+1}^* = \mu_{t+2}^*$ because the μ_{t+1}/μ_t map does not intersect the ray at A, but only at C, as shown in 5.2d. Points A and B are therefore not equilibria in the sense of a fixed point, but are a periodic equilibria pair in period 2. (This particular equilibrium will be demonstrated in detail with Figure 5.3, at which point we will elaborate further on 5.2d.)

Let us further investigate point C (the exercise will prove insightful into the dynamics of chaos). At C, $\mu_{t+1}^* = \mu_t^* = \mu_{t+2}^*$; therefore C is an equilibrium point. But is it stable? Observe that the μ_{t+1} map intersects the ray from above in the decreasing section of the map; that is, the map is negatively sloped at C. The negativity of the slope of μ_{t+1} at C can also be shown mathematically from $(2-k)<0$, $k>3$; that is, the time path of μ_{t+1} is oscillatory at C. Furthermore, the time path diverges at C since $|2-k| > 1$, $k>3$. C is simply an unstable equilibrium point (recall it was weakly stable in 5.2b at $k = 3$); that is, any initial μ_t, close to μ_t^* but not equal to it, will lead to a divergent time path away from μ_t^*. However, the time path does not continue to diverge away from C indefinitely but settles into a two period cycle, namely A and B. Phrased otherwise, the unstable fixed point C has given birth to two stable periodic points (A and B) which are stable.   The map (μ_{t+1}) is said to bifurcate (generate two new equilibria) at this value of k with the unstable equilibrium generating a two period stable equilibria.   Note finally that C remains a fixed point notwithstanding A and B; that is, there is a $\mu_t^* = \mu_{t+1}^* = \mu_{t+2}^*$ · · · . at C and a $\mu_0 \neq \mu_t^*$, which generates $\mu_n^* = \mu_{n+2}^* = \mu_{n+4}^*$ · · · ·· The bifurcation process is further demonstrated in Figure 5.3 below

Figure 5.3   The graphs of μ_{t+1} and μ_{t+2} are plotted at $k>3$. μ_{t+2} intersects the ray three times with a stable cycle occuring at A & B. Point C is an unstable fixed point. Note that μ_{t+2} and μ_{t+1} intersects the ray at C.

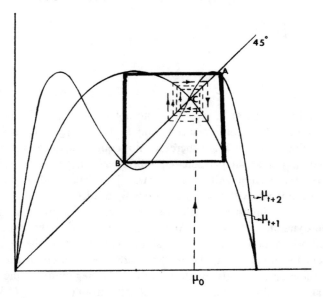

In Figure 5.3, the graphs of μ_{t+1}/μ_t and μ_{t+2}/μ_{t+1} are plotted to further illustrate the dynamics of the iteration process. Let us start with an initial $\mu_t = \mu_0$, close to μ^*_t, which generates C'; then, $\mu^*_t = \mu^*_{t+1} = \mu^*_{t+2}$, and the trajectory is reflected by the μ_{t+1} map onto the 45° ray where it is then reflected to the map μ_{t+1} at $\mu_t > \mu_0$ and then back to the 45° ray which next reflects it to μ_{t+1}; (μ_{t+1}) moves in an explosive manner away from μ_0 and μ^*_t, the initial and equilibrium membership grades, respectively). But, the trajectory does not continue to diverge *ad infinitum*, rather, it settles into the path (marked with a heavy solid line on the diagram) around the points *A* and *B*. Thus two possibilities exist: if the membership grade is initially at μ_t, an equilibrium exists at *C*; otherwise, if the membership grade is initially close to but not equal to μ^*_t, it will diverge further from μ^*_t, with each iteration until it settles into the periodic equilibria of period 2, at *A* and *B*.

The periodic equilibria can be obtained mathematically, with points *A* and *B* being the solution (roots) to the equation $\mu^*_{t+2} = f(\mu^*_{t+2})$, $4 > k > 3$ and $n \geq 0$. Also the slopes of μ_{t+2}/μ_t at *A* and *B* are equal and negative as shown in 5.3. (This can be demonstrated mathematically, but the note below should suffice for present needs.[23])

As the value of *k* increases further, the two period cycle (bifurcation), becomes unstable, and gives way to a 4 period steady state: each steady state bifurcates to two steady states which in turn becomes unstable as *k* increases and gives way to further bifurcations. Manifestly, the likelihood of these values applying to a real world competitive oligopoly industry extending from one long−run equilibrium to another, etc. is virtually zero.

At $k > 3.8$, 3 period cycles occur ($\mu_1 = \mu_4$), which bifurcate to 6, 12, 24, 48, ... period cycles at higher *k* values. Cycles of periods 5 or 6 appear beyond $k > 3.8$. Specifically, stable periodic points of period 5 or 6 result from a weakly stable fixed point in the same manner of the period's doubling bifurcation, as shown in Figure 5.3. As noted in the previous paragraph, these chaotic values are quite improbable for the competitive oligopoly economy visualized in this book.

At $k < 4$, 'strange attractors' appear: time paths never leave a certain region with no time path ever replicating itself. Thus, no periodic fixed points appear, though they get closer and closer to each other within a given region (attractor) and never leave the attractor. The time paths approach each other such that a computer originated picture of the time path in the 'strange attractor' will show a dark strip at a high number of iterations instead of distinct lines because of graphical technical inabilities to completely and precisely depict thousands of iterates. Again, the last two paragraph conclusions also apply here.

One final thought is relevant, the belief function membership grade loses its meaning when $k>4$, for this causes some membership grades to escape [0,1]; for example, let $k = .5$, $\mu_t = .4$, then $\mu_{t+1} = r(.4)(1-.4) = 5(.4)(.6) = 1.2$. But according to the basics of fuzzy math, the possibility measure (belief level) or $\mu(r)$ cannot be greater than 1. In summary, the relevant k values for competitive oligopoly industries, in general, are those <3.

OLIGOPOLY EQUILIBRIUM WITH FUZZY CHAOS

Consider a 'tuning' parameter which generates oscillatory explosiveness. But during one peak (boom) expansion of the industry, is it not likely that a new k will arise because of entry. And then, is it not likely that the membership grades will also change? But random shocks will also prevail, and thereby interfere with the chaotic world, where by 'chaos' we technically and rigorously mean the law of the lawless! Is it not further conceivable that a growing sophistication will arise among the entrepreneurs in a given industry who are subject to full competitive entry or exit, which in turn brings the k values and the membership fuzziness into closer harmony with the lawlessness that approaches 'the lawful'. This, then, is our basic conception of (1) competitive oligopolistic industries, (2) in an interdependent set of economies, under (3) the rules of a lawful universe. It serves furthermore in effect to support and to herald our own philosophical conception of life, which philosophy will be provided directly below − − that is, before the conclusion section of this chapter. Moreover, it supports the validity of an economics science that is predicated on the variational reactions of human beings to stimuli which are often influenced by the diverse chaotic underpinnings that over time are converted into different patterns by the random shocks which derive from Mother Nature as well as from Institutional, Human Origins.

What it boils down to is this: Real world existence implies equilibrium results for survivors. Human beings, in general, go from excesses towards normality. If they fail to reach that normality, they must exit, which exit holds whether we are thinking of the human being in the role of a decision—making entrepreneur whose firm goes under or an exit from the world when we are thinking of the human being in terms of her or his health. Phrased differently, all humans are subject to random disturbances (for example, car accidents, a stray bullet, etc.); but beyond probabilistic events, and especially for those who enter in the role of entrepreneurship, the individual is additionally subject to chaotic perturbations. It is, in fact, the chaos of the business world which inexorably moves potentially viable oligopolists to the strange attractor, while the non—viable counterparts who are accident prone and/or whose decisions err and/or are just plain unlucky are repelled. This repellent applies, of course, from the market's fixed points which would otherwise have ultimately moved the firm to its long—run oligopolistic equilibrium.

It is manifest that what was just proposed above represents this writer's philosophy of life and of human action. This philosophy includes views of people who are lucky, have great skills, and those who have bad luck, inadequate skills, *ad infinitum*. Indeed, the *ad infinitum* in the preceding sentence is itself an all encompassing inclusion, limited only by one's imagination of the many occurrences and events which define the human existence. It is within this overall conception of life that the present writer views the viable firms of oligopolistic industries as members of the sets which move chaotically to the long—run equilibrium, as described in static terms in Chapter 4. My overall conception of life applies particularly to free—enterprise entrepreneurs who are engaged in interdependent competitive activities.

SUMMARY

Our static view of oligopoly markets (Chapter 4) and the present chapter's dynamic analysis demonstrate that with technical and allocative efficiency requirements being met in the long run, a stable deterministic long—run oligopoly equilibrium must result. Moreover, it is our conceived of reality that fuzzy chaos underlies the competitive business world, which world is itself marked by oligopolistic industries in free enterprise economies. Fortunately from the predictive standpoint, the universe is essentially orderly (witness the revolution and rotation of the earth, its moon, the planets, and the outer universe). And this orderliness permeates the fuzzy, chaotic world of business activities in the sense that our tendencies towards the extreme (say Hitler and Stalin) are moderated over time and the firms in the free market economy whose entrepreneurs are (and were) the most skillful and perhaps, even more importantly, the luckiest will be the survivors. The consequence is the long—run equilibrium that was set forth in Chapter 4.

NOTES

1. We will demonstrate that the long—run equilibrium is theoretically tractable; however, in practice, due to round—off computational error, precise and complete specifications of the long—run equilibrium path is impossible, especially in the truly distant future ($t=\infty$). This practical intractability does not in any way void the method or limit the scope of the present approach or theory. It is our contention (as demonstrated in Chapters 2, 3 and part of Chapter 4) that in practice approximate (inexact) reasoning is the tool of the 'human' entrepreneur. Exactness and precision are best left to the entrepreneur's inferior — the calculating machine.

2. At the cost of repeating our main thesis, it warrants emphasis that although the results may appear to be prearranged, especially in the sense of being in sharp contrast to the majority—held view of oligopoly markets, the relevance of our assumptions and method should be considered. Our approach and theory employs traditionally accepted tools and principles: specifically, an average cost envelope in the long run (a long—run requirement for all markets); marginal cost/revenue equalities (profit maximization); average revenue/cost equality (zero profit); and the shadow—opportunity cost—imputation of all inputs (including those of the entrepreneur). In addition, the method and results obtained herein are affirmations and extensions of many prior works in the field of spatial microeconomics.

3. Also see Poincaré (1880, 1892).

4. The change in future membership grades and the complexity of estimating these grades n periods from the present is consistent with human nature: it is easier to predict the instant future $t + 1$ than to predict $t + n$, $n > 1$. Analogously, the immediate past can be predicted with greater accuracy than the distant past: the decision-maker is like the captain of a ship who sails further and further from a port as the ship moves closer to its destination, with the point of departure becoming less clear while the destination is approaching the visible (that is, it becomes crisp). Of course, the ship that is in the middle of its voyage, in mid-sea, can neither see its point of departure nor its point of arrival, yet the skilled navigator charts the course of the ship.

5.   Denote the fuzzy r by $\tilde{r}$, where $\tilde{r}$ is a time invariant fuzzy number. For the purposes of this chapter we assume that $\tilde{r}$ is a continuous fuzzy number or set. Let $\mu_t(r_t) \in [0,1]$ represent the strength of the entrepreneur's belief that $r_t \in \tilde{r}$ at time t.

6.   The selection criterion proposed here is not binding. Alone required is consistency in the selection method: when two crisp elements correspond to a membership grade at $t+1$, one element is selected in accordance with a specified rule; such as the max, min or average of both elements, and the rule is then followed throughout the system's dynamics.

7.   Results based on studying a logistic map can be generalized to a full family of quadratic difference equations. Devaney (1987) devotes over a hundred pages to its study. The logistic map is also the focus of May (1976), Jensen (1987), Baumol (1989) and Butler (1990).

8.   Many varying definitions of chaos are employed by mathematicians without agreement on one strict definition. We utilize the definition provided by Devaney (1987, p.50) and Barnsley (1990).

9.   Technically speaking a periodic equilibrium is defined as $P_0 = P_n$, $n > 0$. We choose to distinguish above between the successive or immediate equilibrium of period $n=1$ and the n period equilibrium where $n > 1$.

10.   The rate of change in the market entropy may accelerate or decelerate through time due to additional uncertainties; therefore k may increase or decrease during the system's motion.

11.   Because of the significance of entropy in determining our analysis, we provide a detailed account of the entropy change in the next section of this chapter. For the present we claim that the heterogeneous economic space precludes two markets from possessing the same entropy.

12.   It is our belief that in oligopoly markets possessing extremely high entropies (uncertainties), the oligopoly market dynamic long-run equilibrium is best depicted in the region of strange attractors. Our rationale for this belief will be manifest later in this chapter. However, it suffices presently to state that a heterogeneous landscape is constantly changing and hence future events tend not to duplicate past events perfectly, oligopolistic industries not being the exception.

13.   Although we observe the case of some duopolists who produce approximately perfect substitutes with prices remaining constant over extended periods, we stress that these prices are not necessarily fixed since each duopolist offers discounts, specials, coupons, etc. which make the effective (final) price to the consumer different in one period from another, as in the case of the soft drink and automobile industries.

14.   Physicists have proven that once the change in entropy occurs in a physical system, the process is irreversible; that is, the system never returns to its original state. The irreversibility of the change in entropy is due to the fact that it takes an extremely long period of time for the system to return to its original state in which case the observation of a decrease in entropy becomes practically impossible. Thus, the entropy never decreases.

15.   See Chapters 3, 4 of this work for this accounting.

16.   If the traditional costs do not allow the relocation of the firm within the spatial market, exit of the high total cost (inclusive of the entropy cost) producer must ultimately occur.

17.   Note $k=0$ would imply no change in the market entropy; therefore, the system is static, as evaluated in Chapter 4. Moreover, negative values of k are not permitted in our model. As stated previously in this chapter, entropy does not decline; a negative k simply implies a decrease (that is a negative change) in a market's

entropy. For the purposes of this chapter, k is always viewed as being greater than zero.

18. We re-emphasize that $\mu_t \in [0,1]$, therefore μ^*_t (the equilibrium membership grade) cannot exceed 1 or decrease to a negative value.

19. At $k=0$, there is zero change in the market entropy, thus the motivation for the dynamical system ceases to exist. In other words, as mentioned previously, the static analysis of Chapter 4 suffices for the subject industries with other industries disappearing in time or not being competitively oligopolistic.

20. The fixed point at $k=2$, $|f'\mu_t)| = 0$, is called a critical point because the 45° ray crosses the hill (map) at its peak. The equilibrium thus occurs at $\mu^*_t = .5$, where the strength of belief equals the strength of disbelief that r_t is the true (crisp) market r. The equilibrium is convergent, and therefore stable.

21. The careful reader will recognize that in prior discussions on periodic points, for example, $z_{n-4} = z_{n-2} = z_n$, we were essentially discussing what we shall henceforth refer to as a bifurcation.

22. The slope of μ_{t+1} with respect to μ_t is

$$\frac{\partial \mu_{t+2}}{\partial \mu_t} = \frac{\partial \mu_{t+2}}{\partial \mu_{t+1}} \cdot \frac{\partial \mu_{t+1}}{\partial \mu_t}$$

Recall from the fixed point definition $\mu_t = \mu_{t+1} = \mu_{t+2} \ldots$, thus, at C,

$$\frac{\partial \mu_{t+2}}{\partial \mu_t} = \frac{\partial \mu_{t+1}}{\partial \mu_t} \cdot \frac{\partial \mu_{t+1}}{\partial \mu_t} = \left(\frac{\partial \mu_{t+1}}{\partial \mu_t}\right)^2 \text{ and } \frac{\partial \mu_{t+n}}{\partial \mu_t} = \left(\frac{\partial \mu_{t+1}}{\partial \mu_t}\right)^n .$$

This means that

at $k<3$, $|\partial \mu_{t+1}/\partial \mu_t| < 1$, $\partial \mu_{t+2}/\partial \mu_t$ is also less than 1

Moreover, since the 45 ray intersects the μ_{t+1}/μ_t map on the declining side of the map

$$(\partial \mu_{t+1}/\partial \mu_t < 0)$$

and in addition the slope of μ_{t+2}/μ_t at the same point is

$$(\partial \mu_{t+1}/\partial \mu_t)^2$$

then the slope of μ_{t+2}/μ_t is positive at C; that is to say, the μ_{t+2}/μ_t map is rising at the intersection point. Of course, a plot of μ_{t+3}/μ_t will show that the map is falling at C.

23. In order to keep the analysis on an intuitive level instead of becoming a mathematical exercise in the solutions of difference equations, it suffices to note that the slopes of A and B must be identical, otherwise the time path will deviate (either converge or diverge) from the stable two period cycle.

6. Various Applications of Fuzzy Math to Economics

The reader may have wondered how fundamental the impacts of fuzzy math would be on the science of economics beyond restricting the use of calculus and converting from short–run oligopolistic fuzziness to a crisp long–run equilibrium solution. Clearly, the answer to the basic question will involve decades of research, innovation, and development. For the purposes of this book, we provide three special examples of fuzzy math impacts on applied economics.[1] Our initial special example demonstrates how a long accepted, basic tool of analysis in economics would be altered. The second and third examples indicate how standard applications by economists of accepted economic principles would be changed when fuzzy math is utilized in place of ordinary math. In particular, we first center our attention on the oligopoly market's demand–supply paradigm. Our second and third examples evaluate antitrust instruments that have been generally accepted in the United States as evidence of monopoly power or a certain market structure.

FROM THE OLIGOPOLISTIC FIRM TO THE OLIGOPOLISTIC MARKET

Fuzziness has no place in the world of perfect competition. Of course, perfect competition has been said to provide a workable background for policy analysis and even for some economic–based aggregate decisions. Notwithstanding, oligopoly theory is probably the most applicable in practice if that theory can prove to be definitive. Let us accordingly extend our application of fuzzy math to the oligopolistic industry's supply–demand paradigm; then, as mentioned previously, we shall apply fuzzy math to antitrust policy.

For the supply−demand application, recall from Chapter 3 the derivation of O^*, and the basic O^* components of a 'few,' 'interdependent' firms producing 'similar' products. Related to any oligopoly industry is the entropy measure $d(O^*)$ that was described in that chapter. Of course, the oligopolist may be a member of more than one industry because of multi−product lines; the firm may be just a trivial insignificant competitor or a major producer in one or more industries, and thus have a membership grade ranging from 0 to 1 in any given industry. Whatever the case, an additional entrepreneurial return is associated with rational decision making in the presence of oligopolistic uncertainty. It is against this overall background that we now propose the demand−supply framework for an oligopolistic firm and its industry.

From Fuzzy Utility to the Fuzzy Demand Curve

Throughout Chapters 3 and 4 we have stressed that the products produced by rival firms are not identical, but similar. That is, a product produced by a firm may not be an exact replica of the product produced by a rival firm. Also, a firm may produce basically the same product but in different varieties and shapes. We generally, in the present example, delineate the consumer's demand curve given the inexact identity of products in a market.[2]   In other words, we investigate the demand curve of a consumer for a group of similar products that deviate slightly from some average or call it basic product.

Consider two basic product groups, x and y, where x is a product umbrella under which falls all the similar products produced in a subject market and y is, similarly, an umbrella product for all the y similar products of another market. For example x is apple cider and y represents potato chips. We delineate only the similarity of products in x keeping in mind that the same explanations apply to y.

A market firm may produce one or more similar products x_{ij}, where i and j refer to a firm and its product respectively. Let $x_{ij} \in$ (similar products) and refer to the set of similar products by X_s, where X_s is a fuzzy set whose membership grades describe the compatibility of the set elements with the basic product. Recall that X_s contains x the homogeneous or generic product as a special case. The same definitions apply to y and establish Y_s.

Let us accept the neo−classical assumption that the consumer can precisely determine the bundles of x and y which provide the same crisp utility. We do this with one reservation: Crisp determination of the (x, y) bundles is only possible when both x and y are homogeneous in their product categories. However, when the consumer is at best faced with (x_s, y_s) where $x_s \in X_s$, $y_s \in Y_s$, only approximate determination of these bundles is possible. We accordingly present the neo−classical rationality assumption as a special case in a more general and realistic scenario.[3]   That is to say, a crisp utility is obtained by an approximate bundle of x_s, y_s.

Figure 6.1   The crisp indifference curve

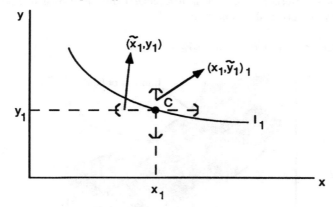

Next consider the crisp indifference curve I_1 in Figure 6.1 above, constructed under the neo−classical assumptions of product homogeneity and crisp bundles. A point such as C on I_1 provides the same level of utility to the consumer as any other point on I_1. Let C be the crisp bundle (x_1, y_1) of x and y.

In a market of x_s (similar x products), and y (homogeneous products) the consumer chooses $(\tilde{x}_1, y_1)$ as the bundle at C which is equivalent to (x_1, y_1) in utility; that is to say, $(\tilde{x}, y_1) \approx (x_1, y_1)$ where $\tilde{x}_1$ is a fuzzy number whose value is based on the assumption that y is a homogeneous product. Thus $\tilde{x}_1$ is a conditional possibility distribution, as defined below:

$$\tilde{x}_1 = \{x_s, \mu(x_s) \in [0, 1] \mid y_1 \in y\} \tag{1}$$

Similarly, assuming the homogeneity of the x product, the bundle $(x_1, \tilde{y}_1)$ can be obtained to yield the same utility as (x_1, y_1), that is, $(x_1, \tilde{y}_1) \approx (x_1, y_1)$. The fuzzy number $\tilde{y}_1$ is defined below:

$$\tilde{y}_1 = \{y_s, \mu(y_s) \in [0, 1] \mid x_1 \in x\} \tag{2}$$

By definition $(\tilde{x}_1, y_1) \approx (x_1, y_1) \approx (x_1, \tilde{y}_1)$. We obtain $(\tilde{x}_1, \tilde{y}_1)$ by the extension principle

$$\mu_{(\tilde{x}_1, \tilde{y}_1)}(x_s, y_s) = \vee [\mu_{(\tilde{x}_1, \tilde{y}_1)}(x_s, y) \wedge \mu_{(x_1, \tilde{y}_1)}(x, y_s)] \tag{3}$$

Thus, different bundles of (x_s, y_s) can be obtained to derive $\tilde{I}_1$, the thick indifference curve or indifference band, as shown in Figure 6.2 below — given the continuity of I_1.

Figure 6.2 The fuzzy indifference curve

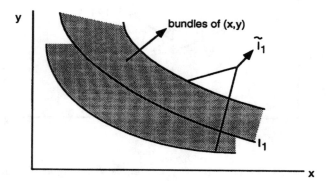

The indifference band $\tilde{I}_1$ intuitively suggests that, given the slight differentiations of products in a real−world market, the consumer utilizes approximate numbers to describe different bundles which provide the same utility. In still other words, $\tilde{I}_1$ is 'approximately I_1'. The crispness of I_1 is therefore elasticized to describe (x_s, y_s) instead of (x, y). Moreover, given the I_1 continuity, $\tilde{I}_1$ is also continuous and consists of many indifference curves with different certainty levels (membership) grades. A crisp indifference curve can thus be obtained from $\tilde{I}_1$ at a certain possibility level.[4]

A fuzzy indifference map would be constructed by repeating the above procedure for higher levels of utility.   From the fuzzy indifference map and a crisp budget constraint, we can derive a fuzzy demand band for x_s.[5]   At a crisp price P_x, the fuzzy quantity q_x that is demanded can be obtained with some certainty.   Also, any crisp quantity of x would command a fuzzy price.   The fuzzy demand curve is shown in Figure 6.3 below.

Figure 6.3   The fuzzy demand curve

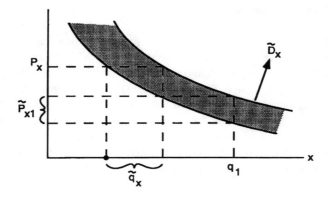

Note that q_1 is a crisp quantity that is demanded of x.   For this amount, the consumer is willing and able to pay the fuzzy approximate price $\tilde{P}_x$.   On the other hand, at a crisp price the consumer is willing and able to purchase various quantities of $\tilde{q}_x$ at different certainty levels.   By the extension principle, we obtain, as before, the fuzzy price and quantity pair from the joint distribution of the two conditional distributions.   The crisp demand curve is, of course, a special case of the fuzzy demand $(\mu_{(P,X)}(P,X) = 1 \Rightarrow$ homogeneous product).

The market demand curve would in turn be derived by the horizontal summation of all consumers' demand curves.   The fuzzy quantities demanded by different consumers at a given fuzzy price would be added by use of the extension principle.   The market demand curve is fuzzy whenever any consumer's demand curve is fuzzy.

The fuzzy quantity demanded relates to a price and in concert describes what economists have always known; namely that the demand curve is an approximate demand curve which should never be construed as an exact estimate of actual demand. Our market demand involves many crisp curves at different degrees of confidence. Furthermore, unlike stochastic models, no specific distribution is assumed here. Instead, subjective possibility distributions apply which are generated by people in accordance with their subjective criteria.

The Fuzzy Market Supply Curve

Even though the oligopolistic firm may produce only a single product, its production costs are fuzzy in the short run.[6] This fuzziness arises from the similarity (non−homogeneity) of variable inputs in a given input class. Specifically, a laborer is realistically describable by some fuzzy linguistic variable, such as 'hard worker', 'intelligent', 'dedicated', 'more or less hard working', etc. All inputs within a category are at best similar, not identical. Because of this condition, uncertainty arises in the use of inputs which translates to an uncertainty in the cost of producing any output (the extension principle again).[7]

It follows from the fuzzy costs of the product in the set of similar products that the average and marginal costs of each firm are also fuzzy. Manifestly, the necessary and sufficient condition for fuzziness in costs is that at least one of the variable inputs is fuzzily determined. It further follows that the membership of each firm in O^* intersects with the fuzzy marginal costs of production. The fuzzy marginal costs of the firms in the industry are then summed to obtain the industry's MC, doing this in a manner similar to that involved in deriving the fuzzy market demand. In general, ascribing variably all differential rents as well as the implicit costs for uncertainty onto any firm's fuzzy MC curve establishes the representative firm's adjusted MC curve. The aggregation of these curves provides the industry (market) supply curve. This curve in concert with the fuzzy market demand curve generate fuzzy price−quantity sets by the extension principle. The intersection yields the fuzzy optimal output. Note that the fuzzy equilibrium set of P and Q is determined by

$$\underset{\text{equilibrium}}{\mu(P,Q)} \quad = \quad \vee \quad [\quad \underset{\text{demand}}{\mu(P,Q)} \quad \vee \quad \underset{\text{supply}}{\mu(P,Q)} \quad]$$

Furthermore, if the price and quantity demanded are fuzzy numbers and the price and quantity supplied are also fuzzy numbers, the equilibrium price and quantity are obviously fuzzy numbers. The equilibrium in process is describable as approximately P and Q, a softly deterministic equilibrium, that we demonstrate below in Figure 6.4. We include in this figure, at the same time, a Robinsonian correspondent to the market demand curve; the ΣMC included thus consists of only the explicit costs plus differential rents, but not the cost of behavioral uncertainty.[8]

Figure 6.4 The oligopoly market supply and demand model

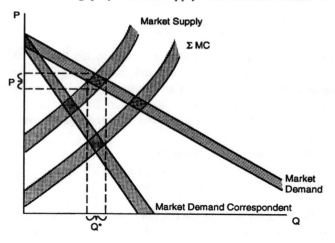

Our model allows the firms not to profit—maximize in the short run (a market fact claimed in many empirical studies). Rather significantly, when fuzzy sets are used for the supply and demand curves instead of continuous crisp numbers, discontinuities must arise and from this we would obtain the sticky price paradigm.[9] Also, consider the relevancy of the described equilibrium in the context of the Austrian school of thought: namely, a set of points applies to the equilibrium of a market, not an exact point. Need we emphasize that pursuant to our model the fuzzy r capacity is imputed at the optimum–optimorum output level of each firm with the market equilibrium being crisp, that is completely deterministic in the long run as all viable firms in the long run operate at their most efficient technical costs.

THE ANTITRUST TOOLS FUZZY APPLICATION

One of the areas to which fuzzy sets are readily applicable is the problem of determining the market structure of an industry. These structures are ordinarily resolved in the United States by use of the Herfindahl–Hirschfield Index (HHI) or the Lerner Index.[10] The HHI is defined as the summation of market shares, as given below

$$HHI = \sum_{i-1}^{n} S_i^2 \qquad (4)$$

where s_i is the proportion of firm i's sales to the total sales in the industry. Specifically, if the industry has only one seller (pure monopoly), the HHI is 10000; if an industry were purely competitive, the HHI value would be zero. In between lies the vague area of imperfect competition and the imperfect judgements of the antitrust authorities.[11]

The Lerner Index (LI) is given by

$$LI = \frac{P - MC_i}{P} \qquad (5)$$

where P is the market price for the homogeneous product and MC_i is the marginal cost of firm i. The LI value therefore measures the price–marginal cost differential relative to the price. At $P = MC_i$ (marginal cost pricing), the $LI = 0$ and the firm is said to be efficient (in the sense of perfect competition). At $LI>0$, the firm is considered to be an inefficient provider of consumer welfare (an oligopoly or a monopoly). The higher the LI value, the greater is the monopoly power of the firm.[12]

Determining the HHI and LI is a difficult and troubling practice. Consider the determinants of an industry's market structure, the prices of its producers' outputs, the possibility of potential entry, and the scope of existing and potential substitutes. All of these are fuzzy realities, to say little about the special features of an industry which are at best softly (fuzzily) deterministic, which is to say that precise data are simply not available. But if in fact market data were available, they would either be too costly to obtain or impossible to translate into a realistic model that would provide a meaningful index for the industry and its structure. Indeed, even if all required elements were readily obtainable and determinable, which of course means we could provide a crisp number to the scope of existing and potential substitutes, etc., a problem still applies: namely, the opinion of the investigator is needed, which fact naturally leads to subjective interpretations of the results of the research. Moreover, deletion of any datum which, if included, may have established some alternative *a priori* assumptions about the market manifests a side problem that generally exists.[13]

At the cost of being pedagogical, we shall address the problem of fuzzy market data in detail below. But first, let us recognize that each market feature must be delineated individually regardless of interrelatedness. Specifically, let us consider several identical factors:

(a) The Price: Each firm in an industry may produce a product (in different sizes, shapes, options, etc.), and not an identical standardized product. Associated with the product group would be a set of prices which may or may not mirror those by the firm's competitors in the short run. Therefore, a single crisp price may not apply. Moreover, in addition to the product group dissimilarities any average market price would ignore the quality of each product having been perceived by individual consumers. The consequence is overestimation or underestimation of a crisp market price which may lead the market investigator to overestimate or underestimate the monopoly power of a market firm.

(b) Potential Entry: Market entry by possible competitors is not a uniformly distributed characteristic among all potential entrants. Some firms may be better equipped to enter the market immediately after a price change, while others will require a longer time period to have their plants renovated and their machinery retooled. Furthermore, entry may occur only when the market prices are beyond a certain range. Otherwise, when the prices are within the range, entry is deterred. Different sets of time, prices, and products must accordingly be used to define potential entry. Failure to accurately include potential entrants will overestimate the monopoly power in the market.

(c) Substitutes: Correct estimates of the sales of substitutes is vital to determining an industry's members and structure. Moreover, when some product substitute(s) is excluded, a firm's market share is overestimated, and hence the HHI. The opposite of course also applies. It is manifest that the exact scope of substitutes in a market is difficult to determine in practice: Some products are considered as substitutes for a given product group only within a price range; beyond that range they cease to be substitutes. Also, different products have different substitution elasticities for the product group. In fact, 'good' substitutes may become 'poor' substitutes as consumers perceptions of product characteristics are revised: 'Distant' substitutes may become 'close' substitutes. The need to re−estimate market size and the potential shares of firms is always present.

(d) Special Features: Due to the heterogeneity of economic space, every industry has its own special features, such as franchises, shipping costs, product spoilages over long distance hauls, etc...These features may determine a certain market structure as the optimal structure for that unique industry. Exclusive of relevant features from market structure studies adversely affects the objectivity of the results.

(e) Input Prices: The multiplicity of both inputs and their classifications prohibits exact determination of the prices of the inputs. Furthermore, the firms in the industry may themselves be (a) purely competitive buyers of the inputs, or (b) oligopolistic buyers, or (c) a monopolistic purchaser. The structures of input markets must be determined in order for objective input−price estimates to be made. Otherwise, a correct crisp MC_i, if not disclosed *accurately* by firm i to the researcher, is a meaningless value.

While the aforementioned practical market realities may appear to be forbidding, still another market feature which often concerns economic theorists must be addressed: namely, the conjectural variations of the entrepreneurs in the industry. Clearly, the level of conjectural variations among entrepreneurs as to behavioral characteristics of rivals varies from one industry to another. Also, the conjectures of industrial rivals do not necessarily remain unchanged in the short run. In still other words, each rival in the market may have a different view from that of others as to how the different firms will react to a new product, to a new price, to changed shipping strategies, to different output levels, locations, etc., especially as initiated by a given (or other) firm in the industry. The oligopolistic behavioral uncertainty in the short run, and the opportunity cost that arises therefrom is certainly different for all entrepreneurs in an industry. Indeed, to further compound the problem of defining the industry, or say the market size, a manager's conjecture are in fact based on the individual's expertise and the individual's observational and theoretical skills.[14]

Based on all of the above, we conclude that all of the determinants of what is an industry and what monopoly power exists therein are fuzzy. It follows that any description of a market must of course use a deterministic set of values to cope with and solve the prevailing vagueness problem; otherwise, such index as the HHI or Lerner index is *per se* irrelevant and inapplicable. Most vitally, a stochastic model relegates fuzziness to random stochastic chance and a market structure becomes an accident of history, not the purposeful interaction between those who are and those who are not part of an industry. We shall propose below how fuzzy math would be applied in an economy whose antitrust authorities want to use the LI or HHI or a similar index.[15]

Role of Conjectural Variations

Assume, w.o.l.o.g., a linear fuzzy demand for firm i, and that the number of firms in the market is a 'few' firms, a fuzzy set whose support is n firms, $n \in N$. Also, let the costs of production be fuzzy. Then, in a 'similar' product market, each firm charges a price $P_i \in \{\tilde{P}\}$, where $\tilde{P}$ is the fuzzy set of possible market prices, and P_i is defined as

$$P_i = f\,[q_i,\ C_i(q_i),\ \sum_{j \neq i}^{n}\ q_j\ \underset{j \neq i}{\vee} C_j(q_j)]$$

That is, each firm's price is not only dependent upon the demand for its own product, but also on the demands for other firms' products, defined by the set 'similar'. Furthermore, we include the market cost structure as a determinant of each firm's product price. In other words, we allow for mark−up pricing possibilities (cost plus pricing, which exists in business practices), and the possible interrelationships between the firms' production costs.

Under imperfect information, q_i, q_j, $C_i(\cdot)$, $C_j(\cdot)$ are all fuzzily deterministic, that is, subjectively but expertly estimated. Given the complexities of each market or industry, the expert's best guess is an approximation.

We recognize that (1) is viewed as an element in the intersection of the fuzzy supply and demand curves of the industry. Thus, in the short run each firm aspires to be within the equilibria set and behaves as such. The prices or outputs of the other firms, as well as the firm's own price and output are basic to the representative firm's strategy choice. Each firm's decision − valuation set is weighted by its own perceived membership in O^*. More specifically, each entrepreneur, manager, or for that matter student of an industry has a view of the elements of O^*. Let O_i^* be the set of industry rivals, as perceived by firm i. The individual's view of O^* is described by the set O_R^*. For O_R^* to equal O_i^*, the elements and their respective membership grades in each $O_{(\cdot)}^*$ must be equal.

We can suggest a set of firms ($k > n$) for each firm in the industry the managers of which firms would be asked to indicate their respective memberships as well as those of other firms in $O_{(i)}$; each manager would use a membership grade from 0 to 1. Then the manager would be asked to assign a maximal grade to a varying rival or the rivals which it perceives to hold the greatest impact on its own market. Each set would be normalized. The responses could then be grouped by the max−min composition rule to form O_I^*, which to recall is the industry set (membership definition) that encompasses all views. A set of rivals would then identify their industry. However, the investigator may have a set $O_R^* \neq O_I^*$, where O_R^* is the researcher's own subjective evaluation of the rivals' membership in an industry. Again the max−min composition would be applied to O_R^*, O_I^* to obtain a final set O^*.

Next, each competitor in O^* would be given a set of prices P and asked the following questions

(1) Given the set P (usually a large set), indicate (from P) your profit maximizing price if the industry is very competitive, that is, are there numerous rivals? We call this price P_{ic}, where i refers to a firm

in O^*, C = the purely competitive concept of economic theory. Alternatively, P_{ic} may be viewed as the minimum possible price.

(2) Given the set P, indicate your profit maximizing price if the industry is a pure monopoly — that is, are you the only producer in the market? We call this price, P_{im}, the maximum possible price anticipated by i. Of course, since the price and cost functions are fuzzily estimated, as we assumed earlier, the TR/TC are also fuzzy. Thus, different marginal equalities may exist at different presumption or possibility levels.

Questions (1) and (2) determine the minimum and maximum bounds of the firms' prices. These bounds are not identical for heterogeneous firms. Furthermore, the maximum or minimum prices may themselves be fuzzy numbers, in this case, a singular number is obtained for each bound via multiplication of the possibility — cardinality ratio by the support of the fuzzy number; that is,

$$\overline{x} = \sum_{i-1}^{M} w_i x_i \quad i = 1,...,M$$

is the number of elements in the support of the fuzzy number, $\overline{x}$ is the crisp price obtained from the fuzzy price $\tilde{x}$ and w_i is

$$\frac{\mu_{\tilde{x}}(x_i)}{\sum \mu_{\tilde{x}}(x_i)}$$

Of course, the $\mu_{\tilde{x}}(x_i)$ are obtained from each manager by asking him for the possibility distributions of his maximum and minimum prices.

After establishing the range, the researcher then asks each manager of a firm in O^* to assign a membership grade to the prices that fall between P_{ic} and P_{im}, given the present state of the industry (oligopoly). Each respondent may assign a possibility of 1 to an ideal price(s) and lower possibilities to prices that deviate from the ideal on either side. Thus, each manager's possibility distribution of the approximate price is established for the market investigator.

Suppose the researcher obtains $\tilde{P}_i$, $i \in n$ for every firm in the industry. The prices are identical in their supports but differ in the respective membership grades assigned by the entrepreneurs to each element in the support.

The fuzzy average price $P_{Average}$ for the industry is obtained by the extension principle. This price is necessarily a fuzzy number which quantifies all the uncertainties about the industry determinants.

Now to the (LI), note that with fuzzy parameters $(P_{Average} - MC_i) / P_{Average}$, LI is also a fuzzy number whose support and domain is the 0, 1 interval. The numerator establishes the per unit conjectural variation cost to firm i which must equal r/Q_i^*, where r is the imputed behavioral uncertainty cost and Q_i^* is firm i's optimum long−run capacity. At the equality points, the firm is viewed in its long run equilibrium. LI is of course never 0 or 1 since LI = 0 would signify perfect competition and LI = 1 implies pure monopoly. A fuzzy LI is accordingly the best predictor of the so−called monopoly power of a firm. It must never be viewed as clear cut evidence of monopoly power, but only as approximate (subjective) evidence of a firm's market power.

The HHI Fuzzy Intersections

The Department of Justice is likely to challenge a merger − as indicated in its 1982 Merger Guidelines − if the premerger HHI of the market is greater than 1800 and the post merger HHI is greater than 1900; that is, if the proposed merger increases the HHI of the market by 100 points or more. If the merger(s) increases the HHI by an amount greater than 50 points but less than 100 points, other factors are then considered by the Department of Justice to determine whether it needs to challenge a merger or not. If the HHI falls between 1000 and 1800, then a merger challenge is 'unlikely', unless the increase in the HHI is ≥ 100; and 'more likely than not' if the increase in the HHI$>>$100; that is, the structural impact is significantly greater than 100. Finally, if the HHI of a market is less than 1000, a merger challenge is deemed 'unlikely'.

Due to the softness of market data, the HHI is a fuzzy measure which reports a vaguely defined market. Each firm's market share is at best a fuzzy estimate described by 'approximately S_i', 'close to S_i', 'approximately between S_i and S_j', 'more or less S_i' etc ... The vagueness around the exactness of S_i may arise from the inexact observability of firm i's sales or the fuzziness of the total market sales (Q). Either way, the outcome is a fuzzy S_i.

The questions that follow are these: given a fuzzy HHI, how would it be represented and how could it be interpreted if one desires to continue the use of such a measure? To proceed with our answers, consider the universal set H over the interval [0, 10000], with 0 representing a perfectly competitive market and 10000 the pure monopoly market. Define the fuzzy HHI by $\tilde{h}$, a fuzzy measure of market concentration, and specifically, $\tilde{h} \subset H$ where $\tilde{h}$ is a fuzzy HHI value and H = [0, 10000] interval.

Next define a linguistic variable X which contains many linguistic terms that describe the different market structures. Here $T(x)$ will connote the fuzzy sets of the linguistic variables (that is, the linguistic terms of $x \in X$). Specifically

$T(x) =$ {'pure competition', 'very competitive', more or less competitive', 'almost oligopolistic', 'oligopolistic', 'almost beyond oligopolistic', 'more or less monopolistic', 'monopolistic', 'pure monopoly'}

Each term of x is a fuzzy set. Pure competition is a fuzzy set whose only element is $h = 0$ at a $\mu_{\tilde{h}}(h) = 1$ that is if $h = 0$, then the market structure is purely competitive with a 100 per cent certainty. If $h =$

Figure 6.5 The Fuzzy HHI

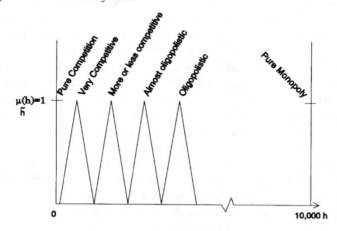

10000, $\mu_{\tilde{h}}(h) = 1$, then the market is a pure monopoly with 100% certainty. The remaining linguistic terms fall in the open interval (0, 10000). These sets are represented in Figure 6.5.

The support for each of the fuzzy sets would be determined along with the membership grades by market decision makers.[16] Each fuzzy set represents the type of competition in the market. We propose that emphasis be given to the intersection of the actual $\tilde{h}$ calculated via the fuzzy market data with the individual fuzzy sets in [0, 10000]. The market structure of an industry is then determined by the set closest to $\tilde{h}$ that is, the one which has the greatest representation in a term.

Suppose that the set $\tilde{h}$ intersects the two sets 'almost beyond oligopolistic', and 'more or less monopolistic'. Then the researcher finds the resulting intersection from $\tilde{h}$ with 'almost beyond oligopolistic' and the intersection of $\tilde{h}$ with 'more or less monopolistic'. This sets are then ranked in accordance with their magnitudes.

To determine the type of the market via a fuzzy $\tilde{h}$, the decision maker intersects $\tilde{h}$ with the set of fuzzy labels. If $\tilde{h}$ falls between two sets without intersecting either then it is labeled by the closest fuzzy predicate; if $\tilde{h}$ is exactly the same distance between two sets, A and B, then the market is labeled as not A and not B; that is, $\tilde{h}$ falls in the complementarity of their negations, where 'not' and 'and' have their usual set theoretic meanings, and if $\tilde{h}$ overlaps two sets in the [0, 10000] interval then $\tilde{h}$ is said to belong more to a set than another if its intersection area with that set is higher. Division of the intersection area of $\tilde{h}$ with a set in $T(x)$ by the area of the set itself indicates the degree of compatibility (agreement) between $\tilde{h}$ and the set. This latter determination is valid only after the incidence of $\tilde{h}$ has been determined. Note that the compatibility degree with a set may not be unique. We demonstrate this method with an example.

Let the sets 'almost beyond oligopolistic,' and 'more or less monopolistic', be A and B where A and B are triangular fuzzy numbers (TFNs) whose numerical values are the triplets (1600, 1800, 1900) and (1700, 2400, 2500), respectively. Also, let the $\tilde{h}$ for a market, approximately estimated due to the softness of market data by an expert, be the triplet (1400, 2300, 2600), that is, 'approx. 300'. All three fuzzy numbers are graphically shown in Figure 6.6 below

Figure 6.6   The intersections of three TFNs (approx. 1800, approx.
  2300, approx 2400)

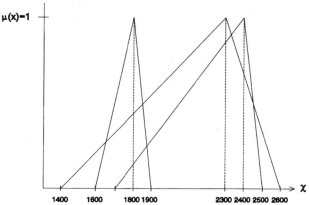

To obtain the intersection areas $\tilde{h} \wedge A$, and $\tilde{h} \wedge B$ we derive the membership functions of A, $\tilde{h}$ and B from the respective triplets of the sets as below

$$\mu_A(x) = 0 \qquad\qquad\qquad x \leq 1600,$$

$$= \frac{x - 1600}{200} \qquad 1600 \leq x \leq 1800,$$

$$= \frac{-x + 1900}{200} \qquad 1800 \leq x \leq 1900,$$

$$= 0 \qquad\qquad\qquad x \geq 1900.$$

$$\mu_{\tilde{h}}(x) = 0 \qquad\qquad\qquad x \leq 1400,$$

$$= \frac{x - 1400}{900} \qquad 1400 \leq x \leq 2300,$$

$$= \frac{-x + 2600}{300} \qquad 2300 \leq x \leq 2600,$$

$$= 0 \qquad\qquad\qquad x \geq 2600.$$

$$\mu_B(x) = 0 \qquad\qquad\qquad x \leq 1700,$$

$$= \frac{x - 1700}{700} \qquad 1700 \leq x \leq 2400,$$

$$= \frac{-x+2500}{100} \qquad 2400 \leq x \leq 2500,$$
$$= 0 \qquad x \geq 2500.$$

We solve first for area $(\tilde{h} \wedge A)$ by describing the surface of the intersection and then integrating over the intersection surface.

Figure 6.7 The intersection of $\tilde{h} \wedge A$

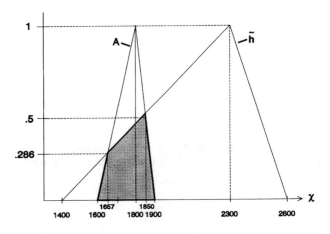

$$\frac{x-1600}{200} = \frac{x-1400}{900}$$

$$x = 1657.14,$$

$$\mu_{\tilde{h}}(x) = \frac{1657-1400}{900} = .286$$

$$\frac{-x+1900}{200} = \frac{x-1400}{900}$$

$$x = 1850$$

$$\mu_{\tilde{h}}(x) = \frac{1850-1400}{900} = .5$$

Thus, the intersection points of the sets are $x = 1657.14, 1850$ at $\mu_{\tilde{h}}(x) = .286$ and $.5$, respectively. For clarity, only the intersection of $\tilde{h}$ and A, is shown in Figure 6.7.

In the figure, the shaded area indicates the intersection surface of both $\tilde{h}$ and A. The area of $\tilde{h} \wedge A$ is obtained as follows

$$area(\tilde{h} \wedge A) = \int_{x-16000}^{1657} \frac{x-1600}{200} dx + \int_{1657}^{1850} \frac{x-1400}{900} dx + \int_{1850}^{1900} \frac{-x+1900}{100}$$

$$= 8.151 + 46.2 + 12.5$$

$$= 66.851$$

For the area $\tilde{h} \wedge B$, the surface $\tilde{h} \wedge B$ is obtained at

$$\frac{x-1700}{700} = \frac{-x+2600}{300}$$

$$= 2330,$$

$$\mu_B(x) = \frac{2330-1700}{700} = .9$$

$$\frac{-x+2500}{100} = \frac{-x+2600}{300}$$

$$= 2450,$$

$$\mu_B(x) = \frac{-2450+2500}{100} = .5$$

$$area(\tilde{h} \wedge B) = \int_{x-1700}^{2330} \frac{x-1700}{700} dx + \int_{2330}^{2400} \frac{x-1700}{700} dx + \int_{2400}^{2450} \frac{-x+2600}{100} dx$$

$$+ \int_{2450}^{2500} \frac{-x+2500}{100} dx$$

$$= 380$$

Clearly area $(\tilde{h} \wedge B)$ is greater than $(\tilde{h} \wedge A)$, then we conclude that the market belongs more to a 'more or less monopolistic' than to 'the almost beyond oligopolistic' market type. Note that the degree of compatibility with B is (area $\tilde{h} \wedge B)/ = 380/600 = .63$, that is, compatibility $[(\tilde{h} = \text{approx. } 2300) \wedge$ 'more or less monopolistic'$] = .63$; a partial truth.

Based upon the above method, one could determine if a merger raising $\bar{h}$ by 50 or 100 points would move the structure further from one competitive state to an undesirable one. Manifestly, consistent guidelines would have to be set by the antitrust authorities. Let us further recall from the α−cuts that the membership of an industry in a market structure set could be crisply obtained at different degrees of confidence. Once the elastic bounds and the distribution for each market type is defined via a membership function, a consistent method for investigating a market structure would be on hand.[17]

> That market power is an elusive quality requires no demonstration ... it is not
> possible, nor will it ever be possible, by calculating market shares ... or other
> hocus pocus, to present an unambiguous measure of the degree of monopoly
> (Mason, 1956, p. 480).

There is no tool which can 'gauge with accuracy the degree of power that may be exercised by individual producers or groups of producers.' (U.S. Chamber of Commerce, 1957). Thus if a tool is to be used to measure market structure, it must utilize fuzzy sets.

APPENDIX

The Figure 6.8, taken from the lectures of M.L. Greenhut, helps explain Figure 6.4 of this chapter and related materials. It contains the long and short−run cost curves of oligopolists who are producing homogeneous goods. The envelope $LRAC_{00}$ in this figure refers to the optimal−optimorum set of large firms whose lowest of all average cost outputs is Q_{00}^*. $LRAC_0$ is, in turn, the envelope of a smaller size set of firms whose optimal (lowest technological cost) output is Q_0^*. Note that $Q_0^* < Q_{00}^*$. In the larger envelope, which as mentioned is drawn lower than $LRAC_0$, the short−run technological cost curves of two sets of firms are conceived. Specifically, $SRAC_{00}$ refers to the most efficient of the large capacity set of firms, an efficiency related to superior managerial skills. The cost curves $SRAC_1$ refer to other large firms of average efficiency and $SRAC_2$ refers to the marginal firm whose optimal production capacity also involves quantity Q_{00}^*. Ascribing all differential rents for the $SRAC_{00}$ and $SRAC_1$ firms bring

Figure 6.8 The long and short—run cost curves of the oligopolists with rent differentials

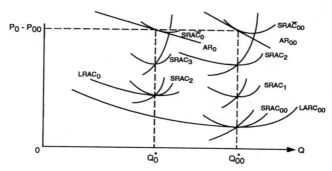

them to the $SRAC_2$ level. Correspondingly, $SRAC_0$ represents the optimal set of firms whose capacity is at Q_0^* and $SRAC_3$ the marginal firm besides the others whose differential rents raise the firms of this size (that is, capacity output Q_0^*) to the level of the marginal firm at that size. For simplicity, we can now conceive the $SRAC_3$ and $SRAC_2$ as the set of small and large size firms respectively, or say Firm 2 and Firm 1. Note that $SRAC_3$ and $SRAC_2$ include all rent differentials and are at the same classical average cost level as that which is derived and depicted in standard neo—classical economic theory. Simply put, when all differential rents in a market are ascribed, the lowest technological explicit plus implicit average costs at such outputs as Q_0^*, Q_{00}^* are identical.

NOTES

1. This chapter draws substantially from drafts of a paper this writer is coauthoring with M.L. Greenhut. I wish to thank him for his permission to draw freely from that paper herein. Even materials not included in that paper which are included herein have benefitted considerably from his editorial suggestions and help.

2. The primary focus of the analysis in this chapter is subjective (horizontal, or Lancastrian) product differentiation. Of course with vertical differentiation the caveats and method of Chapter 4 apply.

3. Unfortunately the present analysis as stated earlier, cannot relate to the world of perfect competition, whose domain and predictions lie in the abstract, never to be observed, world of theory.

4. The above procedure expands the scope of experimental economics to include brand names instead of identical products in the choice space of the consumer. Also, linguistic responses such as 'good', 'very good', etc. can be quantified and precisely translated into mathematical models of consumer choice by utilizing the procedures outlined in this book.

5. Our results are unchanged under the assumption of a fuzzy budget constraint. Only the procedure differs since a fuzzy budget constraint is a generalization of the crisp scenario. The extension principle readily applies here.

6. In the long run, the technical production costs are necessarily crisp under the basic assumption presented previously in Chapter 4.

7. Chen and Yu (1989) derive a fuzzy isoquant under more general conditions.

8. For full details on different cost curves, including imputing Marshallian rents only *vis à vis* imputing all implicit costs, see Greenhut, Norman, Hung *op cit*, pp. 325 – 340, also see the short appendix to this chapter.

9. Gordon (1993, p. 213) describes sticky prices via a monopoly model. Our model, descriptive of an oligopoly industry, is clearly more suitable for macro purposes than the aforementioned.

10. Another tool is the market concentration ratio (CR4) which sums the sales of the four largest market sellers relative to total sales by all firms in the industry. Also, there are concentration ratios for the largest eight, twenty and fifty sellers. Since the CR4 does not provide information about the rest of the market, concentration tables are usually given for all of the firms in the industry and not only the leading sellers. However, even explicit tables are usually problematic in providing summary data which attempt to provide concise information.

11. We will delineate in a later part of this section the conclusions derived by antitrust law courts and economists about market structures over the range $0 < HHI < 10000$. For the present, our brief presentation serves as a definition.

12. In the short run it is feasible to expect an oligopolist to produce at $P > MC_i$ due to under-utilization of plant capacity and other inefficiencies.

13. See Scherer and Ross (1990, Chapter 11) for an excellent survey of empirical investigations of market structures, and a conclusion similar to the subject one in the text above.

14. Antitrust laws (the Sherman Act (1890), the FTC and Clayton Acts (1914), the Robinson-Patman Act (1936) and the Celler-Kefauver Amendments (1950)), which have prompted the study of market structures, are a major source of fuzziness to antitrust investigators. The vague language of these laws has straitjacketed economists as well as lawyers and judges. (Judge Robert Bork demonstrates in his book *The Anti—Trust Paradox* (pp. 58 – 61, 1978) that 'competition' has at least five meanings in antitrust laws).

15. Lest confusion exist on the part of some readers as to the advocacy by the subject writer of the HHI index, let it be noted quickly that nothing contained herein is designed to support use of either indices by the antitrust authorities. Rather, the reality is only that the HHI and LI are used and accepted by many; it is this fact alone which prompts the use of these indices as an example of how fuzzy math would alter the range of values accepted as acceptable or not acceptable by authorities.

16. For the theory and a method to determine the membership grades and the linguistic modifiers (very, almost, more or less etc...) see Chapter 1 of this book. Also, see Zadeh (1973, 1988, 1989) where a membership function is suggested and detailed under the above linguistic modifiers.

17. See Weir (1993) for a recent study of the inconsistent subjectiveness of antitrust legislators.

References

Banon, G. (1981), Distinction Between Several Subsets of Fuzzy Measures, *Fuzzy Sets and Systems* Vol. 5, pp. 291−305.

Barnsley, M. (1987), *Fractals Everywhere*, Academic Press, Inc., San Diego.

Baumol, W.J. (1987), 'The Chaos Phenomenon: A Nightmare for Forecasters', *L.S.E. Quarterly* 1, No. 1, March (1987), pp. 99−114.

Baumol, W.J. and J. Benhabib (1989), 'Chaos: Significance, Mechanism, and Economic Applications', *Journal of Economic Perspective*, Winter 1989, pp.77−105.

Becker, Gary S. (1971), *Economic Theory*, Alfred A. Knopf, New York.

Belman and Giertz (1973), 'On the Analytic Journalism of the Theory of Fuzzy Sets', *Information Sciences*, Vol. 5, pp. 149−150.

Benson, B. (1980a), 'Spatial Competition: Implications for Market Area Delineation in Antimerger Cases', *Antitrust Bulletin*, Vol. 25, No. 4, pp. 729-749.

—(1980b), 'An Examination of U.S. v. Philadelphia National Bank in the Context of Spatial Microeconomics', *Industrial Organization Review*, Vol. 8, No. 1, pp. 27-65.

Blin, J.M. and K.S. Fu, A.B. Whinston, and K.B. Moberg (1973), 'Pattern Recognition in Micro−Economics', *Journal of Cybernetics*, Vol. 3, No. 4, pp. 17−27.

Bollingen Boulakia, J.D. (1971), 'Ibn Khaldun: A Fourteenth Century Economist', *Journal of Political Economy*, Oct. 1971, pp. 1105−1118.

Bork, R. (1978), *The Antitrust Paradox*, Basic Books, Inc., New York.

Buckley, J.J. (1986), 'Portfolio Analysis Using Possibility Distributions' in E. Sanchez and L.A. Zadeh's (1987) *Approximate Reasoning in Intelligent Systems, Decision and Control*, Pergman Press, Great Britian.

Butler, A. (1990), 'A Methodological Approach to Chaos: Are

Economists Missing the Point?', *Federal Reserve Bank of St. Louis*, pp. 36−49, March/April.

Chamberlin, E.H. (1933) 1946 1962, *The Theory of Monopolistic Competition* (5th Edition), Harvard University Press, Cambridge, Mass.

Chang, S.S.L. (1977), 'Application of Fuzzy Set Theory to Economics', *Cybernetes*, Vol. 6, pp. 203−207.

_and H.O. Stekler (1976), 'Fuzziness in Economic Systems, It's Modelling and Control', *Workshop in Stochastic Control and Economics*, National Bureau of Economic Research, Palo Alto, CA, May.

Coase, R.H. (1937), 'The Nature of the Firm', *Economica*, Vol. 4, pp. 386−405, November.

Cournot, A. (1838), *Recherches Sur Les Principes Mathématiques de la Théorie des Richesses* (Chapter 7) English Translation: Researches into the Mathematical Principles of the Theory of Wealth, 1897, N.T. Bacon, New York.

Debreu, G. (1959) 1975, *Theory of Value: An Axiomatic Analysis of Economic Equilibrium*, Yale University Press, New Haven and London.

Deloche, R. (1975), 'Theories des Sous−Ensembles Flous et Classification en Analyse Economique Spatiale', Working Paper, *IME*, Vol. 11, Fac. Sci. Econ. Gestion, Dijon.

De Luca, A. and Termini, S. (1972), 'A Definition of Non-Probabilistic Entropy in the Setting of Fuzzy Set Theory', *Inf. Control*, Vol. 20 pp. 301−312.

Demsetz, H. (1959), 'The Nature of Equilibrium in Monopolistic Competition', *Journal of Political Economy*, Vol. 67, No. 1, pp. 21-30.

_(1967), 'Monopolistic Competition: A Reply', *Economic Journal*, Vol. 77, No. 306, pp. 412-420.

_(1968), 'Do Competition and Monopolistic Competition Differ?', *Journal of Political Economy*, Vol. 76, No. 1, pp. 146-148.

_(1972), 'The Inconsistencies in Monopolistic Competition: A Reply', *Journal of Political Economy*, Vol. 80, No.3, pp. 592-597.

Devaney, R. (1987), *An Introduction to Chaotic Dynamical Systems*, Addison−Wesley Publishing Company, Inc., Redwood City.

_(1989), 'Dynamics of Simple Maps', *Proceedings of Symposia in*

Applied Mathematics, Vol. 39, pp. 1−24.

Dubois, D. and H. Prade (1978a), 'Operations on Fuzzy Numbers', *Int. J. Scyst. Sci.*, Vol. 9, No. 6, pp. 613−626.

__and H. Prade (1978b), 'Fuzzy Real Algebra: Some Results', in *Fuzzy Algebra, Analysis, Logics, Tech. Rep.* TR−EE 78/13. Purdue Univ., Lafayette, Indiana. [*Int.J. Fuzzy Sets Syst.* 2, 327−348, (1979).

__and H. Prade (1980), *Fuzzy Sets and Systems: Theory and Applications*, Academic Press, New York.

__and H. Prade (1982), 'A Class of Fuzzy Measures Based on Triangular Norms − A General Framework for the Combination of Uncertain Information', *Int. J. of General Systems*, Vol. 8, No. 1.

Ekeland, I. (1988), *Mathematics and the Unexpected*, University of Chicago Press, Chicago.

Friedman, J. (1983), *Oligopoly Theory*, Cambridge University Press, Cambridge.

Fustier, B. (1985), 'The Fuzzy Demand', paper presented at the First International Fuzzy Systems Association Congress, Palma de Mallorea, Balearic Island, Spain, July 1−6, 1985 and printed in *Fuzzy Economics and Spatial Analysis*, Edited by Ponsard, C. and Fustier, B. pp. 29−45.

Gale, S. (1972), 'Inexactness, Fuzzy Sets, and the Foundations of Behavioral Geography', *Geographical Annals*, Vol. 4, pp. 337−349.

Goguen J.A. (1967), 'L−Fuzzy Sets', *Journal of Mathematical Analysis and Application*. Vol. 19, pp. 145−174.

Gordon, Robert J. (1993), *Macroeconomics*, Sixth Edition, Harper Collins College Publishers.

Greenhut, M.L. (1956), *Plant Location in Theory and in Practice*, University of North Carolina Press, Chapel Hill, N.C.

__(1970) 1974, *A Theory of the Firm in Economic Space* (2nd printing), Lone Star Publishing Co., Austin, Texas.

__(1978), 'Impacts of Distance on Microeconomic Theory', *The Manchester School*, Vol. 46, No. 1, pp.17-40.

__(1981), 'Spatial Pricing in the U.S., West Germany and Japan', *Economica*, Vol. 48, pp. 79−86.

__and M.R. Colberg, (1962), 'Factors in the Location of Florida Industry', *Florida State Studies*, No. 36.

__and W. Lane (1989), 'A Theory of Oligopolistic Competition', *The*

Manchester School, Vol LVII, No. 3, September 1989.

___and C.S. Lee and Y. Mansur (1991), 'Spatial Discrimination, Bertrand vs. Cournot: Comment'. *Regional Science and Urban Economics*, 21, pp. 127−134.

___and Y. Mansur 'Oligopolisitic Behavioral Uncertainty and the Long-Run Equilibrium: An Application of Fuzzy Set Theory', Working Paper 91−21, *Dept. of Economics, Texas A & M University.*

___and Y. Mansur 'Oligopolisitic Behavioral Uncertainty: An Application of Fuzzy Set Theory', Working Paper 91−22, *Dept. of Economics, Texas A & M University.*

___and G. Norman and C.S. Hung (1987), *The Economics of Imperfect Competition*, Cambridge University Press, London.

Heblebower, R.B. (1954), 'Toward a Theory of Industrial Markets and Prices,' *American Economic Review*, Vol. 44.

Hey, J.D. and Martina, R. (1988), 'Reactions to Reactions and Conjectures About Conjectures,' *Scottish Journal of Political Economy*, Vol. 35, No. 3.

Jain, R., H.H. Nagel (1977), 'Analyzing a Real Worldscene Sequence Using Fuzziness', *Proceedings 1977 IEEE Conference on Decimination and Control*, pp. 1367−1372.

Jensen, R. (1987), 'Classical Chaos', *American Scientist*, Vol. 75, pp. 168−181.

Kandel, A. (1986), *Fuzzy Mathematical Techniques with Applications*, Addison−Wesley Publishing Co., Massachusetts.

Kaufman, A. and Gupta, M. (1988), *Fuzzy Mathematical Models in Engineering and Management Science*, Elsevier Science Publishers B.V., North Holland, Amsterdam.

___and Gupta, M. (1985), *Introduction to Fuzzy Arithmetic.* Van Nostran Reinhold Co. Inc., New York.

Klir, G. and T. Folger (1988), *Fuzzy Sets, Uncertainty, and Information*, Prentice Hall, New Jersey.

Knight, F.H. (1921), *Risk, Uncertainty, and Profit*, Houghton-Mifflin, Boston, Mass.

Lancaster, K.J. (1966), 'A New Approach to Consumer Theory', *Journal of Political Economy*, Vol. 74, pp. 132−157.

Lane, W.J. (1980), 'Product Differentialtion in a Market with Endogenous Sequential Entry', *Bell Journal of Economics*, Vol. 11, pp. 237−60.

Leland, H.E. (1977), 'Quality Choice and Competition', *American Economic Review*, Vol. 67, pp. 127–135.

Kosko, B. (1992), *Neural Networks and Fuzzy Systems: A Dynamic System Approach to Machine Intelligence*, Prentice Hall, New Jersey.

Maiers, J. and Y. Sherif (1985), 'Applications of Fuzzy Set Theory, IEEE Transactions on Systems', *Man and Cybernetics*, Vol. SMC–15, No. 2, Jan–Feb 1985.

Marshall, A. (1910), *Principles of Economics*, 6th Edition, Macmillan and Co., Limited, London.

Mason, E.S. (1956), 'Market Power and Business Conduct: Some Comments', *American Economic Review*, No. 2, May, p. 480.

May, R. (1976), 'Simple Mathematical Models with Very Complicated Dynamics,' *Nature*, Vol. 261, pp. 459–467.

Minkowski, H. (1903), 'Volumes and Oberflache', *Math. Ann.*, Vol. 57, pp. 447–495.

Nahmias, S. (1977), 'Fuzzy Variables', *Fuzzy Sets and System*, Vol. 1(2), pp. 97–100.

Nahmias, S. (1979), 'Fuzzy Variables in a Random Environment' in *Fuzzy Set Theory and Applications*, M.M. Gupta, R. Ragade, R. Yager, eds., Amsterdam, North Holland, pp. 165–180.

Negoita, C. (1979), *Management Applications of System Theory*, Birkhauser Verlag, Basel and Stuttgart.

Ohta, H. (1976), 'On Efficiency of Production Under Conditions of Imperfect Competition', *Southern Economic Journal*, Vol. 43, No. 2, pp. 1124-1135.

—(1977), 'On Excess Capacity Controversy', *Economic Inquiry*, Vol. 15, No. 2, pp. 153-165.

Parker, S. (1978), 'Categorical and Probabilistic Reasoning In Medicine', *Artificial Intelligence*, Vol. 11 pp. 115–144.

Poincaré, H. (1880), 'Sur Les Courbes Definies par Les Equations Differentielles,' *C.R. Acad. Sci.*, Vol. 90, pp. 673–75.

—(1892), *Les Methodes Nouvelles de la Mecanique Celete I, II, III.*, Paris: Gauthier–Villars, Dover, New York, 1957.

Robinson, J. (1961), *The Economics of Imperfect Competition*, Macmillan & Co., Limited, London.

Rothschild, K.W. (1947), 'Price Theory and Oligopoly,' *Economic Journal*, Vol. 57.

Roux, J., R. Simoyi, and H. Swinney (1983), 'Observation of a Strange Attractor', *Physica*, 8D, pp. 257–266.

Ruelle, D. and F. Takens (1971), 'On the Nature of Turbulence', *Commun. Math. Phys.*, Vol. 20, pp. 167–192.

Samuelson, P.A. (1939), 'Interactions Between the Multiplier Analysis and the Principle of Acceleration', *Review of Economics and Statistics*, May 1939, Vol. 21, pp. 75–78.

Scherer, F.M. and Ross, D. (1990), *Industrial Market Structure and Economic Performance*, 3rd edition, Boston, Houghton Mifflin Co. p. 446.

Shortliffe, E. (1976), *Computer Based Medical Consultations: MYCIN*. Elsevier Science Publishers B.V.

Simon, H. (1957), *Models of Man*, New York.

Smithson (1987) *Fuzzy Set Analysis for Behavioral and Social Sciences*, Springer–Verlang, New York.

Stegeman, K. (1989), 'Policy Rivalry Among Industrial States: What Can We Learn from Models of Strategic Trade Policy?' *International Organization* Vol. 43, No. 1.

Swinney, H. and P. Szolovits (1985), 'Observations of Order and Chaos in Non–Linear Systems', *Physica*, 7D, pp. 3–15.

Sugeno, M. (1974), *Theory of Fuzzy Integrals and Applications*, Ph.D Thesis, Tokyo Inst. of Technology.

Szolovits, P. and S. Parker (1978), 'Categorical and Probabilistic Reasoning in Medicine', *Articifical Intelligence*, Vol. 11, pp. 115–144.

Terano, I. and M. Sugeno, (1975) 'Conditional Fuzzy Measures and Their Application', *Fuzzy Sets and Their Applications in Cognitive and Decision Processes*.

U.S. Chamber of Commerce (1957), 'The Significance of Concentration Ratios', *Measurement of Economic Concentration*, No. 1, June 1957.

Weir, C. (1993), 'Merger Policy and Competition: An Analysis of the Monopolies and Mergers Commission's Decisions,' *Applied Economics*, Vol. 25, pp. 57–66.

Yager, R. (1980), 'On Modeling Interpersonal Communications', *Fuzzy Sets: Theory and Applications to Policy Analysis and Information Systems*, Edited by Wang, P. and Chang, S. (1980), first Edition, Plenum Press, N.Y.

Zadeh, L.A. (1965), 'Fuzzy Sets', *Information Control*, Vol. 8, pp. 338−353.

__(1972), 'A Fuzzy Set Theoretic Interpretation of Linguistic Hedges'. *Journal of Cybernetics*, Vol. 2, No. 3, pp. 4−34.

__(1973), 'Outline of a New Approach to the Analysis of Complex Systems and Decision Processes', *IEEE Transactions*, Vol. SMC3, pp. 28−44.

__(1975), 'The Concept of a Linguistic Variable and Its Application to Approximate Reasoning', Parts 1, 2, and 3, *Information Science*, 8, pp. 199−249, 8, 301−357, 9, 43−80.

__and K. Fu, K. Tanaka, M. Shimura (eds.)(1975), *Fuzzy Sets and Their Applications to Cognitive and Decision Processes*, Academic Press, New York.

__(1978), 'Fuzzy Sets As A Basis For A Theory of Possibility', *Fuzzy Sets and Systems* 1, pp. 3−28.

__(1988), Fuzzy Logic, *IEEE Computer*, pp. 83−89, April 1988.

__(1989), 'Knowledge Representation in Fuzzy Logic', IEEE (Invited Paper), *Transaction on Knowledge and Data Engineering*, Vol. 1, No. 1, March 1989, pp. 89−100.

Zimmermann, J.J. (1985), *Fuzzy Set Theory and Its Applications*, Kluwer−Nijhoff, Boston.

__(1987), *Fuzzy Sets, Decision Making and Expert Systems*, Kluwer Academic Publishers, Boston.

Index

189